PLANT WITCHERY

Also by Juliet Diaz

Witchery: Embrace the Witch Within

The above is available at your local bookstore,
or may be ordered by visiting:

Hay House USA: www.hayhouse.com

Hay House Australia: www.hayhouse.com.au

Hay House UK: www.hayhouse.co.uk

Hay House India: www.hayhouse.co.in

Juliet Diaz

Plant Witchery

Discover the Sacred Language, Wisdom, and Magic of 200 Plants

HAY HOUSE, INC.
Carlsbad, California • New York City
London • Sydney • New Delhi

Published in the United States by: Hay House, Inc.: www.hayhouse.com® • *Published in Australia by:* Hay House Australia Pty. Ltd.: www.hayhouse.com.au • *Published in the United Kingdom by:* Hay House UK, Ltd.: www .hayhouse.co.uk • *Published in India by:* Hay House Publishers India: www.hayhouse.co.in

Cover + Interior design: Karla Baker
Interior illustrations: Regina Milan

Cataloging-in-Publication Data is on file at the Library of Congress

Hardcover ISBN: 978-1-4019-6020-9

E-book ISBN: 978-1-4019-6021-6

Audiobook ISBN: 978-1-4019-6022-3

10 9 8 7 6 5 4 3 2 1

1st edition, October 2020

Printed in the United States of America

SUSTAINABLE FORESTRY INITIATIVE
Certified Chain of Custody
Promoting Sustainable Forestry
www.sfiprogram.org
SFI-01268
SFI label applies to the text stock

For Mother Earth, who is always guiding me on my path and spirituality. For your unconditional love, powerful medicine, and enchanting spirit that has helped me become the awakened being I am today.

Let this book be your guide as you step
into your innate gifts of connection and
communication with our Mother Earth.
Embody the Plant Witch in all her Magic.

CONTENTS

List of Rituals, Spells, and Potions   xii

Welcome to Plant Witchery   xiv

PART

·❧ 1 ❧·

WHAT IS PLANT WITCHERY?

The Exchange   3

What Is Magic?   4

Real Magic   5

What Is a Plant Witch?   6

Becoming a Plant Witch   8

Learning from My Elders   11

We Are Nature   12

PART

·❧ 2 ❧·

THE SECRET LANGUAGE OF PLANTS

Plant Language   17

Plant Wisdom   18

The Sun and the Moon   21

The Seasons   29

How to Develop Your Relationship with Plants   32

Daily Practices for Connection with Plants   33

PART
·❧ 3 ❧·

A COMPENDIUM OF PLANTS

Abre Camino *Koanophyllon villosum*   44

Acacia *Acacia*   46

Adder's Tongue *Ophioglossum vulgatum*   47

African Violet *Saintpaulia ionantha*   49

Agrimony *Agrimonia*   50

Ague *Aletris farinosa*   51

Air Plants *Tillandsia*   53

Alfalfa *Medicado sativa*   55

Allspice *Pimenta dioica*   56

Alocasia *Alocasia*   58

Aloe Vera *Aloe vera*   59

Altamisa *Ambrosia peruviana*   61

Althaea *Althaea officinalis*   63

Angelica *Angelica*   64

Angel Wings *Caladium*   66

Apple *Malus domestica*   67

Areca Palm *Dypsis lutescens*   69

Arrowhead *Sagittaria latifolia*   70

Ashwagandha *Withania somnifera*   72

Avocado *Persea americana*   73

Banana *Musa*   76

Basil *Ocimum basilicum*   78

Bay Laurel *Laurus nobilis*   79

Bayberry *Myrica*   80

Belladonna *Atropa belladonna*   81

Bergamot *Citrus bergamia*   83

Birch *Betula*   84

Black Cohosh *Actaea racemosa*   85

Blackthorn *Prunus spinosa*   88

Bleeding Heart *Dicentra*   89

Blessed Thistle *Cnicus benedictus*   90

Bloodroot *Sanguinaria canadensis*   92

Blue Lotus *Nymphaea caerulea*   93

Borage *Borago officinalis*   94

Burdock *Arctium*   96

Butcher's-Broom *Ruscus aculeatus*   97

Cactus *Cactacae*   100

Calamus *Acorus calamus*   103

Calathea *Calathea*   104

Calendula *Calendula officinalis*   105

Caraway *Carum carvi*   106

Carnation *Dianthus caryophyllus*   108

Cat's Claw *Uncaria tomentosa*   110

Catnip *Nepeta cataria*   111

Cattail *Typha latifolia*   113

Cedar *Cedrus*   114

Centaury *Centaurium erythraea*   116

Chamomile *Chamaemelum nobile*   118

Cherry Blossom *Prunus serrulata*   119

Chickweed *Stellaria media*   120

Chicory *Cichorium intybus*   122

Chinaberry *Melia azedarach*   123

Chinese Evergreen *Aglaonema*   124

Cinnamon *Cinnamomum verum*   125

Cinquefoil *Potentilla*   127

Clove *Syzygium aromaticum*   129

Clover *Trifolium*   130

Coltsfoot *Tussilago farfara*   131

Comfrey *Symphytum*   133

Copal *Protium copal*   134

Cornflower *Centauria cyanus*   135

Croton *Codiaeum variegatum*   136

Daffodil *Narcissus*   138

Daisy *Bellis perennis*   139

Damiana *Turnera diffusa*   140

Dandelion *Taraxacum*   143

Datura *Datura*   144

Devil's Shoestring *Viburnum alnifolium*   146

Dill *Anethum graveolens*   147

Dogbane Hemp *Apocynum cannabinum*   149

Dracaena *Dracaena*   150

Dragon's Blood *Daemonorops*   151

Dumb Cane *Dieffenbachia*   152

Echinacea *Echinacea*   154

Elder *Sambucus nigra*   155

Elm *Ulmus*   156

Enchanter's Nightshade
Circaea lutetiana   158

Eucalyptus *Eucalyptus*   159

Eyebright *Euphrasia*   160

Fennel *Foeniculum vulgare*   163

Fern *Polypodiopsida*   164

Feverfew *Tanacetum parthenium*   165

Fiddle-Leaf Fig *Ficus lyrata*   167

Foxglove *Digitalis*   168

Garlic *Allium sativum*   170

Gentian *Gentiana*   171

Geranium *Pelargonium*   172

Ginger *Zingiber officinale*   173

Ginkgo *Ginkgo biloba*   175

Gladiolus *Gladiolus*   176

Goldenrod *Solidago*   177

Grape *Vitis*   179

Hawthorn *Crataegus*   180

Hazel *Corylus*   182

Heather *Calluna vulgaris*   183

Hellebore *Hellebore*   185

Hibiscus *Hibiscus*   186

Hickory *Carya*   188

High John the Conqueror
Ipomoea jalapa   190

Holly *Ilex*   191

Hollyhock *Alcea*   193

Honesty *Lunaria annua*   194

Honeysuckle *Lonicera* 197

Hops *Humulus lupulus* 199

Hoya *Hoya* 200

Hydrangea *Hydrangea* 201

Hyssop *Hyssopus officincalis* 202

Iris *Iris* 204

Ivy *Hedera* 205

Jack-in-the-Pulpit *Arisaema triphyllum* 206

Jade *Crassula ovata* 208

Jasmine *Jasminum officinale* 210

Juniper Berry *Juniperus communis* 211

Lavender *Lavandula* 213

Lemon Balm *Melissa officinalis* 214

Lemongrass *Cymbopogon citratus* 215

Lilac *Syringa* 216

Lipstick Plant *Aeschynanthus radicans* 218

Liverwort *Hepatica* 220

Lovage *Levisticum officinale* 222

Lungwort *Pulmonaria* 223

Magnolia *Magnolia* 224

Mandrake *Mandragora* 225

Maple *Acer* 227

Marjoram *Origanum majorana* 228

Mint *Mentha* 229

Monstera *Monstera deliciosa* 231

Moonwort *Botrychium lunaria* 232

Morning Glory *Ipomoea* 233

Motherwort *Leonurus cadiaca* 236

Mugwort *Artemisia vulgaris* 237

Mulberry *Morus* 238

Mullein *Verbascum* 239

Myrtle *Myrtus communis* 241

Never-Never Plant
Ctenanthe oppenheimiana 242

Nutmeg *Myristica fragrans* 243

Oak *Quercus alba* 245

Orange *Citrus sinensis* 246

Orchid *Orchidaceae* 248

Oregano *Origanum vulgare* 250

Orris Root *Iris* 251

Oxalis *Oxalis* 252

Parsley *Petroselinum crispum* 253

Passionflower *Passiflora* 255

Pau d'Arco *Tabebuia avellanadae* 256

Peace Lily *Spathiphyllum* 258

Pennyroyal *Mentha pulegium* 259

Peony *Paeonia* 260

Pine *Pinus* 262

Pipsissewa *Chimaphila umbellate* 263

Poinsettia *Euphorbia pulcherrima* 265

Ponytail Palm *Beaucarnea recurvata* 267

Pothos *Epipremnum aureum* 268

Prayer Plant *Maranta leuconeura* 269

Primrose *Primula vulgaris* 271

Queen Anne's Lace *Daucus carota* 272

Raspberry *Rubus strigosus* 274

Rose *Rosa* 276

Rose of Jericho *Selaginella lepidophylla* 277

Rosemary *Salvia rosarminus* 278

Rowan *Sorbus aucuparia* 279

Rue *Ruta graveolens* 282

Sacred Fig *Ficus Religiosa* 283

Saffron Crocus *Crocus sativus* 284

Sage *Salvia officinalus* 287

Sago Palm *Cycus revoluta* 288

Saint John's Wort *Hypericum perforatum* 290

Sandalwood *Santalum* 291

Sarsaparilla *Smilax ornata* 292

Sea Buckthorn *Hippophae* 293

Shepherd's Purse
Capsella bursa-pastorsis 295

Sicilian Sumac *Rhus coriaria* 296

Skullcap *Scutellaria* 298

Slippery Elm *Ulmus rubra* 299

Snapdragon *Antirrhinum* 300

Solomon's Seal *Polygonatum* 301

Spider Plant *Chlorophytum comosum* 303

Star Anise *Illicium verum* 304

Stinging Nettle *Urtica dioica* 305

String of Pearls *Senecio rowleyanus* 307

Sunflower *Helianthus annuus* 308

Tansy *Tanacetum vulgare* 310

Tea Tree *Melaleuca alternifolia* 311

Thyme *Thymus vulgarus* 313

Tobacco *Nicotiana tabacum* 314

Turmeric *Curcuma longa* 316

Valerian *Valeriana officinalis* 318

Venus Flytrap *Dionaea muscipula* 319

Violet *Viola sororia* 320

Willow *Salix* 321

Witch Hazel *Hamamelis virginiana* 323

Witchgrass *Panicum capillare* 324

Wolf's Bane *Aconitum napellus* 325

Wormwood *Artemisa absinthium* 326

Yarrow *Achillea millefolium* 328

Yerba Buena *Clinopodium douglasii* 329

Yerba Maté *Ilex paraguariensis* 331

Yucca *Yucca filamentosa* 332

ZZ Plant *Zamioculcas zamiifolia* 334

Continuing Your Journey 337

List of Plants by Essential Properties 339

About the Author 343

LIST OF RITUALS, SPELLS, AND POTIONS

Rituals

Book Anointing Ritual   xvi

Plant Meditation   38

Ague Root House Protection Ritual   52

Altamisa Cleansing Dream Bath   62

Black Cohosh Manifestation Bath Ritual   87

Cinquefoil's Incense Blend to Banish Negativity   128

Dill Visualization Bath   148

Healing Hibiscus Waters Ritual   187

Honesty Self-Reflection Scan   196

Morning Glory Cleansing Footbath   235

Queen Anne's Lace Spirit Bath   273

Saffron Blood Magic Purging Ritual   286

Tea Tree Resetting Foot Bath   312

Yerba Buena Clarity Bath   330

Yucca Root Cleansing Bath   333

Spells

Sun Spell   23

Apple Manifestation Spell   68

Blue Lotus Protection Spell   94

Butcher's-Broom Ice Cube Banishing Spell   98

Cactus Self-Sabotage Protection Spell   100

Centaury Banishing Spell 117

Damiana Love Box 141

Honeysuckle Banishing Steam 198

Jack-in-the-Pulpit Protection Jar 207

Juniper Berry Dirt to Ward Off Evil 212

Lilac Finding Answers Spell 217

Lipstick Plant Movement Spell 219

Parsley Spirit Communication Chocolate Cake 254

Rowanberry Third Eye Jam 281

Slippery Elm Truth Spell 299

Turmeric Passion Bowl Spell 317

Potions

Abre Camino Opening Pathways Floor Wash 45

Allspice Bringing in Abundance Foot Soak 57

Avocado Self-Love Tea 75

Banana Creativity Potion 77

Eyebright Third Eye-Opener Potion 162

Feverfew Hair Mask 166

Hawthorn Meditation Tincture 181

Hickory Strength Syrup 189

Orange Creativity Spray 247

Pipsissewa Repelling Potion 264

Sea Buckthorn Luck Spray 294

Tobacco Clearing Spray 315

WELCOME TO PLANT WITCHERY

Dear Reader,

I am a Plant Witch, a healer, a seer, and an Indigenous Taino from the island of Cuba. I know the truth of what I speak. We are all connected to each other, and to the Earth that holds us. That Magic is available to us all . . . but we have to decide whether we want to grasp it with both hands and bring forth our power to make a difference in this world.

This isn't easy! It takes commitment and faith—faith in the work that you do, and in the power that you have. Despite coming from a family of practicing Witches, I have struggled with that commitment and faith from time to time myself, as I hit challenges, even devastations, in my life: the things that come to us all. But each time, Magic pulled me through. Plants helped me overcome my fears, sheltering me, encouraging me, loving me, as they spoke to me with the voice of Mother Earth, the voice that echoes through us all.

You can do the same. You can close your eyes and find an inner silence, and hear what our Mother is whispering to you. She is saying, *You are powerful. You are Magical. You are a being of light and fire and peace and darkness, and you are beautiful in all your contradictions.*

That is what a Witch is, someone who is unafraid of complexity, and unafraid to shine in her pure light. And a Plant Witch takes this one step further, by seeking a deeper connection to Mother Earth through all her living beings, working with them, befriending them, and loving them. As a Plant Witch grows her practice, she raises her power—and just by doing that, she raises the power of Mother Earth.

Our Mother needs our help. She is being attacked every day. Her seas are dying, her trees are burning, and her creatures are going extinct. It is our sacred duty to love and protect her, as she has always loved and protected us.

So how do you know if you are a Plant Witch?

If you have chosen this book, then it's likely that you are already a Plant Witch. You are already called by Mother Earth to work with her Magic . . . and you are likely working your own Magic every day, without realizing it.

The Plant Witch is one with the Earth and acknowledges the sacred self. She's the protectress of her Mother, and the embodiment of Magic. The Plant Witch acknowledges the seasons and the messages, lessons, and wisdom they bring as they visit us. She sees beauty in the cycles of life, death, and rebirth. The Moon and the stars are her divine compass, helping her navigate her path with pure heart. The Plant Witch practices with natural Magic, as she works with nature to ground, balance, and shift her life, using natural elements to heal herself and to heal others. She cherishes the environment as she cherishes herself.

This is me. This is you, if you choose it. Walk this path with me, and together we will raise the vibration of the world, loving and protecting and empowering all life on Earth.

Love,

Juliet

Book Anointing Ritual

In my first book, *Witchery: Embrace the Witch Within*, I asked my readers to anoint the book to awaken a spell I hid within its pages. This allowed them to connect to the book, and transformed it into an oracle that could guide them through their Magical journey.

With this book, I wanted to do something slightly different. This ritual will awaken and amplify your connection to both our Mother Earth, and to your inner self. The book will then become a symbol of the pact you have made with the Earth—a promise to walk the path of the Plant Witch. This path honors the wisdom, medicine, and Magic that lives within our Mother Earth, and that we carry within us always. The spirits of our ancestors speak to us through the Earth, through the mountains, rivers, oceans, skies, caves, rocks, stones, animals, trees, plants, dirt, bones, roots . . . and the self.

WHAT YOU NEED

All you need for this ritual is the Earth. This can be a space in your garden, or if you have an indoor garden, a pot filled with dirt.

Prepare something for planting—any seed that calls to you for any kind of plant will do. Trust your instincts, and choose what feels right for your practice as a Plant Witch. What represents the kind of Magical work you want to do?

WHAT TO DO

+ Allow yourself a quiet space. If you are in a park, or the woods, or your backyard, find a comfortable seat on the Earth. If you're indoors, open your windows and sit on the floor beside your pot. Clear your mind of all noise. Take a deep breath in and relax the body.

+ Place your seed on top of your book and rest your hands over it. Close your eyes and take three deep breaths.

+ On your fourth exhale, release your breath with an audible hum. Choose a pitch that is comfortable for you, and visualize green light beaming out of your hands and into the seed. Allow that green light to spread into a huge glove of vibration, surrounding the book and yourself. Hum in this way three times.

+ Sitting within that green light, pick up your seed. Whisper to it, "I am you and you are me. I am devoted to myself, the Earth, and the powers that be."

+ Gently and lovingly plant your seed.

+ Hold your book against your heart. Whisper, "Together we are aligned in purpose and in journey. Bring me guidance, as I am devoted."

This book is now your plant oracle.

If you can't feel our ancestors vibrating
through all the plants, trees, rivers,
oceans, mountains, and yourself . . .
then you can't feel your truth.

1

WHAT IS PLANT WITCHERY?

Let's explore further and gain a deeper understanding of what it means to be a Plant Witch and how to walk this path you have already begun to follow. The first step is to become conscious of how every single being in this world speaks to and interacts with each other, as their spirits intertwine.

Nature does not hurry, yet
everything is accomplished.

— LAO TZU

THE EXCHANGE

There is an exchange happening in the world all around us every day. Flowers provide bees with nectar and pollen, and bees provide flowers with the means to reproduce. This exchange is beneficial, even vital, for both.

The same is true with people, as every connection is an exchange.

In my culture, we believe that everything has a spirit and everything is alive just as humans are. Our expansion, our evolution, and our healing happens through exchanges, for when we're giving, we are also receiving. The exchanges are unique to each experience, however there is always an exchange that needs to take place—we can't just take and not give back. To do so would be rude and disconnected with the natural exchange of life. You wouldn't just walk into someone's home, open their fridge, eat their food, and walk out without ever saying, "may I come in?" or "thank you," would you?

An exchange can come in many forms, like saying simple "thank you" after you receive a message from a plant, hugging a tree who gifted you shade from the hot sun, praying to the river who welcomed you with her embrace, or tending to the land by cleaning up garbage that has been left on it. When you create an exchange with nature you are creating a relationship. This relationship becomes stronger and more intimate with each exchange, a beautiful bond and understanding as you pass energy back and forth.

When I grow anything in my garden, I have a small ritual to thank the dirt, the sun, the rain, and the seeds for all their efforts as they create and manifest an abundant garden. I also thank the crops once I am ready to pick them, for the nourishment they will provide me and my family. I never take from the Earth—not even a branch—without asking for her permission first and then thanking her. That is the exchange.

This sacred exchange with Mother Earth is the way life is meant to be felt and experienced—it's as natural as the flowers and the bees. Walking the path of the Plant Witch will help you to live your life in tune with this exchange and reconnect with the very essence of who you truly are as you balance reality with spirituality.

WHAT IS MAGIC?

I t is the eternal question. Is Magic real? What is Magic?

The simplest answer is, "Yes. And Magic is *you*."

We are Magical beings; we are this first, before we are flesh. Magic is the language that speaks our truth. It's our heart in spirit. It is what animates us, what feeds our emotions, our love, our passion, and our gifts.

And so, the truth is that Magic is very personal, and so it is different for everyone. For me, Magic is unconditional love. It is love that reverberates from my soul, echoing with my family, my ancestors, the Earth beneath my feet, the wind in my hair, and the blades of grass brushing my fingers.

Ask yourself, what is Magic for you? There are no wrong answers, for Magic is your truth. Never doubt that you are Magic. Magic is not something that belongs only to a select few, nor is it something that shows up only when you have all the "Witchy tools." Magic is available to all of us, for Magic lives within us all.

Magic lives within you. *It is you.*

You need nothing outside yourself to access your Magic—all you need is within you, if you ignite your power. How do we ignite our power? We embody our truth. We start by healing our minds, bodies, and heart. If we connect to all that is, we open our world to unlimited possibilities. I've inspired thousands of Witches all over the world to wake the Witch within, and not once did I say that it was a special gift that only I have, that no one else can access.

Magic is waking up to the real powers you already hold—to become who you truly are.

In my first book, *Witchery: Embrace the Witch Within*, I go into detail about how to awaken Magic in your life. I explain that if you know who you are, if you accept and acknowledge every wonderful and not so wonderful shade of what makes you, loving every part of yourself as best you can, then your Magic can work at its fullest potential. You can do the most extravagant spells, potions, mantras, setting of intentions—but none of these will work to their full potential if the energy within you is not at a positive state, if you aren't connected to your truth.

Real Magic

I feel I have a responsibility to bring to light what Magic really is, how it really works, and where it actually comes from. As a little girl, I didn't have much of anything at all. My parents were immigrants from Cuba and everything we owned for quite a few years were secondhand, thrift store finds, or hand-me-downs from the community. So how did my mother, a true Witch, practice? She used whatever she had available. She would send me outdoors to pick flowers, sticks, pinecones, mushrooms, grass, plants, branches, as well as stones from a river, resin off trees, and herbs from her garden. I would forage for what she needed. This opened my eyes to see that nature is all around us, and nature is all we need to make Magic.

Plant Witchery helps you access that truth, that delightful interplay between nature and Magic. There are so many different ways to practice as Plant Witchery—and I hope you will explore them all—but the simplest and most direct method is to work with individual plants. This book will introduce you to 200 of my most beloved plant friends and guides, explaining the medicinal and Magical properties of each of them. You will learn how to connect with them, incorporate them into your spellwork, and make them a part of your daily life. As you learn, your Magic will evolve, expand, and become an integral force in your life—but only if you accept yourself and your part as a piece of a greater whole.

Come back to yourself, to your true home. To your natural religion, Earth.

WHAT IS A PLANT WITCH?

Plant Witchery is more than just a path or practice—it is a devotional pact between Mother Earth, Earth spirits, and the inner self. It is a promise to walk a path that honors the wisdom, medicine, and Magic that lives within our Mother Earth and ourselves. The Earth holds the spirits of our ancestors; they speak to us through nature. The mountains, rivers, oceans, skies, caves, rocks, stones, animals, trees, plants, dirt, bones, roots, and the self—these are the ways a Plant Witch communicates with Magic.

The Plant Witch is one with the Earth and acknowledges the sacred self. She also honors the seasons, as well as the messages, lessons, and wisdom they bring. She sees beauty in the cycles of life, death, and rebirth. The Moon and the stars are her divine compass, and they help her to navigate along her path with a pure heart and truth in her soul. The Plant Witch practices with natural Magic. By working with nature to ground, balance, and shift her life, she heals herself and others. She cherishes the environment as much as she cherishes herself.

Plant Witchery is not an appropriative practice—while this book references Indigenous and cultural practices from all over the world, it is never my intention to call those practices my own, or claim a right to them that I do not have. I myself am an Indigenous Witch, but I am not taking from Native American culture or practices and mixing it into a "new" path and calling it my own. A Plant Witch would never do this, for a Plant Witch respects the identity of others. The practice I am introducing you to here is one that belongs to all the children of the Earth. There are no set rules, no right or wrong ways to practice Plant Witchery. It is meant for you to mold and adjust to fit who you are as an individual.

The purpose of this book is to empower people to step into their innate gift of being able to connect and communicate with our Earth—to embody the Plant Witch in all her Magic.

This book goes far beyond just teaching about the medicinal and Magical properties of plants, as it holds information you can get only from me, including my experiences with plants and what they taught me, along with their wisdom and ways to use them as companions in your craft and daily life. Plants, herbs, and roots aren't just their properties, they are living, breathing, and chatty Magical creatures. I want to teach you how to communicate with plants, to learn from them, and work with them. How can you tell if a plant is happy or not? How can you hear what it has to say? In this book, you will learn how to understand their language through energy and connection— through Magic.

Plant Witchery will help you discover the truth hidden within our Mother's heartbeat, a drumming only heard when you reach into your core and wake your true wisdom. You will learn to embrace nature like never before, as you become one with all of its creatures and amplify your Magic to its fullest potential. Plant Witchery is for those who are serious about taking their practice to a deeper spiritual path, for those who want to connect to the wise energies living within nature.

Becoming a Plant Witch

I am a Plant Witch. I've always had a profound connection with plants and the Magic that they possess. I first learned of my gift around the age of six. I was in class and my teacher was talking to us about seeds. She proceeded to lift a plant from its vase. She pulled on the roots and I yelled, "Stop it! You're making her cry." My teacher gave me a confused look and asked me, "Now how does a plant cry, Juliet? I'm not hurting it; I'm simply showing you its roots." I said, "Don't you see her smoke? Don't you hear her? She doesn't like you pulling at her hair." I used to call the tops of plants "hair," and I see smoke coming off plants when they are being harmed—for instance, if they are infected with pests, when grass is mowed, when people cut flowers or pull them from the ground. I've come to realize it's a scent plants release to alert other plants of danger. I smell it, but I also see a mist of energy that comes out of them. My teacher put the plant back down and took me out of the class to speak to me. She told me that if I kept making up stories the other children would make fun of me and she didn't want that to happen. I obeyed, and for a long time never spoke to anyone but my family about my adventures with plants and the stories they told me.

The thing is, I knew what I saw and felt was real. This knowledge, this Magic, runs in my blood, and has been true of every generation of my family, from my mother to my grandmother, my great-grandmother, and onward. It is a part of my heritage. My ancestors, the Taíno people of the Caribbean, were known for being communicators with plants. Indigenous people in general are in tune with nature, but the level reached by the Taíno is unusual—so much so that healers from other tribes would come to learn from them. My ancestors had the gift of communicating with plants—this helped them understand which plants, herbs, and roots to use for healing and Magical purposes. This gift was passed down to me. Today, I am known as the plant whisperer in my community.

But despite what I knew and believed, I had a really rough childhood. Part of that was because I could see things that other children couldn't, and I wasn't able to relate to other children or to communicate with them—and they saw me as "other."

I was also going through physical and emotional abuse. We lived in public housing, and there were always fights—always some kind of crime going on. My father, a drug dealer, was murdered when I was five years old. For most of my childhood, I lived in fear.

So I retreated. My siblings and I weren't allowed to go to friends' houses after school—I didn't have any friends, anyway, being that weird girl who talked to plants—and I was afraid to hang out around our apartment building. Honestly, the only time my siblings and I would go outside and play was when it rained or stormed. My mother believes in the Magic of a storm, and the good cleansing of the rain. She *always* sent us outside to play and dance in heavy rainfalls and among the huge puddles that accumulated at the bottom of a hill where we lived.

Most days, I went to the only place I could—to the cemetery nearby. That was my playground, and it was beautiful. There was a huge forest, trees, flowers . . . and tombstones. I often saw ghosts as a child (and still do) but rarely there. I didn't feel haunted there. The cemetery was the most peaceful place I knew.

Like many children with my kinds of gifts, I had imaginary friends—but for me, they were the plants I found in nature or in pots in our apartment. I was always having conversations with them. I thought these exchanges were all in my head, but as I grew older I realized it wasn't my imagination: that those conversations were real, and those friends had been taking care of me for years. Those plants and trees saved me. That cemetery, filled with so much natural life, was my mystical safe space, a healing retreat.

I remember hearing plants, as they spoke to me so clearly. For instance, I remember the first time I smelled cut grass. It was a spring day, and I was about six years old, hanging around the cemetery as I often did. As the groundskeeper rode around in his mower with its big spinning blades, leaving behind shreds of cut grass, I was struck by an awful numbness that left me unable to move or speak. Time slowed down, and the sharp sounds of the blades echoed through the air. The pieces of grass seemed to float, falling slowly onto the ground, and when the smell of the cut grass reached my flesh, all I could feel was STOP!

I ran toward the groundskeeper as fast as my little legs could take me. Halfway there I had to stop to vomit, gasping for air and trembling with fear. I didn't know what was happening to me, but I knew he needed to stop, I knew he was hurting the grass. When I finally reached him, he yelled, "What the hell, have you lost your mind?" I screamed back, "Stop, you're hurting the grass!" He was so confused, but he definitely didn't want to get into a conversation with a crazy child, dirty and running around a cemetery alone. He ignored me and kept mowing.

I felt hopeless. I dropped to my knees and held on to the dead pieces of grass in my little hands, sobbing, screaming in agony. I cried myself to sleep that night, confused about life, humans, and who I was and why no one would listen to me. As I grew older, the plants and tree elders taught me that they alert others of danger, and when all living beings are truly connected, they each feel each other's pain, love, happiness, and, yes, they feel the warnings as well. I had been feeling the warning the grass was sending out to others. To this day, I refuse to cut my grass or pluck a flower from the Earth, as I can still hear them screaming. If someone I dated brought me flowers, I knew we weren't meant to be!

Of course, now I know that some flowers, like roses, need to be cut, and oftentimes plants need to be pruned in order to keep growing and remain healthy, but I listen to them for their needs and never harm them.

LEARNING FROM MY ELDERS

My mom makes medicine and Magic with the guidance of plants. When I was a little girl, she would converse with them. This was normal for me, especially since I could hear the plants respond, just as clearly as I could hear my mother talking. She never told me that this was something rare, that not everyone spoke to plants or could understand them. She allowed it to be a natural part of our lives.

So now, if I'm doing a custom spell for someone, doing a healing session, or even just providing them with guidance, I always ask our Mother Earth to work with me. I tap into the energy of the person before me, and allow my connection to nature to come through and provide me with insight. There is no one more powerful than a Witch who uses her own self and the Earth to dance in the web of Magic.

Because I wanted to go deeper and gain a broader knowledge base, I researched and educated myself on herbalism—I have three certifications in herbalism, as well as a master of science in herbal medicine. And as I studied, I learned that my intuition has always been right—for while I learned and grew so much as a healer during my studies, nothing could ever teach me as well as listening directly to my plant relatives.

The same will be true for you. You don't need a degree or any other piece of paper to become a Plant Witch. You can use your intuition, and learn by *doing*.

WE ARE NATURE

To me, Mother Earth is my religion, and she isn't judgmental. All her children are equals and sacred beings.

Just for a moment, think about the natural world. All living things depend on each other. We all breathe together. We live, die, reemerge, and work together to enrich and assist other living beings. It's a give and take, a flow, a magnificent cycle. We belong to this Magical cycle.

Our bodies eventually die, and the flesh is taken by the Earth into the soil where it will create new life. We become that life, and our wisdom, lessons, love, and experiences live on forever. Our ancestors live on through nature, teaching us, guiding us, and loving us—they live on through us.

Just like plants, we are seeded in the womb of our mother, in the darkness that cradles our existence. Her love fills our spirit and her body feeds the creation of our vessels. Through the umbilical cord, we are rooted directly to her, to her breath, her heartbeat, her emotions, her thoughts, and her spirit. We are one, connected, waiting to emerge from the womb and into the light.

Plants need the same things we do to survive, heal, grow, and blossom. We all need just the right amount of water, the right amount of light, the proper food, as well as mindful care and love. These similarities exist because *we are nature*. We are earth, air, fire, and water—and when we acknowledge this truth, we come into harmony with the world inside us and around us.

Nature is not something separate from us. Our relationships with all living things—including our relationship with ourselves—is the key to truly knowing who we are. It's how we know what helps us heal and prosper, what hurts us and slows our growth, as well as the reason for our existence here on this Earth.

Plants bring us back to who we are. They bring us back to this place of meaning. We are important. We are connected. We are sacred. We are everything we need. All we have to do is awaken our remembrance to this truth: We are nature.

You and the tree in your backyard come from a common ancestor. A billion and a half years ago, the two of you parted ways. But even now, after an immense journey in separate directions, that tree and you still share a quarter of your genes.

— RICHARD POWERS, *THE OVERSTORY*

2

THE SECRET LANGUAGE OF PLANTS

Let's explore further and gain a deeper understanding of what it means to be a Plant Witch and how to walk this path you have already begun to follow. The first step is to become conscious of how every single being in this world speaks to and interacts with each other, as their spirits intertwine.

Avoid gurus, follow plants.

— Terence McKenna

PLANT LANGUAGE

Plants talk to each other all the time.

Sounds crazy, right? But it's true, and it's backed up by scientific evidence. Of course, we don't need research to prove something humans have understood for eons—my ancestors certainly never needed a scientist to tell them what they already knew. But the science geek in me loves reading about how the whole world is awakening to the truths hidden within our Mother.

For example, two studies published in 1983 demonstrated that willow trees, poplars, and sugar maples can warn each other about insect attacks. The first study was done by zoologist David Rhoades from the University of Washington, and he found that the Sitka willow could literally change the nutritional content of its leaves, so that harmful caterpillars infesting it would be less interested—but the truly amazing thing was that nearby willows who were *not* infested also altered their leaves. A similar study published later that same year by Ian Baldwin and Jack Schultz from Dartmouth University placed healthy poplar and sugar maple seedlings next to infected saplings...and the healthy seedlings began producing anti-herbivore chemicals.

These trees somehow knew what their neighbors were experiencing and reacted to it.

Plant language is real, and you can learn to speak it.

As you connect to the plant's energy, that energy becomes a language you translate within yourself. This language will be different for every person, and yours is unique to you. I will help you begin to talk with plants by sharing with you the medicinal and Magical properties each plant offers, as well as the wisdom they offer me. This will get you started, as you learn to connect with plant energy and grow fluent in this language.

The reality is that we are as much a part of the Earth as plants are. Once upon a time, we could speak their language just as well as the bees could. But we have lost touch with that part of ourselves, the part of us that knows why we're here—really, who we are.

PLANT WISDOM

Plants are chatty Magical creatures. I can't tell you how often they strike up a conversation—I have to surround my workspace with the quietest plants I know so I can get something done! Many moons ago, while I was on a date, I went to a beautiful restaurant with a lovely garden. The space was filled with spider plants, snake plants, huge monstera towering over the tables, and cacti as centerpieces. I said hello to every one of them as we sat down.

My date started talking about his previous relationship—never a great conversation to be having on a first date! As he went on and on about all the things his ex had done wrong, I knew he needed to take more time to mourn this last relationship. I cringed in my chair and eventually retreated to sharing space with the plants all around me. As I did, the cactus on the table pricked me at the base of my spine. It startled me so much that I jumped—not that my date really noticed. The cactus told me I had better things to do than listen to this man talk about someone else. And you know what? He was right. I suggested my date have dinner with his ex instead, and I left.

Yes, I have full-on conversations with plants, trees, nature, and all her spirits. I am lucky to have a lineage of family of Witches whose Witchcraft, spirituality, and culture revolve around plants—but this kind of connection is available to everyone. All it requires is remembering that you are also part of nature, you are one with the plant. You will build your own unique language as you implement the Plant Witchery path into your life.

Plants touch us, speak to us, and teach us in different ways. They are wisdom keepers, the natural healers of the world. Think about it this way: When a plant is sick, we don't change the plant, we change the environment around it. Nothing is wrong with the plant itself—instead, we look at the amount of water it is receiving, the amount of light, or even its placement. We consider whether it is receiving love. Does any of this sound familiar? As humans, we tend to look within, thinking the problem must lie within us, but just like plants, there is nothing wrong with us—it's our environment that needs to change, our lifestyle, the way we eat, the love we receive. We can learn to implement plant wisdom into our own lives.

When I was seven years old, I had an overwhelming feeling of not wanting to live anymore. My life felt unbearable. The elevator in our seven-floor building was broken, and so I climbed my little self up all seven flights of stairs, gasping for air by the time I reached the roof. The air was numb, time was still, and the silence was deafening. I walked to the edge of the roof, shaking in my skin, and looked down at the biggest drop I've ever seen in my life. I stood there, closed my eyes, and leaned my little body forward, bracing for my fall. All of a sudden, a gush of wind hit me like a freight train, so hard my body flew back about six feet! I lay on the roof, stunned, and opened my eyes to the most amazing sight— dozens of daisies falling from the sky. They were floating above me, slowly, then landing on my body. The wind brought them there, to cover me in a blanket of embrace. I cried. A lot. And then I heard, "You belong here, turn over." And so I turned over onto my belly, only to find moss growing out of the tar roof-top. My tears dripped onto the moss, and as they flowed, watering the moss, my despair—the feeling of not wanting to be here—disappeared. The moss absorbed all my pain, all my fear. I owe my life to our Earth.

We can learn from how plants break through hard times. They adapt to circumstances and shift accordingly. Challenges don't keep them from being determined—think about a flower growing through a crack in a city sidewalk. Plants also don't set limits for themselves. They want to thrive and grow as much as possible. A plant never thinks to itself, *I've grown enough, this is my safe place, I'll stop growing now.* No, it unapologetically continues to flourish and thrive, as we all should. We deserve to be limitless.

Plants do not allow obstacles to
take their focus off the Sun.

THE SUN AND THE MOON

Just like plants, our entire being is intimately connected to the natural rhythms of the Earth, including the celestial bodies that influence her: the Sun and the Moon. There is power intertwined in this connectivity, a source of wisdom, medicine, and Magic living within the cycle of life.

Before I go into practicing Magic with plants, I want you to focus on the fundamentals of existing with our Earth and utilizing them for self-healing and growth. The messages, lessons, language, and wisdom of the plants, the Sun, the Moon, and the Earth will all be unique to everyone. I want to inspire you to build a practice that includes mindfulness and compassion to all that is, including yourself. And this starts with connecting to the wisdom waiting to be given.

We have lost touch with our connection to nature and all that is. This shows up so clearly to me when I think about our fears of aging and death, the constant pushing instead of flowing through life, and our disconnection from who we are and our purpose on this Earth.

The truth is, we are eternal beings, living in all places, in all things, all at once. When the Sun rises, so does our soul, and when the Sun sets, the Moon takes us into the deepest parts of our being. We are never alone, never lost, and never unloved. We are every color of the rainbow, the sparkles gleaming above the snow, the flutters of a butterfly, and the howling of the wolves. We are everything. We are sacred.

The Sun

I invite you to dive into your senses for a moment. See yourself standing in an open field surrounded by flowers. Your feet are bare, your toes are digging into the dirt, and your eyes are closed. It's dark, cool, and quiet. It's the moment right before the Sun starts to rise. As the Sun edges over the horizon, enveloping you with warmth and happiness, you naturally lift your chin up toward its embrace. You stand taller, stronger, more confident. The Sun literally lifts you up, inspiring you to rise and grow. Now take your senses to the field of flowers around you. What are they doing? What are they feeling? Yes—they are moving just as you are, reaching, growing, and embracing the Sun the very same way.

What does the Sun say to you? What lessons does it have in store for you? In my journey, the Sun has taught me many great lessons, insights that have changed my perspective on my own importance. All my life I have wanted to give, help, and serve. I want to make a difference in this world, to change lives. In this way, I can look to the Sun. The Sun is a giver. It never asks anything in return, and it doesn't have an ulterior motive. Its fire connects to the fire within me. If I live a life during which I give and serve with purpose, I have lived a life worth living, a life ignited by a genuine force connected to the flames of our universe.

The Sun has also taught me to rise above it all. I was diagnosed with Lupus in early 2019. I was falling apart fairly quickly, barely able to get out of bed. My body and spirit were withering before my eyes. As a mother of two human boys and three precious cats; as a wife, a boss, a creative, a healer, and an activist, I felt like my life was being taken away from me. All the achievements, miracles, and goals I worked so hard to manifest into my life felt like they were all for nothing.

Lupus didn't come in and gently introduce itself to me, it straight up grabbed a baseball bat and came in swinging. For a moment, my faith in my purpose seemed like a lie. And then, like a diamond rising early in the sky, the Sun beamed through my windows as it never had before, shooting its warm embrace straight at my feeble body. *Get up! Get out of bed, my dear. You're not wasted or dead nor broken or useless. You're meant to rise above it all.*

I saw my entire life play before my eyes—the struggles, the pain, the falls, the obstacles. I saw how I got through them all, and how I always found a way to not only survive but to actually live. The Sun reminded me of my strength, of my undeniable fire to live, and of how capable I truly was, no matter the circumstance. I got up. I understood at that moment, standing with my legs shaking in pain, that rising above it all didn't mean physically climbing to the top. Rising above it meant setting my spirit free, allowing it to soar to the highest of peaks without trapping its potential.

Sun Spell

The Sun's energy is always available to us, night or day, on the cloudiest day or in the brightest light. This spell will help you harness that energy and hold it deep within you, so that you can use it when you need it most.

WHAT YOU NEED

A handful of sunflower seeds, for eating

A handful of sunflower seeds, for planting *(they look almost exactly the same, but make sure it's a seed packet from a garden store)*

A small pot of dirt or space of earth

WHAT TO DO

+ Take an edible sunflower seed and a plantable sunflower seed and hold one in each palm. Focus your intentions on the seeds, asking them to grow for you, to stretch toward the Sun.

+ Plant the plantable seed, and eat the edible seed, thanking them both for their service.

+ Repeat with the remaining seeds, then water them. Take a big sip of water, feeding the seeds within you.

+ Every day for 7 to 10 days, water the seeds, always drinking water yourself. Speak your intentions each day, whispering to every seed you planted.

+ When each seed has sprouted, thank them once again. As they continue to grow, so will the Sun energy you carry within you.

The Moon

Oh, the beauty that is La Luna. Majestic, brilliant, and Magical. When I was a little girl I was obsessed with her light. I remember the first time I noticed the disappearance of the Moon. I was about six years old. I looked out my window, and when the Moon wasn't there, I sneaked out and wandered the streets, searching the entire sky. Nothing. Where did she go? I thought something terrible had happened. I ran back upstairs and barged into my mother's bedroom. "Mommy! *La Luna! La Luna no esta en el cielo!*" My little heart was racing, my lungs barely able to keep up with my anxiety.

"The Moon isn't gone, amor, it's just a phase. The dark Moon."

I had seen the Moon changing sizes, but this was the first time I realized there were times when she was simply not there. I was terrified—the Moon was my night-light, the God I prayed to every night. My mother walked me back to bed and she lay down with me while she explained the different phases of the Moon. My crying stopped, and as I calmed my breath, the most Magical thing happened. My mother gasped, "Ay dios, mira!" Out my window, sparkling bright flickering dots rose, floating right there. We watched in awe. My mother took a deep breath. "This is a gift from the Moon, letting you know she's still there for you. She sent lightning bugs to light you up."

After that, at every New Moon I would collect a few lightning bugs and place them in a big jar on my windowsill, and then let them go in the morning, thanking them for their light.

The Moon is always listening, eager to connect with you, and eager for you to connect with her. She taught me to take my time, to honor the changes in my life, and to be patient in the timing of the divine. The cycles of the Moon create a ritual, one we have been a part of since we were in the womb of our mother.

The Moon rules everything that flows on the Earth, including you. Your moods and emotions, your sense of being and spiritual presence. As she does the oceans, plants, animals, and even the soil. Working with the Moon has been in my practice since I was a little girl. It has helped me become more in tune with my spirit, body, and my own biochemistry. I've learned to understand myself better, my emotions, my thoughts, my body and what it needs, and how to ground and balance myself through each phase. She is always there, always present, even when we don't see her watching over us. Each phase holds significant physical and spiritual meaning and influence.

Working with the Moon in an intimate way can open your heart and mind to incredible wisdom. The Plant Witch lives in harmony with the Moon, as well as with the Sun and seasons. The Earth is her religion, her Magical ceremony. We have the power to tap into the Moon's energy in each of her phases.

PHASES OF THE MOON

● New Moon

This is a time to go within, a sacred exploration of the inner self. In this phase, at the start of the lunar cycle, we sort the seeds and choose which ones we want to cultivate, putting in motion the things that we desire and need for the month ahead. Each New Moon allows us to reset. It is a new beginning that brings us endless possibilities. This is an ideal time to plant seeds, both literal and metaphorical, as the Earth is at her most fertile during this time.

EFFECTIVE SPELLS: *new beginnings, self-love, peace, creativity*

PLANTS TO WORK WITH: *avocado, African violet, peace lily, never-never plant*

Waxing Crescent Moon

Around 3½ to 7 days after the New Moon, the growing Crescent Moon urges you to begin to tend to your planted seeds. The plans and intentions that you planted during the New Moon require you to gather information and observe. Be mindful of shifts and things moving in your favor. The ever-brightening light of the Waxing Crescent allows you to peer deep inside and see how you truly feel about what's happening in your life, from your work to your relationships.

EFFECTIVE SPELLS: *awareness, reflection, clarity, self-awareness*

PLANTS TO WORK WITH: *bloodroot, fern, cedar, iris*

 First Quarter Moon

We reach the First Quarter 7 to 10½ days after the New Moon. This is a time when the Moon is beginning to bask in her power, and she can help you draw in whatever you need to fulfill your intentions. What are you looking for? What do you feel like your life has been missing?

EFFECTIVE SPELLS: *luck, abundance, manifestation*

PLANTS TO WORK WITH: *arrowhead, birch, cactus, holly*

 Waxing Gibbous Moon

The Waxing Gibbous Moon occurs 10½ to 15 days after the New Moon. In this phase we are called to fully trust in the universe and in the self. This is the time to ask yourself the hard questions: Do I need to refine my intentions? Change them? Do I need to redirect them altogether? There is no need to fear shifting tides, for wherever you feel pulled to go or whatever you feel pulled to do, there is no right or wrong. Trust that it will always work out the best way to serve you.

EFFECTIVE SPELLS: *truth, self-awareness, healing, clarity*

PLANTS TO WORK WITH: *adder's-tongue, bay laurel, garlic, liverwort, fern*

Full Moon

The Moon reaches climax—full and brilliant—15 to 18½ days after the New Moon. This is the time of illumination. With her light fully shining over you, you are able to bask in your complete power. If there are any spells you've been preparing, now is the time to put them into action.

EFFECTIVE SPELLS: *spiritual development, healing, luck, abundance, psychic ability, opening the door between realms*

PLANTS TO WORK WITH: *oxalis, blackthorn, mullein, cattail, belladonna*

 Waning Gibbous Moon

This phase occurs 3½ to 7 days after the Full Moon. Waning Gibbous, also known as the Disseminating Moon, allows you to see clearly, to determine what no longer serves you, and to reveal the truths all around and within you. This is a time to prune away what you no longer need or want. Look at your accomplishments with beaming eyes, and celebrate.

EFFECTIVE SPELLS: *clarity, unblocking, truth, abundance, amplification*

PLANTS TO WORK WITH: *prayer plant, bleeding heart, goldenrod, lovage*

 Third Quarter Moon

This final quarter of the Moon, 7 to 10½ days after the Full Moon, pushes us to heal the self and share that healing with the world by being compassionate and allowing our light to shine brightly. Now is the time to release the things we are scared to let go. Forgiveness is key in allowing yourself to step into the truth of your being, to live as your best self. Release things that haunt you, so that there is space for new and better things.

EFFECTIVE SPELLS: *banishing, energy clearing, healing, peace*

PLANTS TO WORK WITH: *datura, ginger, apple, moonwort*

Waning Crescent Moon

Approximately 10½ days after the Full Moon, the Waning Crescent, also called the Balsamic Moon, allows you to dig deep. In the previous phase, you worked to find what you need to release . . . now ask yourself, what is left? There are always secrets that we hide even from ourselves, fears and limiting beliefs that stand in our way. Do some divination work at this time, and pry away all that no longer serves you.

EFFECTIVE SPELLS: *new beginnings, awareness, self-awareness, intuition*

PLANTS TO WORK WITH: *ZZ plant, pothos, agrimony, hawthorn*

THE SEASONS

The seasons are the almighty elders of the Earth. Winter, autumn, spring, and summer are the original timekeepers, the natural rituals of life. When we let the seasons guide us, we are living in tune with the Earth. We become vessels in which the Earth can transmute her wisdom and medicine. We become aware of being part of a bigger whole, allowing our fears and need to control things float away into nothingness.

Our ancestors knew that the seasons guided life in ways that were vital to survival, healing, and growth. The seasons teach us about the beauty of aging, death, and rebirth. The Plant Witch within us remembers that from the moment we are born, we are beautiful, dying things. The leaves that fall to the ground nourish the Earth. They nourish the insects and provide burrows and homes for the creatures that live in the forest.

Think about the breath you take in, inhaling the oxygen that a tree has given you. Think about the breath you give out, feeding the trees in return. This is the exchange, the eternal gifting and receiving of life and energy. Death is a part of that exchange.

We can learn a lot about ourselves by paying attention to how we feel and act during each season. For example, during the summer, I used to turn into a hot mess, literally. I couldn't stand the heat, the brightness, but I wanted badly to try and connect with summer. I wanted to feel what others felt about that season, to tap into its joy, playfulness, and fire. So I sat and meditated on it. I called in summer and had long conversations about how she made me feel and how I so desperately wanted to understand her. Do you know what she told me? She said, "You *are* me. You are all the seasons; you just need to find balance." So I did just that. I focused on cooling and releasing energy when summer came to visit. I ate more melons, drank more water, and did exercises that helped release my excess energy, such as kundalini, tai chi, and chanting. I meditated before the sunrise and did yoga after sunset. I went through trial and error to find what helped me.

Spring

This classic time of rebirth and renewal is a time to celebrate. Your Magic is at its most fertile at this time, as you are able to harness the power of Mother Earth as she gives birth to another cycle of life. Set your intentions, work in new and creative ways, and simply allow the childlike energy of spring to inspire your imagination.

EFFECTIVE SPELLS: *creativity, happiness, new beginnings, purification, wishes*

PLANTS TO WORK WITH: *morning glory, ivy, air plant, valerian*

Summer

This vibrant season is full of passion and power. If you can harness summer's fire, instead of letting it weigh you down, you can use it to burn away anything that has been blocking you and ignite your creative fire. Like summer, you contain abundance and Magical energy. What are you capable of creating?

EFFECTIVE SPELLS: *creativity, love, abundance, manifesting*

PLANTS TO WORK WITH: *rose, orchid, bergamot, witchgrass*

Autumn

This is my favorite season. As Mother Earth begins to tilt away from the Sun, we grow colder, darker. Autumn is a time to peer inward, to look at your own shadows and see them for what they truly are. Speak with and honor your ancestors and spirit guides as the veil between worlds grows thin. What messages do they have for you?

EFFECTIVE SPELLS: *spiritual development, shadow work, self-awareness, reflection, psychic ability, opening the door between realms, balance*

PLANTS TO WORK WITH: *Solomon's seal, datura, mint, elder*

Winter

While Mother Earth sleeps, take this time to rest and rejuvenate. Reflect on what it is you have to offer the world, and what it is the world has given you. Embrace a sense of gratitude, and begin to do the work, laying preparations for Magic to come. Purify your spirit and cleanse yourself of all that you have been carrying as you make ready for a new beginning. The cycle continues always.

EFFECTIVE SPELLS: *self-love, purification, protection, peace, healing, energy clearing, clarity*

PLANTS TO WORK WITH: *lavender, cedar, pine, tobacco*

Conversations with the Seasons Journal

I keep a journal for each season, and recommend you do the same! It will help you keep track of how you feel throughout the year, what you experience, and any lessons, messages, and wisdom you may receive.

Use your journal to have a conversation with each of the seasons. What do you love? If you love autumn like I do, think about the comfort and rest she brings you—and then ask yourself how to balance that with the energy you receive from summer. What do you experience with winter? What do you experience with spring?

Pay attention to how your body reacts to each season. How is your appetite? What foods make you feel better or worse? What plants do you notice, and which of them are calling to you, offering you messages? How can you use each of the seasons to balance the others?

How to Develop Your Relationship with Plants

Sometimes it feels as if being a "plant lover" just means participating in a social media competition about who has the most lavish and beautifully photographed collection of plants. Plants are more than just decoration. They are living beings with feelings, thoughts, language, and personality. Growing or owning a plant makes you a plant parent—you are now responsible for a living and breathing being. You are responsible for its care, love, and attention.

Don't be intimidated by this! You don't need to have experience with plants to be an amazing plant parent. I'll give you plenty of practical tips on how to connect with your plants and develop a loving relationship with them. But before I do, let's think a little more about that idea of connection.

If you're reading this book, you likely already have a relationship with nature, or want to create one. In a world that prioritizes the appearance of things rather than the spirit of things, we tend to stop our connection at a mundane level. We go to the park and look around at the beautiful flowers and trees, maybe sit on the grass, and then that's as far as it goes. We know that nature makes us feel better, taps into something deeply, and wakes us up from reality, but we don't consider why or how to bring ourselves to dwell in this knowing and go beyond the surface—how to dig into the roots.

True connection is a spiritual relationship with nature. It is an intentional bond that impacts your entire life. When tapped into on this deeper level, nature fills an empty space within you that cannot be reached in any other way, because the relationship you have with the Earth is a reflection of the relationship you have with the self.

The way to cultivate this deep connection is by practicing it! These daily practices will help you create an authentic and meaningful relationship with your plants.

DAILY PRACTICES FOR CONNECTION WITH PLANTS

Commit to connecting with nature

If this isn't something you are already used to doing, you'll need to plan ahead. First, set a clear intention: *I want to connect with and build my relationships with plant Magic.* Plant Witchery is a practice, and a practice should be part of your lifestyle. Make it a part of your life by literally adding it to your schedule and planner. Carve out some time spent alone with nature. This should be an intimate and personal time, so that you can build an intimate and personal relationship.

Record your experiences

As you deepen your relationships with plants, you may want to keep a journal for recording any experiences, dreams, or insights you receive from the plants, perhaps in the same journal in which you recorded your experiences with the seasons. You're inviting nature spirits into your own spirit—tell them, *"I'm ready to receive and surrender to what it is you need from me."* Pay special attention to how you feel, to energy shifts, the winds, and even storms during your journey in connecting with plants, and write them all down. It's important to record because you are just beginning to create a special language between you—as this language develops, it will come easier to you.

Visit nature more often

Go for a picnic, bike ride, run, or hike. Whatever it is that you like to do, go and do it in nature. Turn off your phone and or leave it behind, unplugging completely. An important step in deepening your relationship with the Earth is to be in her presence as often as possible. If for some reason you can't get out to nature, you can do the same with your houseplants. Sit with your plants, read by them, create by them, have breakfast with them. It doesn't matter what you do, as long as you spend time with them, genuinely and intentionally.

Let nature in

This is especially important for those living in the concrete jungle. Opening your windows and curtains, allowing sunlight and natural air to flow through your home, instantly connects you to the Earth. Your houseplants will love you for it. I especially love to open my windows and curtains to allow the moonlight in. And when it rains or storms, I'm the first to run and allow those winds to rush through my home and cleanse its energies, removing negativity and stagnant energy.

Water plants with intention

Water your plants, your flowers, even trees with love and healing energies. Water absorbs emotions, thoughts, and intentions, so before you water your plants, hold the water and calm yourself. Take a few deep breaths, and then pour all of your love into the water. Think about happy moments, loving moments, or just simply speak love—and then water your plants with it. They will drink up all of your loving and healing energies through the water, connecting you to them.

Observe the elements

Just as plants are unique, so are we. We are each drawn to different elements and places. Are you someone who feels their best when they are near water? Or do you feel best when you're in the mountains? Perhaps you belong in the forest. Try to visit all of nature and take in your surroundings. Notice how you feel in each place. What do you hear? What do you sense? What is your energy like? You can even do this in your backyard around your garden, indoor garden, and/or local park, river, or creek. Start to pay attention to the different elements and branches of nature. This will help you discover which elements speak to you.

Get to know the land

As an Indigenous Witch, I'm respectful of the land. Wherever I go, I want to learn about the place I am visiting. If I go for a hike, I want to know the history of the place—which native tribes may have called this land home, what flowers, plants, and trees grow there, what animals, birds, and reptiles live there. When we do this, we are getting to know the ancestors, nature spirits, and land protectors of a place, creating a meaningful and impactful connection to the land. When we give this kind of care and respect for the Earth, she will do the same for us.

Practice forest bathing

Known in Japan as *shinrin yoku,* forest bathing is a simple but incredibly transformative practice—all that's required is visiting nature and slowly passing through it. You can do this in a forest, or you can simply walk around your own backyard or garden. Obviously, simply being out in nature is healing and Magical in itself, but the difference here is that you are moving slowly and mindfully. This is not about going on a hike or a run or any other form of activity. Forest bathing is simply about being calm and relaxed and walking. It is said to alleviate stress and anxiety, and it is also a great way to be mindful of smells, sounds, and energies coming from nature, all important to Plant Witchery. Listen to the whispers in the wind, and pay attention to any pulls in a certain direction. Become one with nature, and dwell in the dance you create together with your energies.

Surround yourself with plants

If you don't own any plants, now is the time to start! Of course, plants can get expensive, but you can create a meaningful relationship with plants growing near you. So either through purchasing a plant, beginning to cultivate a stronger relationship with a plant you already own, or adopting a plant growing near you, choose a single plant to focus on for one month.

First, introduce yourself. Say hello, and name her! Let her know you are there for her, that you want to connect and will take good care of her. Softly touch her leaves, observe her closely, smell, sense, and get to know her particular energy. Research! I like to use a plant idetification app on my phone when I don't recognize a plant immediately. Learn the basic foundations for how to care for this plant, including the type of soil she needs. Know the anatomy of that plant, learning not only what she needs but *why*.

For one month, create an intimate relationship. Of course, this relationship will go on for longer but for this particular month you are giving her your undivided attention. You may think this is foolish or weird, but remember you are dealing with a living being who deserves this kind of welcome from you, who deserves to be seen as unique and important.

Care for your plants

Simply taking good care of your plants and paying attention to their needs will help you build a better relationship and understanding with nature. Make it a ritual to speak to the plant before you do anything. First say hello, then sit and observe the plant. Is the plant showing signs of dehydration? Overwatering? Does she need to be repotted? Does she look happy? Then turn your attention inward. Hold the plant, close your eyes, and ask her what she needs. Sit for a moment and allow her energy to speak to you. Pay attention to any literal vibrations you might feel (not just energy, although you'll likely feel that, too!). *Are you thirsty?* Listen, feel, and sense. *Do you like the lighting?* Listen, feel, and sense.

Look for messages from nature

Mother Earth is full of possibilities when it comes to messages; there is an entire catalog of wisdom and medicine awaiting your presence. Pay attention to these symbols, as they may show up in ways you don't expect. When a flower catches your eye or a bird starts to squawk around you or a branch gets stuck in your hair while you're walking in the woods—all of these experiences are nature's way of speaking to you. Please pay attention to what you see, what pulls you, what animals you come into contact with, and especially the feelings and energy these beings give you. For example, if you find yourself attracted to a willow tree, consider how this enchanting tree bends in various angles, and poses without snapping. Someone drawn to a willow may need to adjust to life and fully surrender to the change process, rather than fighting the inevitable. Or an encounter with a hawk can indicate a need for increased spiritual awareness and time to surrender, allowing your spirit to rise above.

Meditate

All it takes is 5 to 10 minutes of your time each day to develop a connection through meditation. Find a quiet place where you can sit or lie comfortably. Allow yourself to let go, surrender, and give in to the possibilities of enveloping yourself with the energies and love from the Earth. With time, you'll develop a stronger intuition, understanding, and connection with the green, growing life around you, which will improve your Magical practice.

This plant meditation is something you can do to connect, hear, feel, and sense what each plant wishes to share with you. I recommend doing this meditation with one plant at a time and, as described earlier, to give each plant at least 30 days of undivided attention to build a stronger and more meaningful relationship.

You can perform this meditation either daily or weekly. Each time that you do, you will experience a more profound and deeper connection with the plant, and you will become more patient and mindful in general. Most important, you will stay open and receptive to whatever the Earth has to share with you.

Moving forward, you will find a compendium of Magical plants. I will explain their medicinal and Magical properties, along with the unique wisdom they hold, all of which I have received and experienced myself with each individual plant. As you cultivate your own experiences with each plant, record your findings in your journal.

Plant Meditation

Start by choosing a plant or tree to connect with. If you have multiple plants in your home, or if you want to purchase a new plant and are not sure which to choose first, take a moment to quietly pass by the plants you're choosing among. Move slowly, holding your hands over each one without touching them physically, but instead touching the energy around them.

Wait patiently, and you may intuitively be directed toward which plant is calling to you. It's important to listen carefully, because each plant can guide you through a certain situation or time in your life, and it will let you know it's there to help. Perhaps you already feel deeply which plant you want to spend time with. Follow your intuition and pay attention to signs, as plants communicate with us in a variety of Magical ways.

WHAT YOU NEED

One plant

Sacred smoke (*I recommend mugwort, rue, rosemary, frankincense, myrrh, amber, or copal but you can use what you have available to you or what you feel comfortable with*)

WHAT TO DO

+ I recommend drinking tea 15 minutes before meditation to open up your third eye. Reishi, ginkgo, blue lotus, ashwagandha, lavender, or eyebright are all good choices.

+ Find a quiet place. You can listen to soft music if you like, as long as it does not distract your thoughts for this meditation.

+ Clear the energy and self with sacred smoke.

+ If you're using an incense stick, you can go ahead and light it and rest it in a holder or on a small plate. If you're using resin or herbs, the easiest method is to place a small amount on a charcoal disc, and then light it. Carry your smoke around your space, wafting it into all the corners of the room, and brushing the smoke over your head and shoulders. At this point, you can either extinguish your smoke or leave it burning for the length of your spell.

+ Place yourself in a comfortable seated position or lie down. The key here is comfort. Place the plant in front of you; if you're lying down, place it above your head. Keep your shoulders relaxed, soften your facial muscles, close your eyes, and breathe gently. Lay your hands wherever they feel most comfortable.

+ Take a moment to acknowledge your physical presence. Take a deep breath in through your nose, and exhale out from your mouth. Free your mind from negative thoughts and allow whatever comes to consciousness to just flow away.

In your mind, say, *I'm ready for your medicine and wisdom.* Repeat slowly and with intention three more times.

+ Release all expectations and allow your plant to work with you as she sees best for you. Remember that plants are all loving beings, so if you feel the need to cry, cry. If you feel the need to laugh, laugh. Allow yourself to journey through your emotional roots. They are efficient pathways in visiting all parts of the spirit.

+ Keep your focus on your breath. What colors do you see behind your closed eyes? What shapes? See your spirit in the vast darkness, illuminated with pure light. Focus on your spirit in this form, play with it, smile at it, embrace, and love it. See yourself in this sacred essence, a living being perfect in all ways. Protect your spirit, tell it how you will watch over it and cherish it. How you love and appreciate it. Promise yourself that you will no longer lock your spirit inside for no one to see, and swear to unchain yourself from a negative mind-set.

+ Take a long deep breath in and a long deep breath out. Focus on your breath and connect to its intimate warmth. Let go, surrender, be free. Stay in this space as long as you like while your plant guides you through your journey inward. Your plant will nudge you to remind you she's there with you and there's nothing to worry about. She will spread loving and calming energies all over your body, nourishing you at deeper levels.

+ When you are ready and have released discomfort and fear, focus on one thought. Think about one thing you love about yourself. Just one is enough. Hold on to that thought, then let it flow away, keeping the feeling it raised within you. Take that loving feeling and fill your entire being with it. Take your time—feed your body, mind, and spirit with your love.

+ When you're ready, picture your plant. In your mind, walk to her and touch her gently. Look at her with admiration, love, and gratitude. Fill her with that loving energy you just created for yourself. Watch her bloom, grow, and expand right before your eyes. The more you fill her with love, the more she blossoms. She is now filled with your essence—you are now her, and she is you. Healing, loving, and growing together.

+ Now ask her, *What message do you have for me today?* Listen with every part of your body, spirit, and mind.

+ When you are ready to end the meditation, even if you feel like you didn't receive a clear message, thank your plant. The message is there, and it will reveal itself when the time is right.

When a plant isn't growing or thriving, you don't try to fix the plant itself, instead you fix the environment around the plant. Like a plant, you do not need to be fixed, you simply need to create an environment that nurtures your growth.

PART 3

A COMPENDIUM OF PLANTS

This section offers a guide to the 200 plants that I have found most helpful in my practice, listed alphabetically by common name, followed by Latin name. Each description includes what I see as the plant's primary essential, medicinal, and Magical properties, as well as how she may choose to impart her wisdom. Many entries include a suggested spell, potion, or practice that will aid you in establishing or strengthening your relationships with these wonderful beings.

There are some instances throughout this compendium where I have listed the Latin genus of the plant without a specific species designation. When this is the case, the entire genus possesses the essential, medicinal, and Magical properties I mention, giving you a little more freedom in which plants you get to work with!

ABRE CAMINO
Koanophyllon villosum

ESSENTIAL PROPERTIES

unblocking, energy clearing

Abre camino translates from Spanish to "road opener." This shrub in the sunflower family is found growing in the tropical regions of Florida, Cuba, the Bahamas, and Jamaica. In the Afro-Cuban traditions of Santería, abre camino is considered one of the most powerful plants for working Magic.

MEDICINAL PROPERTIES

You can work with this plant for colds, constipation, headache, muscle cramps, anxiety, and sore throat, and she can be consumed as a tea. But she is primarily good for urinary issues—so if you have bladder stones or a UTI, abre camino will help you through.

MAGICAL PROPERTIES

Abre camino clears obstacles, providing an "open road" for you to pursue your goals and dreams. Whatever has been blocking you, whether it comes from inside you or from outside forces, she will remove that block, leaving your path clear so you can reach what you desire.

PLANT WISDOM

Abre camino is a powerful spiritual plant who likes to be worshipped. Dreaming of abre camino is rare, but when she appears to those who are devoted to her, she comes to show what has been blocking them. In my experience, when something blocks my path or blocks the flow in my home, abre camino warns me about it by creating a high-frequency ringing in my left ear.

Place dried abre camino over your workspace or over your front door to keep the energy in your home flowing freely; if need be, you can also hang her over your bed to remove blocks in your relationship. Growing fresh abre camino inside gives your home a more peaceful and loving atmosphere.

Abre Camino Opening Pathways Floor Wash

Floor washes are powerful ways to remove unwanted influences from your home. This floor cleaner will clear your home of negativity, absorb and banish any personal obstacles that have been preventing you from moving forward, and purify your home.

WHAT YOU NEED

　　4 tablespoons fresh or dried lemon balm

　　4 tablespoons fresh or dried pine

　　2 tablespoons fresh or dried rue

　　6 tablespoons fresh or dried abre camino *(If you're using whole plants, take a small to medium-size piece of abre camino and cut it into smaller portions.)*

WHAT TO DO

+ Bring 4 to 6 cups of water to a boil, add all the ingredients, and allow your plants to steep for 30 minutes.

+ As you're waiting, take this time to open your windows, light a white candle, play some music that will wake up your spirit, and burn some incense.

+ Sweep the entire house. Then, when your floor wash is ready, strain the steeped plants and use this to mop your floors. As you work, make sure to keep your mind free of negative thoughts, and pour your intentions into the act, using both the spirits of the plants and your own inner Magic.

ACACIA

Acacia

ESSENTIAL PROPERTIES

wisdom, protection, opening the door between realms

Acacia plants vary from small shrubs to trees. Most species are found in Australia, but others grow throughout the world. Acacia seeds and leaves are flavorful and edible, and some species produce gum. Acacia's use as a fragrance dates back centuries and the essence of *Acacia farnesia* is still used in the perfume industry today. In Egyptian mythology, the acacia tree is a symbol of everlasting life, and it is said that Moses's burning bush was an acacia.

MEDICINAL PROPERTIES

Acacia's medicinal uses are varied, as it has been explored by several cultures over thousands of years. This plant can be used for pain relief, and gum extracted from acacia can ease stomach pains. It also helps wounds heal, promotes oral health, and can soothe a cough or sore throat. However, overuse can cause hair loss or even stunt growth, so do not consume more than 15 to 30 grams of acacia per day, and, as always, check with your doctor.

MAGICAL PROPERTIES

Burning the dried flowers of acacia can bring you wisdom and insight, though I recommend cleansing your space first to clear any lingering negativity and put some protections in place. Acacia opens communications to the other side, and you don't want ill-willed spirits coming through. My favorite way of making sure acacia keeps me safe is to take a few of her thorns and place them in a glass of water, keeping it near me while I meditate or do any Magical workings with the plant. You can also simply sit and meditate beneath her branches and take in her beautiful aroma and healing energy.

PLANT WISDOM

The first time I dreamed of acacia I woke up in a puddle of sweat, barely able to catch my breath. I had just done meditative work with her, seeking to control my visions, and that same night I saw my higher self. She grabbed my hand and pulled me through what seemed a geometric portal, but my physical body could not handle it and went into shock. I woke up barely breathing. But with a few more months of working with acacia I was finally able to handle the portal spiritually and physically. Acacia is powerful but brutally honest. She will make you do the work before she allows you to connect to her fully, and I respect her for that. The dreams and visions she gives will be personal and unique to you, intended for your highest growth.

Acacia is best kept outdoors, as she is a highly energetic being. I suggest keeping her by the windowsill, perhaps out in the yard, on a balcony or porch, or in the corners inside your home. This way her energy won't interfere with the natural flow, and she will still be able to provide insight and protection.

ADDER'S-TONGUE

Ophioglossum vulgatum

ADDER'S-TONGUE

ESSENTIAL PROPERTIES

healing, love, creativity, shadow work

This unusual-looking fern is so named for its spore-producing stalk, which sticks out of the earth like a snake's tongue. She hides underground for much of the year, dining with the fungi, but sometime in June through August she pokes up in grasslands, meadows, hillsides, and sand dunes.

MEDICINAL PROPERTIES

The roots and leaves of the adder's-tongue can heal wounds, and also serve as an antiseptic. Like most ferns, adder's-tongue is edible, though you'll want to cook her first to denature the plant's thiaminase content, which can leach vitamin B_{12} from your body. Eating adder's-tongue will help heal bruises.

MAGICAL PROPERTIES

Adder's-tongue is known for healing, love, spiritual growth, and creative enhancement. If I needed to choose just one plant to do shadow work with, she would be it. She naturally dwells in the darkness, and knows her way around the shadows lurking within. She teaches that even that darkness has lessons to give, and gently brings this wisdom into your heart center. Adder's-tongue says, *Do not fear what you cannot see, for my spirit recognizes your spirit. Because we are together, you are never alone.*

You can also work closely with this plant for creativity, especially in writing! I kept her next to me every time I sat to write this book. I love to keep some by my computer, by my writing chair, and in my planner. Place some dried adder's-tongue by your workspace, wherever you do your creative work.

PLANT WISDOM

Adder's-tongue won't intrude upon your dreams unless you ask her to. If you are looking to heal old trauma, do shadow work, or work on strength or creativity, meditate with her before bed and ask her to visit your dreams. Make sure to tell her the reasons why, and try to work on only one issue at a time. When you go to sleep, make sure your room is extremely dark, no lights at all—so make sure to cover any tech lights as well. The darker it is, the better she will see.

Adder's-tongue is best left to grow in the wild, though she can do well in a garden. When she's dried, you can place her in your home just about anywhere you like, particularly in spaces where you like to sit and contemplate.

AFRICAN VIOLET
Saintpaulia ionantha

ESSENTIAL PROPERTIES

self-love, protection

African violets, also called *Saintpaulias,* are native to Tanzania and adjacent southeastern Kenya on the African continent. Their vibrant beautiful blooms instantly bring color and life into any space, but it should be noted that keeping them thriving in your home takes extra care and attention.

MEDICINAL PROPERTIES

African violet flowers and leaves can be eaten, and they have a ton of vitamins, particularly vitamins A and C. Her leaves may be made into a poultice for bruises and wound-healing, and you can also add her to a cough syrup.

MAGICAL PROPERTIES

African violets are the divas of the plant kingdom. They are all about being your best self. Work with African violet if you want to take yourself to the next level both physically and spiritually, for she teaches us that we are constantly reinventing ourselves, and that we should not be afraid to shed the things that no longer serve us—for by releasing them, we are allowing new growth and new abundance into our lives.

PLANT WISDOM

African violet knows how important self-love is, and she wants us to indulge ourselves. She reminds us to see the beauty in all things, and to enjoy every minute of our lives. She believes you deserve to treat yourself, and you should believe it, too. One form of self-care is setting boundaries—African violet wants you to live your best life, and to do that you have to make sure you are careful to keep toxic people or situations out of your life. Her message to you is, "You are sacred, and honoring yourself is the ultimate act of love." Invite her into your dreams to help you see your life clearly—she will show you the aspects of your life that need your attention.

AGRIMONY

Agrimonia

─────────────────────────── ϟ

ESSENTIAL PROPERTIES

protection, peace

Agrimony is a woody herb with tiny yellow flowers. She grows all over North America, Europe, and Asia, and gives off a lovely, soft scent, smelling like slightly spicy apricots. She also produces a nice yellow dye.

MEDICINAL PROPERTIES

Ancient Greeks worked with agrimony to treat eye disorders, as well as issues with the kidneys and liver. In England, she served as an aphrodisiac, and according to English folklore, if you placed a sprig of agrimony under someone's head, they would sleep until it was removed. That's probably not likely, but a tea or decoction brewed from agrimony can help you achieve a gentle rest. Nowadays, agrimony is most commonly used in skin care, as she is very effective at clearing up pimples and acne.

MAGICAL PROPERTIES

Agrimony is protective. You can place her under your pillow to ward off nightmares and intrusive spirits, or you can bury her at the boundaries of your home or garden to offer long-term protection from evil spirits, intruders, and unwanted quests. Agrimony is great to meditate with in times of hardship. Connecting to agrimony allows her to search deep within you for traces of negativity—she dispels what she finds, cleansing you from the inside out. She also helps accelerate spiritual healing, which is my personal favorite way of working with her. I do this by taking a leaf and crushing it, allowing her beautiful aroma to envelop my senses as I meditate. Whatever it is you seek, ask for her help, and remember to thank her after you've finished.

I burn dried agrimony at least once a week to move bad vibes out of my home. I also like to take some crushed dried agrimony and sprinkle a horizontal line in front of my front door when I have guests coming over. This protects me from any spirits that may have latched on to your visitors, leaving them outside.

PLANT WISDOM

When you dream of agrimony, you are receiving a message from her spirit that you are protected, which often imparts a sense of peace and calm. But if you dream of agrimony bleeding, she is trying to warn you that if you don't embody your truth, you will be consumed with ghosts feeding off your spirit. Many years ago, when I was running away from my true path and purpose, this dream came to me multiple times. If you want agrimony to speak to you in your dreams, drink a tea made with just a sprig of agrimony, a teaspoon of lemon balm, and a teaspoon of valerian root.

AGUE
Aletris farinosa

ESSENTIAL PROPERTIES
protection, psychic ability

Ague is also known as unicorn root, colicroot, crow corn, and white star grass. She grows all across North America, particularly in Illinois, and has narrow leaves and a long, tall stalk covered with tiny flower bells.

MEDICINAL PROPERTIES

It's important not to consume too much ague root, particularly raw and fresh, as it can cause abdominal disfunction, even vomiting. But taken in small

Ague Root House Protection Ritual

Ague can help you create a powerful protective shield for your home, both inside and out.

WHAT YOU NEED

2 pieces dried ague, divided

Salt

Chili powder

1 onion, halved

WHAT TO DO

+ Grind up 1 of the pieces of ague root, either with a knife or using a mortar and pestle.

+ Sprinkle the ground-up ague around the outside of your home, keeping your intentions for protection steady as you work. If you live in an apartment, you can sprinkle a cross, star, or circle of ague at your front door—whichever symbol feels best to you.

+ Place the second piece of ague in a large glass of cold water.

+ Add a pinch of salt, a pinch of chili powder, and ½ of the onion.

+ Let the glass sit on a high shelf or on top of your refrigerator for 3 days, so that it can absorb any negativity in your home.

+ After the third day, throw the ague and onion in the trash and dump the water in the toilet. Take the trash out immediately—don't let it sit in your home.

doses, ague can move digestion along and ease flatulence, though she has an extremely bitter flavor. She has also been known to induce calm, and can combat anorexia, anxiety, and depression. A poultice made with ague leaves can ease an aching back.

MAGICAL PROPERTIES

Plant Witches with particular gifts of mediumship and psychic abilities are often drawn to ague. As a seer, I work with ague almost weekly, and having her by my side helps me navigate through my visions while at the same time protecting me while I'm at my most vulnerable. During your Magical workings, drinking a tea steeped with dried ague can induce visions (though again, be wary—fresh ague root acts as a narcotic). Ague root can also be carried as a protective talisman, placed in your circle or altar for protection while you are casting or doing Magical workings. It can also be ground into a paste and used to remove a hex.

PLANT WISDOM

Dreams of ague are very telling. If you eat ague in a dream, it means someone has cursed you, or that you have blocks to overcome in your life. If you are served ague in a dream, it is a warning to cleanse and protect yourself from coming evil, usually from jealousy. If you are planting ague in your dream, she is calling you to work with her.

Ague thrives best outdoors, where she can be wild and free. You can harvest the pieces you need, though always ask permission first and make sure to thank her. Respect these pieces—they hold her spirit. When you bring them inside she will flow through your home, protecting every nook and cranny.

AIR PLANTS
Tillandsia

AIR PLANTS

ESSENTIAL PROPERTIES

purification, balance, freedom from cares

So-called air plants are a lovely group of species that can thrive while literally hanging in midair. These small, silvery, perennially flowering plants are coated with trichomes, a special kind of cell that allows them to absorb moisture directly from the air, rather than through roots. They survive by clinging to whatever is handy—branches of trees, telephone poles, rocks, and more.

MEDICINAL PROPERTIES

This plant has no known medicinal properties.

MAGICAL PROPERTIES

These carefree plants can inspire the same lightness of spirit in you. They thrive on uncertainty, for they do not necessarily have a way of finding the moisture they need—and yet, they are also self-reliant and able to find happiness and ease whatever their circumstances. When mercury is in retrograde, I bust out all of my air plants and hang them all over my home. They bring in a beautiful, carefree flow that feels almost divinely peaceful. I also place them near me in my workspace whenever I am having trouble getting out of my own head, am feeling stuck, blocked from my own stress, or any kind of anxiety— they help elevate my child's mind and open up my imagination, allowing me to relax, release tension, and not worry about the small stuff.

PLANT WISDOM

Want to fly in your dreams? Place air plants above the head of your bed, and before you fall asleep ask them to take you away into the skies. I would advise that you do this during a Full Moon and avoid the New Moon, because when in flight during a New Moon, the spirit likes to travel into the unknown. Flying during a Full Moon is best for beginners who are just starting to connect to this plant and/or flying in dreams, as the experience will be much more peaceful and filled with joy.

Air plants can live everywhere and anywhere! But I love to keep them in my children's rooms to help them stay connected to their pure hearts. Air plants will help them unwind from a long day at school, and amplify their imaginations.

ALFALFA
Medicago sativa

ESSENTIAL PROPERTIES

healing, abundance, manifesting, luck

Also known as lucerne, alfalfa is commonly used for grazing and animal feed. She is technically a legume, with a homey, aromatic scent. Alfalfa plays a critical role in ecology—she is a birthing place to several varieties of insects, and is often grown near more delicate plants, like cotton, that can't handle these insects.

MEDICINAL PROPERTIES

Alfalfa can combat high cholesterol, as she prevents the gut from absorbing cholesterol. She is also helpful with kidney conditions, asthma, rheumatoid and osteoarthritis, as well as diabetes. She is often taken as a supplement because she contains high levels of vitamins A, C, E, and K, as well as potassium, calcium, phosphorous, and iron—she's basically a multivitamin.

MAGICAL PROPERTIES

Being able to cultivate enough food is a sign of wealth. If you consider the lives of our ancestors, imagine what alfalfa meant to them—she signified the ability to raise cattle, enough to feed their families and communities. With this association in mind, alfalfa is often incorporated into prosperity spells, to invite and protect wealth. Keeping a jar of dried alfalfa in your kitchen will ensure your family always has enough to eat, and keeping alfalfa in your pocket can bring you good luck.

Alfalfa is also a powerhouse in manifesting your desires and dreams. When creating a vision board, attach some dried alfalfa onto the board. Or if you are someone who likes to create lists, attach her to your list. Alfalfa will amplify your intentions of manifesting. On a Full Moon, burn some of the dried leaves and take the ashes to a river. Let the ashes flow into the river, and as you let them go, ask that they take all your worries away, releasing you from whatever it is you want to release. You can also spread the ashes on the Earth to call in whatever you need—like abundance, for example.

PLANT WISDOM

Alfalfa is a great companion in meditation and in the dreamworld. If you are not able to control your dreams, opt to meditate with this plant. Sit and envision what you want to manifest, whether it is good health, luck with a test or a trial or life in general. Doing vision work with this plant calls in the energies to manifest whatever it is you are wanting, turning your dreams into reality.

Alfalfa is happiest resting near a window in your home. The breeze of an open window will carry her energies up high, so they can return with protection, love, and peace.

ALLSPICE
Pimenta dioica

ESSENTIAL PROPERTIES
success, courage, luck, abundance

Named for her unusual flavor that somehow combines pepper, cloves, cinnamon, and nutmeg, allspice is used all over the world including in Jamaica (where it is known as pimenta), the Middle East, Germany, and Portugal. Allspice is the dried peppercorn-like berry of the allspice tree, which is an evergreen shrub, though she can grow to be quite tall.

MEDICINAL PROPERTIES

Allspice contains eugenol, a chemical that kills germs and is an analgesic. Historically, allspice oil has been rubbed on the gums to relieve toothaches. She also serves as an effective antioxidant, antiviral, antifungal, and

Allspice Bringing in Abundance Foot Soak

Washing with this allspice soak will remove any blocks from your path, allowing abundance to come forth.

WHAT YOU NEED

½ cup whole allspice

5 to 6 bay leaves

WHAT TO DO

+ Bring 6 to 7 cups of water to a boil.

+ Add the allspice and bay leaves, reduce the heat, and let them simmer for 10 minutes.

+ Let the water cool slightly, then strain it into a bowl large enough to rest your feet in.

+ Allow your feet to soak in this for 5 minutes, then take a washcloth and rub your ankles, calves, and feet with the scented water.

anti-inflammatory. In Central America and the Caribbean, she is used to ease menstrual cramps and calm sore muscles and joints.

MAGICAL PROPERTIES

Allspice invites wealth and success. She is associated with the element of fire, that burning force of creativity and destruction, so work with her should be done with care. She can boost your courage and make you feel more powerful.

You may also keep allspice in your wallet to bring in money, and place it on your altar next to or in a candle to manifest wealth and abundance. I keep my allspice plant in my kitchen, where she amplifies the energies in the space. While I cook, her energies combine with the food, awakening abundance in my home.

When you dream of eating anything containing allspice, this is a warning to pay attention to your finances. Watch what you are spending on nonsense and focus instead on saving. When allspice shows up in dreams, she's reflecting your worries on what you may lack and brings clarity, helping you to be grateful for what you already have.

ALOCASIA

Alocasia

ESSENTIAL PROPERTIES

strength, courage, balance

This lovely, broad-leaved plant prefers indirect sunlight and can grow incredibly fast. In the summertime, alocasia can produce a new leaf once a week, and each leaf will be larger than the previous one.

MEDICINAL PROPERTIES

While alocasias make wonderful houseplants, they are very toxic, as they contain insoluble oxalate crystals (the same crystals that form kidney stones) which, if ingested raw or undercooked, can cause the mouth and throat to swell up and feel like tiny knives are poking you.

Some alocasia species are poisonous, but similar plants serve as a food source and have medicinal purposes—so I don't recommend eating alocasia or dabbling with it in this way unless you have deep knowledge of this plant.

MAGICAL PROPERTIES

Alocasia is a vision of beauty and enchantment. Her energy is strong yet subtle. She is happiest in an open space, where there isn't a lot of clutter. Balance is her essence, and she prefers a space that holds the same. I keep mine near a big window, with a water feature placed near her to add balance to her space. A lovely flow of water makes her happy and amplifies her energies.

PLANT WISDOM

For a sizable plant, alocasia has an airy, majestic look and feel. She teaches us to embody balance and to stand in our power. With her spirit, anything is possible. She asks that you have courage in life, especially during hard times, helping you to understand that even in the hard, softness can be found. When you want to bring in new opportunities, sit and speak with her, meditate with her, and keep her close when you're creating. She helps you seize opportunities as they come, and gives your heart the strength it needs to go after them.

Dreaming of this beauty can signify that there is something off balance in your health or life. I remember once when she grew and grew in my dream. I climbed her to reach the very top and when I looked down, I saw my life below me, like a blueprint. It was darker in some areas and faint in others. I stayed up there with her for as long as I could, and examined where I needed to pay more attention in my life.

ALOE VERA
Aloe vera

ESSENTIAL PROPERTIES

protection

This gentle and loving succulent has long pointy leaves with tiny spikes growing from the edges. She is both ornamental and medicinal, and grows easily and happily with relatively little care (though of course you should always shower your aloe with love).

MEDICINAL PROPERTIES

The soothing effects of aloe vera are widely known. While the gel is easy enough to find at a drugstore, simply asking your plant for permission to take a leaf and rubbing the sap onto your skin allows you to connect more directly with her, receiving her healing without any intermediaries. Aloe vera not only soothes burns and accelerates healing, she is also good for the skin in general, helping to seal in moisture. Aloe vera is also edible, and contains antioxidants and antibacterial properties; she can help treat canker sores or other mouth ulcers.

MAGICAL PROPERTIES

Aloe vera is treasured for her protective nature. Planting aloe vera around the entrance to your home or hanging some dried aloe vera above your door can help keep your household safe. Aloe vera not only protects from outside forces, but also from those of us who are accident-prone. She really wants to help out. I place dried aloe vera in the pockets of my children's clothes before sending them to school, for protection and to prevent injuries. If you have kids—especially boys, like I do!—then you know they can get hurt easily.

I work often with spirits and ancestors, and the practice in my Indigenous culture is to rub aloe vera on the throat space to help with communication with spirits, and on the third eye to help awaken sight during meditation. If you feel you have a curse placed on you, take a stem of aloe vera, lick it, and then burn it, asking it to burn away any evil that may have been placed on you.

PLANT WISDOM

In dreams, aloe vera is very mothering, kind of like a spiritual life coach. She wants to see you grow just as she does, reminding you that there is a special path for you—you are here *on* purpose *for* a purpose. Meditate with her when you need inspiration and empowerment, especially if you are struggling with the meaning of life. Aloe vera grows happily in windows, doorways, and in the center of rooms—these are places where she can do her work and be happy.

ALTAMISA

Ambrosia peruviana

ESSENTIAL PROPERTIES

purification, opening the door between realms

Altamisa is a variety of ragweed found in South America, and is quite similar to mugwort. She grows easily in relatively moist environments, and her usual herbal size can expand to a bush in wetter, more swampy locations. She has a strong, almost bitter scent, and a very bitter flavor.

MEDICINAL PROPERTIES

Altamisa is an anti-inflammatory, and her bitter flavor can stimulate the digestive system. She can help regulate menstruation, reduce swelling in the legs, and aid respiratory issues like asthma. She also has a calming effect, and can help relieve stress and anxiety.

MAGICAL PROPERTIES

The Incas embalmed their dead with altamisa to ensure a smooth transition to their next existence. Burning altamisa can purify your altar or sacred space, and can enhance your ability to transport your consciousness during meditation. Sprinkling altamisa into a ritual bath is sacred to the spirit of creation, water, and motherhood.

Altamisa prefers to be in a sacred space, such as your altar, meditation space, or any room that is quiet and has bright light. She brings an energy flow of openness. Wherever she is, you can feel her vibrating with positive energy and purity.

PLANT WISDOM

When working with altamisa, you are to be very respectful. Always ask permission to even touch her and/or speak to her. "Altamisa, may we have a chat please?" Close your eyes and feel for subtle energy—if you feel energy in your

Altamisa Cleansing Dream Bath

This bath will cleanse your body of negative energy and ill will, opening you to visions and connections to other realms.

WHAT YOU NEED

1 tablespoon dried altamisa

1 tablespoon dried mugwort

1 tablespoon dried rue

1 tablespoon dried lemon balm

1 tablespoon dried rose petals

White candle

WHAT TO DO

+ Bring a pot of water to a boil.

+ Add all the ingredients except the candle and allow them to simmer for 10 to 15 minutes.

+ Strain the liquid, let it cool a bit, then add it to your bathwater.

+ Dim your lights or turn them off entirely and light your candle. Soak in your bath for a minimum of 15 minutes.

throat that indicates she is saying *yes,* you may absolutely converse with her. But if you feel that energy anywhere else in your body, especially the stomach, that means she is saying *not right now.* I've seen people work with her without asking permission and their intentions often backfire or simply don't work at all. Altamisa isn't a diva, but she's definitely goddess-like.

Taking a bath with altamisa will open your mind. If you bathe with her before bedtime, she will open portals and help you travel in your dreams, even connecting you with your ancestors and aiding you to communicate with spirit. She doesn't personally appear in your dreams, but her energy does—though this takes practice working with her.

ALTHAEA
Althaea officinalis

ESSENTIAL PROPERTIES

healing, psychic ability

Also known as marshmallow, althaea's blossoms are light, fluffy, and white—hence the name of that puffy thing we put in s'mores. In fact, marshmallows used to be made with eggs, sugar, and the roots of the althaea. Althaea grows in marshes or along the banks of rivers, and prefers moist, sandy soil.

MEDICINAL PROPERTIES

Althaea was considered one of the most important healing herbs in ancient Greece—dubbed "the healer." The root is nutritious and contains a great deal of fiber, making it good for digestive issues. Althaea can soothe a cough or cold, help a sore throat, and calm skin irritations. Today she is a common ingredient in cosmetic treatments.

MAGICAL PROPERTIES

Althaea is a welcoming plant—she attracts benevolent spirits to the home. You can simply place her on your altar, asking her to allow spirits with good intentions into your space for guidance. Make sure to keep a glass of water next to her, as this helps keep the spirits there, not wandering off into the rest of your home. It is also important to burn dried althaea with a resin such as copal, myrrh, or frankincense—this will give you protection when working with these spirits, while at the same time increasing your psychic abilities. When I go to cleanse someone's home or space, I place some dried althaea in my hair, which I always wear up in a bun when I do work. Carry her with you for protection.

When althaea shows up in a dream, chances are you will either be watching her burn or floating in water. These are the only two examples I've gathered in my research with Indigenous peoples and interviews with other plant whisperers. She shows up alongside fire to warn of danger, evil, or bad intentions lurking in your home. When she appears with water, she is healing you. She has attached herself to your spirit, and wants to work with you in healing your old traumas.

Plant althaea at the corners of your home or property for protection and to keep out evil. She also invites the good spirits to help protect the home. Her comforting presence can make your home a happier, more peaceful place.

ANGELICA
Angelica

ANGELICA

ESSENTIAL PROPERTIES
protection, healing, energy clearing

Angelica has a bitter and earthy flavor, and is often used to flavor alcohol, especially gin and the liqueur Chartreuse. Angelica is so-named because she was used to protect against the plague, and is associated with the archangel Michael. The story is that she came into bloom around Michael's feast day, and that he appeared in a vision to explain how she protects against evil. Her flowers spread wide, like a starburst.

MEDICINAL PROPERTIES

Angelica has so many healing properties, but some caution should be used. Pregnant women should avoid her, as she can cause some pelvic tightening which may lead to miscarriage. She also contains Furocoumarins, which can make the skin sensitive to ultraviolet light. But if you're wise and careful, angelica can help treat a cold or other respiratory ailments, speed the healing of wounds, and ease a headache or heartburn.

MAGICAL PROPERTIES

Angelica protects everyone, but especially women. You can grind up her roots into a tonic, or carry her dried root as a protective amulet. Her leaves, if dried and burned, will help dispel negative energies, and if you bathe in water sprinkled with angelica it will remove any harm anyone has wished upon you. I personally have loved working with angels since the day I first saw them, so to me this plant is indeed divinely connected to the angelic realm and the fairy realm. Holding dried angelica in your hands while praying amplifies your intentions, getting your message across loud and clear.

PLANT WISDOM

It is said that when you dream of angelica, you are dreaming of angels. She is protective in dreams; if you are having a nightmare, imagine her and she will come and whisk you away, bringing you to a beautiful dream instead.

Angelica is great at getting rid of negative thoughts, so I place her next to all mirrors—and next to my bed—whenever I feel especially uncomfortable with my naked body. She exudes peace and love, and should be placed anywhere the family gathers so that she can dispel any negativity and help to avoid arguments.

ANGEL WINGS
Caladium

ESSENTIAL PROPERTIES

luck, abundance, love

This lovely plant's sweet, pink- and white-veined leaves do seem as though they could soar in the skies. Angel wings' leaves are light, translucent, and arrow-shaped. They come in a variety of colors, including white, pink, red, and green. Angel wings is native to South and Central America, and enjoys a moist climate, though that's something you can easily re-create in your home.

MEDICINAL PROPERTIES

This plant has no known medicinal properties.

MAGICAL PROPERTIES

Angel wings is known as a "magical charm plant." Indigenous peoples in South and Central America work with her to ensure luck and success in a variety of areas, from hunting and fishing to love and safety. Work with her to bring abundance and luck into your life—but you must be clear on what it is you want. This isn't random good luck; you have to set a clear intention and do the work to prove to angel wings that you do truly want it. She will grant you all the luck and abundance you could need.

If you have been in a long-term relationship that has begun to lose its fire, keep angel wings in your bedroom. And if you've been having trouble communicating in this relationship, keep her in the living room or at the dinner table, so she can bring clarity to your heart and help you pay attention to what is truly important to you. Given that sense of clarity though, you may find you want to break up. In that case, snip one of angel wings' leaves and let it sit out for seven days. On the seventh day, burn it while speaking your intentions for ending the relationship. You will find the conversation much easier than it might otherwise have been.

Angel wings' appearance alone can remind us of the Magic that surrounds us. She looks like she belongs in an enchanting forest fairy tale where she lights the path to a Witchy cottage. She will sprinkle her wisdom into your spirit, clearing the way for you to reach your goals and desires. If she visits you in a dream, you will likely soon experience a new relationship or another form of happiness.

APPLE
Malus domestica

ESSENTIAL PROPERTIES

spiritual development, opening the door between realms, manifesting, abundance

There are thousands of cultivated apples, not surprising as this fruit has been around for thousands of years. Apple's life-giving properties made her an important part of the rituals and practices of a variety of cultures. In Scandinavia and in Greece, it was believed that eating sacred apples would give eternal life—though of course that story was perverted in the fairy tale of *Snow White*. Speaking of "the fairest," it is said that the Trojan War began not with Paris's kidnapping of Helen, but when the goddess Eris threw an apple into a crowd of goddesses, saying that it was for the most beautiful.

MEDICINAL PROPERTIES

"An apple a day keeps the doctor away"—this expression doesn't come from nowhere! Apples are high in fiber and vitamins, and raw apple cider vinegar is one of the most useful and healing condiments in your kitchen cupboard. Placing crushed apple leaves on a wound can prevent infection.

Apple Manifestation Spell

Harness the abundant fertility of apple by placing your dreams in her caring hands.

WHAT YOU NEED

1 apple

1 bay leaf

1 teaspoon cinnamon

1 teaspoon dried basil

1 clove

1 tablespoon honey or olive oil

1 yellow candle *(yellow is for manifesting)*

WHAT TO DO

+ Cut a hole in the apple and scoop out as much flesh as you can.

+ Mix together the bay leaf, cinnamon, basil, clove, and honey, and, if possible, grind them with a mortar and pestle.

+ Take a small piece of paper and write down what you wish to manifest.

+ Place the paper inside the apple, spoon in your mixture, and place the filled apple on your altar.

+ Dress your yellow candle with the remaining mixture. Light it while speaking your desire.

+ Remove the apple once it begins to rot, as you don't want that energy on your altar.

MAGICAL PROPERTIES

Work with apple for spiritual development, though you should be specific, letting her know what it is you want to focus on. This can be as simple as eating an apple before doing a manifesting spell or when trying to connect to your ancestors. You can also peel an apple and rub the flesh on your forehead to wake the third eye, allowing your intuition to develop. Dreaming of apple is a very personal experience, so pay attention to any signs, numbers, colors, animals, or anything else in the dream that may have meaning to you.

Apples are sacred to many cultures and practices and are an important symbol in some religions. The apple is filled with abundant energies, making her a perfect partner in abundance work as well as spells of fertility and love. She is also great for working with your ancestors, as she serves as an offering.

Areca Palm
Areca

ESSENTIAL PROPERTIES
clarity, productivity, success

The areca palm is a wonderful plant for both indoors and outdoors, as she grows quickly, with gently bushing leaves growing in clumps. She does require a little extra care—like most palms, she needs a lot of light, and she also needs some feeding. She can turn brown and get spots if she doesn't receive enough magnesium and iron.

MEDICINAL PROPERTIES

But areca is worth the trouble (as are all plants!) because of the service she provides you in exchange. All plants purify the air by removing carbon dioxide and releasing oxygen, and areca also releases negatively charged ions, which attach themselves to mold, dust spores, bacteria, and allergens, effectively removing them from the air. In addition, areca absorbs harmful gases that can leach into the air, improving your nervous system and mood.

MAGICAL PROPERTIES

Areca is wonderful to work with to improve your career and business. I advise lots of business owners and corporate officers to keep a few of these Magical beings around, to help keep everyone from procrastinating and feeling brain dead. She is the plant that will help you stay on track and get your work done. Writing a book? Have a deal on a project coming through? Need to get to your to-do list? Meditate with her early in the morning and ask her to bring out her qualities within you. And then watch how your day flourishes! Working with areca is like drinking an energy drink for the mind and soul.

PLANT WISDOM

I love to dream with areca palm. I often do so when I need her to help me untangle my thoughts so I can clearly focus on a project or creation. Writers block? Creative funk? She is the one to ask to help navigate your way through these blocks in your dreams.

Areca is best kept in your office or next to your workspace, keeping you focused and creative. You can also keep her in your kitchen, where she'll stop you from ordering in or cooking boring meals. A total plus!

ARROWHEAD
Sagittaria latifolia

ESSENTIAL PROPERTIES

healing, strength, courage, protection

This aquatic tuber has leaves that look like—you guessed it—large arrowheads. These leaves are very long and thin, clumping up above the water, while the tuber below remains immersed. Like many plants, arrowhead contains insoluble calcium oxalate crystals, which can cause extreme pain if eaten raw—so just make sure your pets don't go snacking on it. If arrowhead is cooked properly, the crystals dissolve.

MEDICINAL PROPERTIES

Many Native American tribes have worked with arrowhead to relieve headaches. A poultice made from the roots can treat wounds and sores, while a tea made with dried roots can calm digestion. The leaves can treat skin conditions. Arrowhead tubers are highly nutritional and contain a great deal of phosphorous, which is needed for bone growth.

MAGICAL PROPERTIES

Arrowhead works best in a vision journey, a meditative state that allows you to travel to different realms and spaces. Traveling into the inner universe is her expertise. Allow her to take you into the spaces left untouched, the spaces rotting within you. She will find them, and she will guide you in the journey to mending them.

Arrowhead is best kept in your bedroom to help you heal during the night. If your children are suffering from bullying or any other troubles, she can protect their hearts and heal their thoughts. I also keep a few in my meditation space, for healing work.

PLANT WISDOM

Arrowhead's superpowers are in healing trauma—and giving you the strength, courage, and protection you need to do this healing work. Is healing Magic? Of course it is. Healing is mending, shifting one energy to another, and when we heal ourselves, we amplify our inner power, opening space for the things we desire most of all. This is why many Indigenous peoples believe that healing must come before anything else. Healing leaves you with your truest self, your most powerful self.

Set arrowhead next to you as you write in your journal, meditate with her, and even bring her to the bathroom when you take a self-love bath. She will gently guide you, while at the same time striking viciously at the ghosts that live within you.

Ashwagandha
Withania somnifera

ASHWAGANDHA

ESSENTIAL PROPERTIES

healing, strength, amplification

Also known as winter cherry or Indian ginseng, *ashwagandha*'s name translates literally to "smell of horse," and her root does indeed smell very equine. This small shrub in the nightshade family has been a part of Ayurvedic medicine for centuries.

MEDICINAL PROPERTIES

Ashwagandha can do just about anything. As she is an adaptogen, she can help your body cope with daily stress, adjusting her healing properties to whatever it is you need. She can also treat arthritis, anxiety, depression, fibromyalgia, insomnia, menstrual concerns, liver disease, and asthma. She can improve mental function and can work as an aphrodisiac. The root is generally taken internally, but may also be made into a salve and used externally to treat wounds and skin conditions.

MAGICAL PROPERTIES

Everyone should learn how to work with ashwagandha, for she is as powerful spiritually as she is medicinally. Her presence in your life awakens a life force energy, constantly feeding you strength and healing. If you are able, purchase a plant and care for her; you can also work with her dried roots.

Ashwagandha is particularly helpful when you are in need of grounding. We all need to feel grounded from time to time, especially after doing spell-work. Hold ashwagandha in your hand while meditating or while sipping her tea, and you will instantly feel rooted to the Earth. You can also pour her tea into your bath to cleanse your auric field. As you soak, her healing will permeate through your entire being. Placing her roots on your altar or incorporating them into your spellwork will add longevity to your Magical workings—add ashwagandha to practically any spell, and she will amplify its energies, making it last longer.

PLANT WISDOM

Ashwagandha is such a sacred plant. Her wisdom lives in the spirit of connectivity: She can help you become aligned with both your higher self and the Earth beneath your feet. She can also help you navigate whatever hardships come your way, whispering to you, offering you guidance on your next steps. She teaches how to find the strength you need within yourself, and the knowledge that you can break through even the most troubling of times. Invite her into your dreams by sipping her tea before going to bed. Ask her to join you, and she will fill you with deep healing as you sleep.

AVOCADO
Persea americana

ESSENTIAL PROPERTIES
self-love, love

Also known as alligator pear or butter fruit, the avocado was treasured long before it became ubiquitous on toast as a staple food in Mexico and the Caribbean. There is evidence that it was eaten by our ancestors around 10,000 years ago. The word *avocado* is derived from a Nahuatl word, *huacatl*, which means "testicle." Botanically speaking, her fruit is actually a very large berry with a very large seed. Its smooth, creamy texture and flavor varies from species to species, but is pretty much universally delicious. Avocados are easily grown from seed; you can readily have your own little avocado tree in your home!

MEDICINAL PROPERTIES

Avocados are extremely rich in nutrients, containing healthy fats along with fiber, vitamins C, E, K, B$_6$, and more. Avocados contain lutein and zeaxanthin, which improve eyesight, protecting you from damage from ultraviolet light. They can also improve digestion, lower your risk of depression, treat osteoporosis, and generally detoxify your system.

MAGICAL PROPERTIES

Avocado has a gentle, compassionate, and nurturing spirit. She asks us to be mindful of how we treat ourselves, what we do to our physical and spiritual bodies. "Am I eating as healthfully as I can?" "Am I taking good care of my body, mind, spirit?" She teaches us that the mundane world is just a small part of what makes us who we are, and that we can only embody our true selves when we pay attention and take good care of all of our parts.

Placing a pit of an avocado under your bed will help you find your sexuality, passion, and inner fire. Placing a pair of avocados on each side of the bed will increase the love in a relationship. Use avocado oil in your candle Magic in spells for love and self-love, and also for balance, as balance is key when navigating the space between lust and love.

PLANT WISDOM

When you work with avocado, know that she may share her wisdom in a variety of ways. Some people describe her as a trickster, but in my experience, she's not trying to be tricky, she's simply doing whatever is necessary to get you to open up, to bring your awareness to new levels, and get your spirit flowing. She navigates as she sees fit, and this is to your benefit.

If you dream of avocado, she's making you aware of any poisons you may be feeding your mind, body, or spirit. Allow her to guide you in this dream and take note of both what you feel and where in your body you feel it, so that when you wake up you can apply healing and extra care to those areas.

Avocado Self-Love Tea

This gentle tea will help you feel love for yourself, love that is always there even if it is sometimes hard to access.

WHAT YOU NEED

   1 ripe avocado

   4 cups water

   1 tablespoon honey

   1 tablespoon dried chamomile

   1 teaspoon pepper *(optional)*

   1 teaspoon dried rose *(optional)*

WHAT TO DO

+ Remove the seed from the avocado.

+ Bring the water to a boil, and add the seed. Reduce the heat and let the seed simmer for 5 minutes.

+ By that time, the seed should have softened. Remove it carefully and cut it into small pieces.

+ Return the seed pieces to the pot of water, letting them steep for 10 minutes.

+ Strain your tea, adding honey for more love, and chamomile for a soothing effect on the heart. You can also add pepper if you want to ignite passion, and rose if you seek to heal a loving relationship.

BANANA
Musa

ESSENTIAL PROPERTIES

creativity, abundance

The banana tree is technically a very large herb. There are so many varieties, from the starchy plantain to the sweet apple banana. Bananas actually emit very low levels of radioactivity due to their high concentration of potassium—but they aren't harmful. In fact, they're extremely beneficial! You can eat all parts of the banana, not just the fruit. The leaves and even the peels can be delicious, if prepared properly. Banana leaves are also useful as a kind of ready-made take-out container, or as a wrap for steaming or grilling fish or other foods.

MAGICAL PROPERTIES

Banana's high levels of potassium can help reduce muscle cramps, moderate blood sugar levels, and even offset depression.

MAGICAL PROPERTIES

The best way to work with banana is to cook with her and eat her, Kitchen Witch-style. Add bananas to your food, and set your intentions as you cook. You can also write your desires on a banana peel and then cut it into small pieces to use in your Magical workings—she will add so much abundant energy. You may wish to work with banana for creativity spells as well, and again simply setting those intentions while cooking or eating banana can invoke her Magic.

PLANT WISDOM

Bananas play a role in the spiritual practices of many cultures around the world. Bananas carry a message of living your best life, of going after what you want and what brings you joy. If you are someone who isn't happy in your life,

Banana Creativity Potion

What is it that you want to create in your life? Banana's potent energies will help you manifest your desires and give you the energy you need to do the work to make your dreams come true.

WHAT YOU NEED

1 yellow banana

1 teaspoon cinnamon

1 teaspoon dried damiana

1 teaspoon red clover, fresh or dried

1 sprig of fresh rosemary

3 cups water

Red string or ribbon

WHAT TO DO

+ Peel the banana and set the fruit aside. Take a moment to write your intentions for fertility on the outside of the peel.

+ Mash the banana with the remaining ingredients (except the string), then spread the mixture on the inside of the peel.

+ Roll up the filled peel, tying the string or ribbon around it to hold it together.

+ Place your banana in a bowl and leave it by a window so that it can receive 3 days of sunshine and 3 nights of darkness.

+ On the fourth day, take it outside and bury it in the earth.

work, or relationships, working with banana can help you realize that there is more for you, that you deserve bigger and better things. We often daydream about a better life—banana urges us to take hold of that desire and go after it.

Dreams of banana can indicate health issues around fertility, for either men or women. Work with her to find the underlying causes.

BASIL

Ocimum basilicum

ESSENTIAL PROPERTIES

protection, abundance, self-love, love

This sweet, highly flavorful herb is used in cuisines all over the world. The word *basil* is derived from *basileus* ("king" in ancient Greek). Fittingly, it is thought that basil was once an ingredient in perfumes intended for royalty. There are also stories that say basil was used as an antidote for basilisk poison.

MEDICINAL PROPERTIES

Basil promotes blood circulation, and has also been taken to aid in lactation. Basil essential oil can help clear up acne, and can give you an energy boost as well. And, to lend credence to the basilisk theory, basil can treat snake bites. She's also helpful in lowering blood pressure and, best of all, she repels insects!

MAGICAL PROPERTIES

Gifting a basil plant to a newly married couple is a wonderful idea, as basil encourages happy, easy love—a love that is free from squabbles. It makes a good housewarming present, or to congratulate someone who just got a new job, as basil also invites wealth and prosperity. Basil is sometimes referred to as "the Witch's herb," perhaps because ancient Greeks are said to have used basil to detect Witches. They would burn the herb while speaking the name of the suspected Witch, and if basil "spoke" (i.e., crackled with the flame), then the Witch was confirmed.

Basil is a lovely plant to work with for self-love. Add some basil to your bath to clear negativity and calm your spirit. Basil can also be worked with in powerful candle Magic to bring in wealth and money. Simply dress a green candle with basil and set your intentions. Keeping basil in the corners of the home is a powerful way to keep evil out. If you can't place her in corners due to low light, sprinkle dried basil in the corners of your home instead. Anywhere you place your basil, she will exude a beautiful, loving energy.

PLANT WISDOM

Basil's scent is what most often shows up in a dream. If you smell basil, abundance is on its way. If you happen to see basil herself, expect a love to come forth, or a love you already have to amplify and ignite with new passion.

BAY LAUREL
Laurus nobilis

ESSENTIAL PROPERTIES
abundance, manifesting, creativity, wisdom

Not to be confused with other bays or laurels, many of which are poisonous, the bay laurel is the source of the fragrant bay leaves you can buy at the supermarket. This evergreen tree's Latin name translates to "noble green," and garlands or wreaths of bay laurel were and still are often given to winning athletes.

MEDICINAL PROPERTIES

Bay laurel has antibacterial and antifungal properties, and can be made into a salve or a poultice to help heal bruises or sore muscles. Bay laurel tea is good for general health, particularly for digestion, and adding bay laurel to your bath can treat urinary tract infections.

MAGICAL PROPERTIES

Bay laurel was believed to be such a powerful healer that doctors would wear garlands of bay laurel every day, and it's said that Emperor Tiberius of ancient Rome wore a bay laurel wreath for protection during a thunderstorm. Bay laurel placed beneath a pillow can invite prophetic dreams, and dried bay laurel should be burned to dispel any lingering sickness or negative energy. Bay laurel is a powerhouse at bringing in success, especially in business. Keep her at your office or in your workspace to attract these energies. I find her so helpful at enhancing creativity, bringing focus, and lifting inner wisdom.

PLANT WISDOM

Bay laurel asks that you give her the respect of working with her directly—she will be so much more effective at helping you manifest if you personally grow and care for her. If you don't have that personal relationship, she'll still help, but picture her doing it while rolling her eyes. She prefers to have a direct connection—and honestly, having a personal relationship with all of your plants amplifies their Magical and medicinal uses.

If for some reason you cannot grow bay laurel, even the kind act of holding her leaves and thanking her for working with you will make her spirit happy. I love to meditate with bay laurel, as I sit and allow her to travel within me, filling me with healing love and creative inspiration. Dreaming of bay laurel in food symbolizes good health. If you dream of her growing in the wild, be ready for success and possibly a pay raise. If you see her floating in a pot of boiling water, she is letting you know your spirit is in need of healing.

BAYBERRY
Myrica

ESSENTIAL PROPERTIES

abundance

This is another in the Plant Witch's garden known as "the money plant." Bayberry can grow as a shrub or tree, and while its berries can be eaten, they are more commonly valued for the waxy substance that forms on their outside—thick enough to be used to make candles.

MEDICINAL PROPERTIES

The root, bark, and berries can be used to treat colds, colitis, diarrhea, nausea, and to stimulate the circulatory system. If taken in large amounts, bayberry will cause vomiting, so be sure to be intentional and thoughtful when working with her. The leaves of the bayberry tree are a natural insect repellent.

MAGICAL PROPERTIES

Bayberry is tied to all money magic. She can bring financial abundance and can also create financial stability. She helps distressed spirits to move on and find peace, and also aids in protecting those still among the living.

PLANT WISDOM

If you find yourself worried and stressed over money, wealth, or a general sense of lack, bayberry is for you. She has a soothing and calming effect on the mind, especially for material concerns. She helps you remember what is really important, lifting you from that low frequency into a higher one—into a place where you will surely attract abundance. Dreaming of bayberry symbolizes an internal struggle, so if she appears in your dreams, make sure to find ways to get your head into a quiet state—meditate, take some time off, declutter, or, best of all, spend some time in nature!

BELLADONNA
Atropa belladonna

BELLADONNA

ESSENTIAL PROPERTIES

protection, psychic ability, self-awareness

Belladonna produces a beautiful reddish–dark green, bell-shaped flower. However, it is so poisonous as to be known as "deadly nightshade"—and in this case, the name is no joke. Belladonna's toxicity is so fierce it can cause fever, hallucinations, and even death. It's important that you don't keep or grow her where there are children or pets, or where any outside animals can access her.

MEDICINAL PROPERTIES

For centuries, belladonna was a medicine valued particularly as an anesthetic, to put someone to sleep while they underwent surgery. But belladonna could also be used for cosmetic purposes—Cleopatra took belladonna to dilate her pupils, making them more "seductive." Apparently this was a common practice for hundreds of years, despite overuse causing permanent blindness.

MAGICAL PROPERTIES

You should never ever ingest belladonna. It simply isn't worth it. There are ways to interact with her Magic besides eating her—but you should always use a great deal of care, including washing your hands after handling any part of belladonna. Placing dried belladonna into a small bag or sealed jar (making sure it's labeled properly!) and keeping it near you as you meditate can help your spirit move past where it normally lingers, allowing you to explore the world beyond.

Keep away from those selling it in a flying ointment, as there are so many factors you need to check into, including where and how their belladonna is sourced, how much was used, what the other ingredients are, etc. This product is dangerous, and often does more harm than good. Even if you trust the source completely, a Plant Witch knows that tripping isn't Magic—it's the opposite. Burn some mugwort instead!

PLANT WISDOM

Our understanding of belladonna has been tainted because so many have been working with her incorrectly for so many years. She is actually extremely powerful and protective. She speaks of being present in your whole self, with all the shades of who you are, "bad" and "good." All you truly need is her energy—you don't even have to touch her. She will journey with you if you invite her into your dreams or meditate with her. The most important thing you can do is love her as she is, and she will help you learn to do the same for yourself.

BERGAMOT
Citrus bergamia

ESSENTIAL PROPERTIES

abundance, manifesting, happiness

Bergamot looks kind of like a really bumpy lime, but she is likely a hybrid of lemon and bitter orange. She is edible, but normally isn't consumed or used in cooking—instead, she is used as an aromatic, scenting perfumes and teas (most notably Earl Grey).

MEDICINAL PROPERTIES

Consuming too much bergamot can cause some muscle cramps, but small amounts may reduce LDL cholesterol and lower blood pressure. Bergamot is antibacterial, and the juice can help speed the healing of cold sores. In aromatherapy, bergamot causes a natural uplift, giving you a sense of peace and calm.

MAGICAL PROPERTIES

Bergamot's bright energy can help you move past whatever has been blocking you—whatever you've been afraid of. Her joyful presence helps you see that nothing is really that terrible after all, and gives you the courage to move forward, reaching for what you want. Working with bergamot is perfect for manifesting, bringing in abundance, amplifying happiness, and for your relationship with your true self.

PLANT WISDOM

Bergamot is the guardian angel of the plant world, here to shine a light on your importance in this world. Keep her near you when you're creating vision boards, visualizing your future, and casting manifestation spells. When I'm stressed or overthinking things and have trouble keeping my mood in high vibes, bergamot reminds me that everything is going to be okay. Bergamot shows up in dreams only when invited. When you want her to visit you in the dreamworld, be very specific with what you're looking for from her—for example, if you are feeling sad, ask her to keep you company.

BIRCH
Betula

ESSENTIAL PROPERTIES

abundance, new beginnings, love, protection, strength

Called the white lady of the woods, birch is a tall, thin tree that grows in groups known as stands. This graceful tree has distinctive white bark, visible through the pine trees that often grow near her. The bark and sap have a fresh, wintergreen aroma and flavor. The fluttering of her leaves in the wind creates one of the most Magical sounds in the world.

MEDICINAL PROPERTIES

Birch bark peels away easily and can be soaked in water and placed around a broken arm to serve as a kind of cast. The white lady's leaves contain a high quantity of vitamin C, and tea made from these leaves can act as a diuretic, helping to clear up urinary tract infections. Balms made from the leaves and bark are also good for the skin.

MAGICAL PROPERTIES

The birch tree is one of the first to sprout leaves in the spring, making her symbolic of new beginnings and fertility. Birch's seeming fragility but actual strength makes her a symbol of protection. The psychoactive fly agaric mushroom often grows beneath her branches, and so she acts as a balance, offering protection against psychic forces. Consider writing your fears on birch paper, a piece of softly curling bark, and burning them away. Or create a broom made of birch twigs to sweep out your house in the spring, making way for something new.

PLANT WISDOM

I love birch trees! They have always called to my spirit, catching my soul's eye wherever they are present. And oh, how they love Witches! Especially Witches who are in tune with the Earth. Visit them often, grow them if you can, and keep some bark on your altar during the springtime. Just like us, birch can seem fragile, but she has a profound inner strength. She teaches us how to overcome personal troubles while learning to shed that which doesn't serve us. Birch encourages us to start anew and to take a leap into the unknown, fully trusting in the natural cycles of change and being.

 If you dream of birch, she is calling you to come and heal with her. Now, simply sitting with her won't do—she wants to hear you sing! If you're not a confident singer, don't worry—she just wants to hear your voice, and humming will do. She will take your sound into her leaves and sway it within the winds, stirring your song as if the world is her cauldron and you her ingredients—brewing up a perfect batch of medicine for your soul.

BLACK COHOSH
Actaea racemosa

ESSENTIAL PROPERTIES

protection, strength, manifesting

Black cohosh goes by many names, including bugbane, snakeroot, and fairy candle. Her flowers have no petals, but instead form tight clusters around a tall, thin stem.

MEDICINAL PROPERTIES

Traditionally, Native American tribes worked with black cohosh to treat snakebite and to relieve birth pangs, though this isn't recommended today, as an excess of black cohosh can cause nausea, dizziness, and a lowered heart rate. That said, black cohosh does contain phytochemicals that behave similarly to estrogen, making her a potentially effective treatment for menopause.

MAGICAL PROPERTIES

Black cohosh can be used for protection, as she can undo any negative spells or energy that has been sent your way—and she will also give you the strength to withstand any kind of psychic attack. The root of black cohosh carries the most potent wisdom and Magic, but it will be shared with you only if you grow the plant yourself from seed. As she grows, set your intentions that she will guide you through your Magical practice. Only then can you take the roots when you need them. One root is more than enough for one spell, so place the plant back in the earth, making sure to not kill her.

PLANT WISDOM

A field of black cohosh in your dreams is like having a birthday candle right in front of you, ready for you to blow and make a wish. When you dream of black cohosh, make sure to speak to her about the things you desire and wish to manifest. If you grow this Magical darling, sitting with her and simply chatting about your life, what you feel, and what you wish to manifest will amplify your words into the universe.

Black Cohosh Manifestation Bath Ritual

This bathing ritual will help awaken black cohosh so that she can surround you with her powers of manifestation.

WHAT YOU NEED

2 tablespoons dried black cohosh powder

1 tablespoon dried angelica root

1 tablespoon dried rosemary

1 sliced fresh orange

1 handful of fresh baby's breath

1 handful of fresh red rose petals

1 red candle

WHAT TO DO

+ Fill your bath and bring it to your desired temperature.

+ Add the herbs and plants to your bath and turn the lights out.

+ Light your red candle, and as you do so, set your intentions for manifestation.

+ Soak for at least 15 minutes.

BLACKTHORN
Prunus spinosa

ESSENTIAL PROPERTIES

awareness, protection, shadow work

Also known as sloe, fairy tree, and "dark mother of the woods," blackthorn is a member of the rose family whose small fruits appear similar to blueberries. They have a tart astringent flavor and are often used to infuse gin; they can also be made into jam or wine. Her thorns are serious, and so blackthorn makes a good cattle-proof hedge. The thicker stems are quite sturdy and useful as walking sticks.

MEDICINAL PROPERTIES

A syrup made from the berry can help treat a sore throat, and gargled to help stop a cough. The flower can be applied directly to the skin to treat a rash, and a tea made of blackthorn can help calm the stomach, though it also acts as a strong diuretic, making it good for detoxing if you're careful.

MAGICAL PROPERTIES

Along with making for a good walking stick, the strong wood also serves as a powerful wand. In Irish folklore, blackthorn is so precious, she has her own fairy tribe dedicated to her. Called the Launatsidhe, they curse those who try to cut wood from the blackthorn between the holy days of Samhain and Beltane. You can burn the dried wood or thorns to banish negativity, or keep a dried berry or thorn in a gris-gris or charm bag for protection or as an aid to overcoming adversity. Blackthorn is a gateway to the unseen, and can help you stay aware of all that we don't see in our day-to-day lives.

PLANT WISDOM

Blackthorn is at her most powerful when you are working with her for protection against evil, creating boundaries with others, the unseen, and the self. She helps us confront our own darkness, so that we are able to see right through the shadows to what lurks within—so much so that she is used for exorcisms. She is Queen of the Underworld, and it is best to partner with her in shadow work, healing deep trauma, and getting over fears of one's own gifts. Sit by her or simply hold a piece of her while meditating or doing Magical workings. If you wish for her to show up in your dreams, place her over your head before going to sleep.

BLEEDING HEART
Dicentra

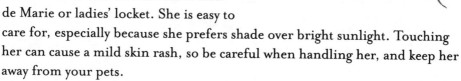

ESSENTIAL PROPERTIES
love, healing

This iconic plant looks just like her name—a heart-shaped blossom that has split open, with a droplet leaking out the bottom. She is also known as fleur de Marie or ladies' locket. She is easy to

BLEEDING HEART

care for, especially because she prefers shade over bright sunlight. Touching her can cause a mild skin rash, so be careful when handling her, and keep her away from your pets.

MEDICINAL PROPERTIES

Bleeding heart can be made into a tincture—she will treat anxiety or grief and give you a sense of calm and well-being. You can also chew on her root to relieve a toothache.

MAGICAL PROPERTIES

Bleeding heart teaches that love is more powerful than we think, that it is a giver of life and bringer of death, and we should recognize the impact our love can have. She is of course great for love Magic, both to attract love and to heal a current relationship.

PLANT WISDOM

Bleeding heart understands what you are going through. She is deeply compassionate and will be there for you no matter how difficult your troubles may seem. She takes the pain from broken hearts and turns it into something beautiful, offering peace and healing in its place. Set your intentions for what you want to let go of, and then burn her petals for release.

If you've experienced a heartache rooted in childhood—if, for instance, your parents weren't there for you, or didn't care for you as they should have, bleeding heart will bring you into her spirit and embrace you with her mothering energy. She draws in those who need her, calling them to her so she can take care of them. She visits only those who need her in their dreams.

BLESSED THISTLE
Cnicus benedictus

ESSENTIAL PROPERTIES
happiness, strength, luck

Like most thistles, blessed thistle grows like a weed, often in places where she is unwanted. And yet these spiky blossoms offer a kind of protection—apparently, in the war between the Scots and Danes, the sleeping Scottish warriors were warned of a Danish attack at dawn when a Dane stepped on a thistle and let out a cry of pain. She's cute and fuzzy, but she can be dangerous, so be careful when handling her.

MEDICINAL PROPERTIES

A tea made from the leaves of the blessed thistle will taste very bitter, but comes with so many benefits. For instance, it will relieve menstrual pain, as well as improve memory and mood. The tea can stimulate the liver, relieve headaches, and support the immune system. It can also improve concentration, as it aids in the flow of blood to the brain.

MAGICAL PROPERTIES

The strength and vitality blessed thistle offers make her an herb of endurance. If you're experiencing a difficult time, blessed thistle will help you make it through. She will also help you release any anger you've been holding, allowing joy to come to you instead. Carry her with you, place her in your pillow, and even in your car if you are easily aggravated in traffic. Sprinkle some dried blessed thistle over a black candle to keep jealousy and hate away, making sure to set that intention while you dress the candle.

PLANT WISDOM

Don't you dare tell blessed thistle lies, for she can see right into the darkest spaces of your heart. But she isn't judgmental—her energy is both mothering and protective. The more sadness she sees, the more she will try to uplift you and bring good things your way. To have her bring you luck in a certain situation, simply meditate with her and ask her nicely. Don't be surprised to see her show up in your dreams as a fairy with a long green gown. Take her hand as she reaches out for yours, and allow her to take your sadness away with Magical visions.

BLOODROOT
Sanguinaria canadensis

ESSENTIAL PROPERTIES

love, self-awareness, courage

Native Americans traditionally take the juice from the bloodroot, which flows a bright red, and use it to dye their bodies and clothes. The juice is also an ingredient in some medicinal remedies, but it needs to be handled carefully, as it is quite toxic.

MEDICINAL PROPERTIES

Bloodroot contains chemicals that can fight bacteria and plaque and can treat inflammation and infection. Native Americans have long worked with her to treat for coughs, to induce vomiting, and to cleanse wounds.

MAGICAL PROPERTIES

Bloodroot can help to strengthen family ties, inviting more harmony into holiday gatherings, or even just in your household. Simply placing bloodroot under the dinner table, over your front door, or carrying her will bring your home more peace. If your marriage is having trouble, some dried bloodroot under your mattress can help bolster your connection . . . and even make bedtime a little more fun! Bloodroot can also be placed over your bedroom door to keep arguments at bay, and to instead attract love into this space.

PLANT WISDOM

Bloodroot brings a message of releasing fears and expanding self-worth, especially for those of us who have this belief that we are hard to love. Most often, our childhood traumas instilled this in us, causing us to be unable to open fully, or to love fully. Bloodroot gets to the root of this and soothes the scars, releases the illusions, and awakens pure love within us. If you dream of bloodroot, there is a message of abundant love coming your way—or perhaps it is a sign of self-love awakening from within.

Blue Lotus
Nymphaea caerulea

ESSENTIAL PROPERTIES
psychic ability, protection

The blue lotus can vary from a very pale blue to a vivid sky blue, fading to a yellow center. Like all lotuses, it rises to the surface of the water it lives in and then blooms over the course of a single day. This variety likely grew along the Nile, and was sacred to both ancient Egyptians and ancient Mayans.

MEDICINAL PROPERTIES

Blue lotus contains aporphine, a psychoactive, which like all psychoactives should be used with extreme caution. Remember, a Witch's goal with plants is not to get high! That said, blue lotus tea is great for stress and anxiety, promoting relaxation and giving a sense of euphoria and ecstasy.

MAGICAL PROPERTIES

It is said that the goddess Isis wore blue lotus perfume, and that Cleopatra bathed in her essences. We can follow their lead and work with blue lotus in aromatherapy and in a bath. She will stimulate the third eye. To awaken your inner wisdom and seek the next steps in your journey, add blue lotus to a footbath and light some blue lotus incense while drinking her cup of tea. I particularly like to use blue lotus with candle Magic, as she has a variety of different meanings in that kind of spellwork. Dress a blue candle with blue lotus for inner healing, specifically of the mind. Dress a white candle with blue lotus for an understanding of yourself.

PLANT WISDOM

Blue lotus illuminates the unseen, the things that lurk in the darkness and within the self. Blue lotus is also a powerful aid to lucid dreaming—invite her into your dreams to induce visions that shine a light on what has been hidden.

Blue Lotus Protection Spell

Blue lotus will create a protective boundary between you and whatever you've asked her to shield you from.

WHAT YOU NEED

Eggshells from 1 egg

1 tablespoon dried blue lotus

Clear glass

WHAT TO DO

+ Add the eggshells and blue lotus to the glass and fill it with water.

+ Tap on the glass 3 times, and whisper into the glass the name of the person or the situation you wish her to protect you from.

+ Keep this glass in a high place for 1 week.

+ Dispose of it at the end of the week and start a new glass.

+ Repeat this process for 3 weeks total.

BORAGE
Borago officinalis

ESSENTIAL PROPERTIES

courage, self-love, psychic ability

Borage, also known as starflower, is a medicinal herb. The leaves and blossoms are edible and taste a bit like cucumber. Borage gets along well with other plants and as it both repels pests and invites bees, it is a welcome addition to any garden.

MEDICINAL PROPERTIES

Pliny the Elder, ancient Roman naturalist and philosopher, believed borage was an antidepressant. Borage serves as a tonic for the adrenal glands, and so can relieve stress; she also is very high in vitamins. Borage can help with eczema, premenstrual issues, ADHD, respiratory issues including cough and cold, and to combat alcohol dependency. She is also great for reducing general inflammation.

MAGICAL PROPERTIES

Borage's anxiety-relieving properties clear the way for your psychic powers, allowing you to see clearly. Drink a tea of borage and your intuition will amplify—this is great to do before a reading, before any Magical workings, or before meditation. I work with borage to communicate with my ancestors, placing her on my ancestral altar and having her by me while I meditate, do any divination work, or chanting. In voodoo traditions, decorating the home with borage blossoms or adding them to a floor wash will help ensure domestic harmony.

PLANT WISDOM

Borage teaches us to accept ourselves just the way we are, to have courage to stand in our light and power, and to ignore the noise of the world that keeps us from listening to our inner selves. Borage is your best source for owning your truth and ridding yourself of any fears that are blocking you from shining bright. She often shows up in dreams, but you may miss her if you don't pay attention. She wants us to see and feel our own beauty, and therefore teaches us to stop and be aware of our surroundings and of our inner world. When you do see her, this symbolizes you are breaking cycles that have been holding you captive. Expect great changes moving forward.

BURDOCK
Arctium

ESSENTIAL PROPERTIES

feminine energy, healing, protection

Burdock has big, wide leaves and thistle-like, bristly heads that are so sticky that they inspired the invention of Velcro and other hook-and-loop fasteners. She grows just about everywhere, and so is easy to wild-harvest. Her beautiful purple flowers can be seen from late summer into autumn. Burdock is often eaten as a root vegetable, as she has a sweet, mild flavor.

MEDICINAL PROPERTIES

A tincture or decoction made from the roots or seeds of burdock is an excellent blood purifier, and a poultice made from her leaves can soothe bruises. Burdock can also combat dandruff and other scalp ailments. She holds lots of vitamins and minerals including potassium, magnesium, iron, and manganese, and is also an effective prebiotic.

MAGICAL PROPERTIES

Burdock's soothing and wholesome nature makes her a wonderful general healing plant, and seeking her out in the wild is a wonderful way to connect with her energies. These energies are protective in nature, much like a lioness. You can place burdock root on your windowsills to keep bad energy from entering; burying burdock root in a pot by your front door will keep your home protected.

PLANT WISDOM

Burdock is a biannual plant—in the first year, her large leaves seem to be growing straight out of the ground, and by the second year those leaves shoot up into stalks. She teaches that there is healing and strength in growth, in being patient in your craft. Burdock is pure medicine to the body, mind, and soul, as everything about her energy and wisdom sings of self-development and spiritual growth.

Burdock has two spirits, not one. The root is its own spirit and the flower another, so when working with burdock, you will feel a sense of balance, as feminine and masculine energies combine to nurture your spirit. I suggest this plant to those who feel lost or alone and want to own their truth. You can ask burdock to visit you in dreams, or you can sit and meditate with her to bring you a sense of who you really are.

BUTCHER'S-BROOM
Ruscus aculeatus

BUTCHER'S-BROOM

ESSENTIAL PROPERTIES
banishing, psychic ability, protection, healing

Butcher's-broom is an evergreen shrub with bright red berries. Its flat and stiff branches were once used to sweep up a butcher's block—and interestingly, butcher's-broom does have antibacterial properties, making her quite good for cleaning these kinds of messes.

MEDICINAL PROPERTIES

Indeed, butcher's-broom is a powerhouse for medicinal properties. She's a laxative and a diuretic, and ancient Greeks believed that adding her to wine would remove kidney stones. She can also reduce swelling and help heal a broken bone. Butcher's-broom benefits the entire circulatory system, especially for those with orthostatic hypotension, and can treat hemorrhoids,

Butcher's-Broom Ice Cube Banishing Spell

Use this spell when you have a series of events, habits, or people you want to banish from your life. You'll be able to be very specific!

WHAT YOU NEED

    2 cups water

    2 tablespoons dried butcher's-broom

    1 teaspoon black pepper

    1 teaspoon valerian

    7 coffee beans

    Ice cube tray

    Salt

WHAT TO DO

+ Bring the water to a boil. Add all the ingredients except the coffee and salt and simmer for 10 to 15 minutes.

+ Let the mixture cool. You can strain it if you want to, but it isn't necessary.

+ Place each coffee bean in a separate slot in the ice cube tray, and as you do, set an intention for each 1—what do you want to banish or release? Be specific, and make your intention clear and detailed.

+ Pour your tea over each coffee bean, filling the ice cube slot. Place the tray in the freezer for 3 days.

+ On the fourth day, remove 1 ice cube. Sprinkle salt on it, and as you do, say "I banish you" or "I release you." Bury your ice in the earth or flush it down the toilet.

+ Repeat this ritual every day until you have banished each ice cube.

gallstones, leg cramps, varicose veins, leg swelling, and so many more ailments.

MAGICAL PROPERTIES

Burning butcher's-broom provides a calming atmosphere, not only for people but for animals as well. She can help you stay focused, improving your psychic abilities. Scattering butcher's-broom twigs into the air can invite a gust of wind, while scattering the ashes of butcher's-broom can cause the winds to move on. I work with butcher's-broom primarily for protection and banishment. Bring a pot to a boil and add a handful of butcher's-broom. Let simmer for 15 to 20 minutes, strain, and let cool. Use this water for your Magical workings on protection or banishment; I also like to add it to my bath when I feel negative energies weighing me down.

PLANT WISDOM

Dreaming of sweeping with a broom made of this plant symbolizes a heavy heart and spirit. You may have had your heart broken and/or you may have lost someone. When I do healing work for my own childhood trauma, I often dream of drowning in a river with butcher's-broom floating all around me. I've learned to invite this being into my healing work, burning it or keeping its water on my altar, to help me keep a calm heart during the healing process. Butcher's-broom sends a message of being present—for the pain, the laughs, the good, and the ugly.

CACTUS
Cactaceae

ESSENTIAL PROPERTIES

protection, healing, clarity, strength

Plant Witches with particular gifts of compassion and empathy are often drawn to the cactus. Cacti are great healers, mothering plants that bring a sense of calmness. They thrive in the most trying of environments, tolerating droughts, floods, extreme heat, and extreme cold.

MEDICINAL PROPERTIES

In Latin America, several varieties of cactus serve as a food staple because of their many healing benefits. Agave is a natural antiseptic, used for cuts and burns, and the prickly pear cactus can help us breathe better, purifying the air, removing toxins and even background radiation. Cacti also help increase our focus, clarity, and productivity, making them ideal for office environments and great for creative minds who need a bit more organization in the brain. Cacti can also treat diabetes, high cholesterol, obesity, and more.

Cactus Self-Sabotage Protection Spell

We all unwittingly sabotage ourselves sometimes. We keep ourselves from growing, rising, expanding, and healing. Cacti can help you combat this tendency. Setting new goals is never easy, and the strength and willpower required to stick to those goals are hard to find in the world we live in today—but this spell will help you stay focused and on track. It can be used to break old habits, addictions, and thought patterns that no longer serve you.

WHAT YOU NEED

1 small cactus with spines

Small bell or holy smoke
(I recommend cedar or mugwort, but you can use what you have available)

Rainwater

Banana leaf, tobacco leaf, or banana peel

WHAT TO DO

+ Set your cactus in front of you. Clear the energy around you by ringing a small bell, or by cleansing with holy smoke.

+ Hold a glass of rainwater in your hands and close your eyes as you speak your intentions. A good example of an intent that I would use for this spell would be "Keep me focused and strong while I heal my body" or "Keep me from breaking my own promises." These are general, so make sure to be more specific to better fit what you are asking for. You are filling this rainwater with your prayer/incantation. Take your time and focus on the energy flowing from your hands into the water.

+ Open your eyes and water the cactus with the rainwater, which now carries your intentions. A little goes a long way, and you can save your jar for the next time you need to water the plant.

+ As you pour the water, ask the cactus to please take your intention and care for it. Use this 1 intention for just this 1 cactus; let this cactus be the bearer of this specific intent. It will now drink it and it will live within it, growing strong, resilient, powerful, and protected.

+ If you need to release something at the same time that will help amplify your intention, take hold of a spine. Speak into it what it is you want to let go of. For example, "laziness," "self-hate," and so on. Place that spine in a banana leaf, tobacco leaf, or banana peel, and then bury it.

+ Place a note with your intention under your cactus to remind you of your spell. Your cactus will continue to keep this spell going for you as long as you care for it. When you are done with the intention and no longer need the plant to assist, simply water it with regular water and thank your cactus for being your companion in this spell. Explain that you no longer need it to keep working.

MAGICAL PROPERTIES

Cacti are very powerful Magical companions, calling to those in need of protection, healing, and personal growth. Just as they remove toxins from the air, cacti also remove toxins from the spirit. The principles of feng shui (the art of arranging your living space to best enhance the flow of energy) state that anything with sharp points, thorns, or spines will bring bad luck—but I do not believe this is true for cacti. They do sometimes stir things up in order to clear out any bad energy, and it can be uncomfortable having a plant dive into the depths of your soul! But remember, this is only temporary, and it's how we truly grow and heal. While that kind of active energy is not something you want in your bedroom (or wherever you go to find peace and relaxation), take advantage of cacti's grounding and protective qualities by placing them at the four corners of your home where they will ward off intruders and ill will.

PLANT WISDOM

When I speak to cacti, they tell me tales of love and peace. They remind me of my strength, and that all beings are pure love with a warrior spirit. Cacti have been a huge support system for me, guiding me and releasing me from old memories and pain. Cacti are great for retrieving things hidden within that are hard to bring out. Cacti thorns can help break unhealthy habits, as the spines can poke through the toughest of issues and open up a new direction, path, or perspective. For all their prickliness, I find cacti very chatty in the mornings—they love the sunrise.

Dreaming of cacti can mean a couple of different things. If you're dreaming of being poked by their spines, this may symbolize something you are facing, or an issue you need to stop ignoring. If in your dream you are surrounded by cacti but not being poked by them, it means you are standing in your power, strong and resilient. Pay attention! Huge opportunities and changes are coming, and you are ready for them.

CALAMUS
Acorus calamus

ESSENTIAL PROPERTIES

control, balance

Calamus, also known as sweet flag, grows tall in the wetlands of Europe, India, Africa, and much of Asia, as well as North America. Ancient Egyptians made perfume with calamus, and she is still a common ingredient in perfumes today, as well as in cooking.

MEDICINAL PROPERTIES

Native American tribes, particularly the Chipewyan people, work with calamus to soothe a sore throat or calm an upset stomach, and she is valued in Ayurvedic and Chinese medicine traditions as well. However, reports of severe vomiting have caused calamus to be banned as an herbal supplement in the United States—thanks to those who don't follow dosages properly.

MAGICAL PROPERTIES

Calamus root chips are an essential ingredient in commanding powder, a mixture founded in voodoo. Calamus root can help you to regain control over a situation—or over yourself. Calamus root brings me back into balance. If you're feeling anxious, or as though you're unable to manage what's going on in your life, burning calamus roots or leaves or adding them to a spell can help you regain a sense of calm and find your inner balance so that you can feel in control once more.

PLANT WISDOM

Calamus root dreams come when you ask for them. You can sit and meditate with a calamus in your hand and ask her spirit to show up in your dreams to help you work out any issues you need help with, particularly a lack of having self-control, wanting to get rid of bad habits, and so forth. Calamus root teaches us to take hold of our inner power, allowing us to be fearless in our mighty strength.

CALATHEA

Calathea

ESSENTIAL PROPERTIES

strength, balance, clarity

Calathea is a wonderful houseplant, and certain varieties, like *Calathea roseoptica*, have red stems and dark-green and light-green patterned leaves. Her leaves close up at night and open in the morning, making a gentle rustling sound. For this reason, calathea is known as a "living plant," though of course all plants would fall under that category. Her strong leaves can be used to wrap fish or to carry other small items.

MEDICINAL PROPERTIES

This plant has no known medicinal properties.

MAGICAL PROPERTIES

Working with this plant is vital in learning how to balance yourself and your Magical practice. For those who admire and respect both light and shadow, this plant is for you. Placing her in your sacred space or on your altar will bring the duality of light and shadow into a perfect, harmonious balance, where neither outweighs the other. Calathea will keep you in the in-between, where I like to say I belong and live.

PLANT WISDOM

If you are seeking clarity, keep calathea near you. Listen to her pull as she sways you to feel and see the truth. Calathea loves to fall into the dreamworld with you. During the day she stands tall, proud, and mighty, but when the Sun falls and goes to sleep, she sleeps with it. Her leaves droop and her energy drops. If you are close to her, if you are caring for her and keeping her in your home, she will join you in your dreams, particularly when you carry a weary heart, or when you are worried about a direction you need to take. She will bring you the clarity you need. She teaches us that although we must wake, stand strong, and do our daily tasks, there is also power in knowing when to rest and reset.

CALENDULA
Calendula officinalis

ESSENTIAL PROPERTIES

happiness, love, opening the door between realms

Calendula, often referred to as marigold, is a charming, bright little ball of sunshine. She can be yellow or an intense orange, and is a wonderful addition to any garden. She acts as a natural pest-deterrent, as many slugs and insects don't want to be around her. Her blossoms are edible and make a wonderful dye.

MEDICINAL PROPERTIES

Calendula has much to offer as a medicinal plant. She can encourage a delayed period to start, and help with the cramps once it does. She can treat a fever, and has been used to combat smallpox, measles, and jaundice. She aids in the growth of new tissue, and so is wonderful for wound-healing—she helped in this way on Civil War battlefields. Nowadays she is most often found in skin care products, as her gentle nature soothes the skin.

MAGICAL PROPERTIES

Calendula can foster communication with those who have passed, helping them stay present in our lives. She is also the traditional "he loves me, he loves me not" flower, and symbolizes love and constancy. Her association with the Sun makes her at her most powerful when picked at noon, so time your spells carefully. Taking a bath with dried marigold will give you good dreams. Her name itself is said to derive from how she blooms new flowers monthly, symbolizing the New Moon.

PLANT WISDOM

I call calendula "Little Miss Sunshine," for she is always positive and brings light to all situations. I love seeing her in a cemetery, growing within an abundant Latinx community. Indigenous peoples, especially from Mexico, believe in placing calendula on the gravestones of passed loved ones, comforting them and helping them to communicate. As you know, I grew up surrounded by the hills of a cemetery, and it is where I played and spent the majority of my time. I definitely saw more spirit activity where these beauties where placed. Grow them in your garden or place them in your home, and they will bring a message and energy of love and light so abundant that even the most negative of people will be lifted by her presence.

I don't recommend asking calendula to join you in your dreams, for although she is a joy in the mundane world, in the dreamworld she likes to be playful—a little too playful. In fact, she can be a bit of a trickster and isn't the best dream companion for anyone looking for a restful sleep.

CARAWAY
Carum carvi

ESSENTIAL PROPERTIES
love, protection, prevent thievery

Caraway is also known as meridian fennel or Persian cumin. What we call her seeds are actually tiny fruits; their licorice-like taste is used to flavor so many different kinds of food, notably rye bread. You can also find caraway in salads, desserts, pickles, and other dishes all over the world.

MEDICINAL PROPERTIES

Caraway is wonderful for digestion, particularly if you're prone to acid reflux or gas. She also can aid in reducing inflammation and promoting weight loss.

MAGICAL PROPERTIES

According to German folklore, caraway sprinkled on the coffin of a deceased loved one protects them from evil spirits. And putting some caraway in your car or your purse or wallet will prevent it from being stolen.

Caraway is most commonly found in love spells. Perhaps because of her stomach-calming and fragrant properties, chewing caraway seeds before kissing someone was said to help them fall in love with you. But caraway's true gift is in helping to strengthen a love that is already present. Placing a sachet of caraway seeds under your bed can improve your marriage, and if your partner is going away on a trip without you, send them with some caraway to keep the connection between you strong.

PLANT WISDOM

Dreaming of caraway signifies a death is among you, most likely someone close to you. However, if you dream of eating caraway, the death is your own—not a literal death but a death of the old. It means a rebirth is upon you—a new you, new life, new direction. Caraway teaches us to believe in the changes, to be confident that a loss isn't really a loss but a new beginning. If you are mourning the loss of someone you love, carry caraway with you and ask her to help you transition and release the pain. If you are wanting to let go of your old self and restart a new you, chew some caraway while creating a vision board of who you wish to embody, the life you desire to manifest. Meditate with her while holding on to her seeds as you envision what you wish to let go of.

CARNATION
Dianthus caryophyllus

CARNATION

ESSENTIAL PROPERTIES

healing, amplification

Carnations, while popular in floral arrangements, unfortunately are often overlooked for their powerful Magical properties and wisdom. And this is a shame, because carnations carry a deep history, dating back more than two thousand years when they were called *dianthus* or "divine flower" by the ancient Greeks. Carnation's symmetrical, wavy petals can hold a wide variety of colors, and each color carries its own individual symbolism.

MEDICINAL PROPERTIES

Carnations can reduce a fever and calm an upset stomach, and can also treat nervous and coronary disorders, as well as anxiety and stress. A cup of carnation tea is known to improve heart health and relax the muscles. Carnations have also been added to vinegars, beers, and wines for flavor as well as healing.

MAGICAL PROPERTIES

Generally speaking, carnation can help amplify your spells and give them longevity. You can add her petals to any Magical working to make it stronger and longer-lasting. I like to place her petals on vision boards and incorporate them into manifestation spells to keep my intentions going. Placing carnations in your home brings a joyous, healing energy, making the air feel lighter and brighter. But more specifically the shades of carnation have a different spiritual and Magical meaning and purpose, allowing you to work with them in precise ways to give your spellwork more definitive intentions:

White: spirit communication, new beginnings

Light red: heart-healing, compassion, self-love

Dark red: passion, love, protection

Purple: banishing, releasing, intuition

Pink: purification, cleansing

PLANT WISDOM

Carnations are wise and observant beings, and they take their relationship with you very seriously. Like all plants, they don't want to be "used"—they want to form a partnership, a true friendship. With carnation, once you've begun to work with her, you will grow a forever relationship, a heartfelt connection like you have with your best friend. This kind of lasting devotion is what makes carnation so great for amplification and healing work. Begin to cultivate your relationship by growing carnation, ideally in all her shades, as she loves to present in all aspects of herself—as we all should!

Dreaming of carnations symbolizes death, either of a person, career, or project—something you treasure and will have trouble letting go of. This may seem surprising given what a supportive plant friend she is, but after all this is what she does best—she comes in to heal the heart, and her warning comes with compassion and love.

CAT'S CLAW

Uncaria tomentosa

ESSENTIAL PROPERTIES

psychic ability, unblocking, abundance

Uña de gato or cat's claw is a woody vine with claw-shaped thorns. The cat's claw vine climbs as nimbly as a feline—hence the name. With the help of three-pronged, claw-like tendrils, she can climb as high as 65 feet!

MEDICINAL PROPERTIES

Cat's claw is found in Central and South America, where for centuries she has been used to treat arthritis and digestive disorders. It's anti-inflammatory properties can help regulate the immune system and has even be used to treat cancer.

MAGICAL PROPERTIES

Tea made from the inner bark or roots of cat's claw is quite bitter, but a little honey will help it go down. Peruvian shamans worked with cat's claw to help bring people back into balance—when there is any kind of unease or sense of inequality in your life, cat's claw can help you find your equilibrium again. Cat's claw is a perfect companion for vision quests, as she amplifies psychic powers and wakes intuition. She can also help clear whatever has been blocking you or causing you to be unbalanced, making her a powerful manifesting machine, specifically in wealth and money. She is resilient and bountiful and can bring this energy and presence into your Magical workings.

Cat's claw bark is perfect for adding to incense blends to increase psychic powers, and you can also add it to your money-drawing spells, or even place it in sachets for attracting money. I like to keep her in my manifesting journal pages when I am writing abundance affirmations.

Grow my dear, grow! And don't you look down, for you are meant to reach the skies, mighty and high. Oh, how cat's claw loves to tell me tales of reaching for the stars and breaking through whatever life throws at me. Just as she is resilient, she ignites this same powerful energy in those who work with her. I work closely with her, and so in dreams where I'm falling, she senses my despair and appears, latching onto me and lifting me back up, even higher than the place I fell from. Because of her, I'm not afraid to take a leap, even when I have no idea of where I will land.

CATNIP
Nepeta cataria

ESSENTIAL PROPERTIES
love, luck, happiness

When we think of catnip, we all think of kittens going crazy or something like that—and it's true, around two-thirds of cats are intensely attracted to catnip, and spend their time rolling around, licking at the catnip, jumping, running around, and purring before falling asleep. Of course, one-third of cats can't be bothered at all, which is very catlike of them.

MEDICINAL PROPERTIES

Catnip is a member of the mint family, and is edible. She can soothe cramps, give you more appetite, reduce a fever, and provide a general sense of relaxation. If you're experiencing morning sickness, try adding some catnip to your ginger tea. To keep her properties, catnip is best simmered rather than boiled. A tea of catnip can help you fall asleep peacefully.

MAGICAL PROPERTIES

Catnip is also called "the women's love herb," as she highlights our good qualities, making us more confident and attractive. Hold catnip in your hand and allow her to warm in your palm, and then shake the hand of someone you want a relationship with—whether a friendship or a romantic relationship. If you store this sprig of catnip carefully, the relationship will be strong and lasting. Growing catnip near your entryway or hanging her above your door will bring good luck and happiness to your home. To awaken self-love, use a red or pink candle, carve your name on it, anoint the candle with rose oil, and sprinkle catnip on it. Light the candle while asking your heart to be present for you.

PLANT WISDOM

Catnip, as you may have guessed, brings a message of happiness and bliss. I see her as a laid-back, chill being, someone you could listen to some oldies with while sipping a glass of wine. She not only teaches us not to sweat the small stuff, she also can help us stay calm and collected even in the face of bigger challenges. I grow her in my garden and have her in my cat's in-home garden, so I'm very familiar with her stress-free energies.

If you have a turbulent relationship at home or have children who are extremely hyperactive, placing her in the windows of the rooms where they sleep will bring in calming energies. Meditating with catnip will invite a sense of peace and calm into your heart and mind. When she shows up in a dream, it symbolizes distress, either within you or within your home.

Cattail
Typha latifolia

ESSENTIAL PROPERTIES

abundance, reflection, manifesting, love

Cattail, with its instantly recognizable thick brown sausage-like flower, stands tall out of the marshes and swamps she loves. Her flower produces a fluff that can be used as tinder to start a fire or for insulation, and is also an effective insect repellent. When dried, the flower can be dipped in tallow or wax to make a torch, and the dried leaves (called rushes) may be twisted to make chair seats.

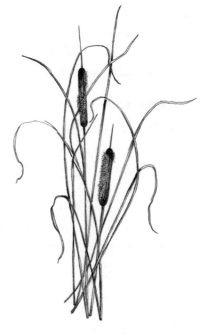

CATTAIL

MEDICINAL PROPERTIES

Cattail is also edible, and her pollen is high in protein. The underground stem of the cattail, called the rhizome—can be eaten in much the same way as maize or rice, and was used as such by Native Americans. The roots may be eaten like potatoes, and young shoots can be boiled until tender and eaten like asparagus. There really aren't that many plants that can be consumed in quite so many ways! Cattail can also be made into a poultice for bruises, cuts, burns, and scars, and when made into tea she helps alleviate upset stomachs and indigestion.

MAGICAL PROPERTIES

Cattail is most powerful when worked with in love and sex Magics. She can amplify passion, so try placing her dried flower in your bedroom. If you're looking to awaken intimacy with yourself, wrap a red silk ribbon around the dried flower, setting your intentions as you do so, and then keep the flower in your bedroom. The dried leaves can also be used in weaving Magic—as you weave, set intentions for manifesting what you desire, or weave to amplify your other Magics, keeping the finished mat in your sacred space. I like to weave cattail leaves into tiny mats for my crystals, to amplify their energies.

PLANT WISDOM

Cattail is the plant of reflection, and is particularly useful when working on personal development. She teaches us to consider whatever is inside that is keeping us from growing, rising, and embodying our best selves. She clears out toxic energies and behaviors. Work with her in collaboration with your healing work, and instantly feel her presence as she pulls the things that need to be addressed to the surface. In dreams she is like a whisper in the wind, softly swaying as if to mesmerize you. She captures your true essence and stops time so that you are in the presence of your truest self.

CEDAR
Cedrus

ESSENTIAL PROPERTIES

energy clearing, spiritual development, protection, healing

Cedar, with her spicy, resinous scent, is native to the mountains of the western Himalayas and the Mediterranean region. Widely known for her enchanting aroma and whimsical presence, she has been used through history for her ability to preserve and for her strength against the elements.

MEDICINAL PROPERTIES

Not only is cedar a natural moth-repellent, she also can repel bacteria and fungi. She can prevent dandruff and soothe the aches of arthritis. She's also a natural sedative, and her scent can help you get a good night's sleep, though for most people her calming presence invites clarity, helping to release all distracting thoughts so you can focus.

MAGICAL PROPERTIES

Cedar is most commonly valued for her ability to sanctify and create a ritual space. Burning cedar can dispel any negativity and turn the most mundane of places (your messy bedroom, the neighborhood park, even your car) into a sacred space. As cedar is also a symbol for longevity, she is useful for healing spells, or you can simply carry her around or keep her in the home to invite a good, long, healthy life. Place cedar over your front door to keep out negativity, especially ill-willed spirits. Burning cedar while meditating raises the conscious mind into high frequency, boosting psychic abilities. Cedar is a great partner when you're communicating with your ancestors, as she will protect and amplify the connection.

PLANT WISDOM

Cedar has been associated with death: In the past, cedar oil preserved the heads of enemies killed in battle, the wood was used to make coffins, and to communicate with the dead. Cedar has taken on this identification with death, but that is not her natural state! She represents life—abundant, joyful, peaceful life. This vibrancy helps you connect to your higher self, to spirit, and to the Earth—in fact, I see her as a triple goddess in the plant kingdom. Ask her to visit you in dreams only if you are physically with the tree itself, as speaking directly to the cedar tree is the only way to invite her in, but once you do, she will then be with you forever, bringing dreams that are vivid and full of messages.

CENTAURY
Centaurium erythraea

ESSENTIAL PROPERTIES

psychic ability, healing, protection, banishing

Centaury grows in meadows and forest clearings, and her flowers open in the afternoon and close at night. She received her name from an ancient Greek story, in which the centaur Chiron—who had been poisoned by an arrow dipped in the blood of the many-headed Hydra—cured himself with this blossom.

MEDICINAL PROPERTIES

Centaury has been used to treat snakebites and to kill worms, and is also an effective blood purifier. Consuming centaury over a period of time is said to reduce appetite and help with weight loss. Centaury can also treat ulcers, stomach inflammation, and liver diseases. She is great for treating high fevers as she induces sweating.

MAGICAL PROPERTIES

Medieval Witches burned centaury to enhance psychic abilities and to induce visions. Centaury will also ward off snakes, both the reptile and human ones. Place centaury in your pocket when going to public places or when meeting people you feel uneasy around, and you can hold it in your hand while on the phone with someone who is being negative to protect your auric field. Keep her in your garden next to rosemary to amplify protection for the home.

PLANT WISDOM

Centaury is a kindhearted plant. If you are a healer, or if your heart needs healing, keep her with you to help alleviate sadness and bring in joy. She is quiet and speaks with touch, rather than sound. If centaury appears in your dreams, that means you have an imbalance in your heart center.

Centaury Banishing Spell

This spell will help you banish any emotion you no longer wish to feel.

YOU WILL NEED

1 bay leaf

2 cups water

¼ cup dried centaury

1 tablespoon **Himalayan salt** *(table salt will also work)*

1 teaspoon pepper

WHAT TO DO

+ Take your bay leaf and a pencil, and write on the leaf whatever emotion it is you wish to be rid of, whether it is sadness, anger, or anything else.

+ Bring 2 cups of water to a boil, add the bay leaf, and then sprinkle in the centaury, salt, and pepper.

+ Let the mixture boil 3 to 5 minutes, and as it's boiling, close your eyes and take deep breaths while envisioning the emotion leaving your body.

+ When you're done, you can simply pour the water down the drain or dispose of it however you like. If you have more than one emotion you'd like to banish, work the spell over from the beginning, addressing only one emotion at a time. You can repeat this spell as many times as you need to.

CHAMOMILE
Chamaemelum nobile

―――――――――――――――――――――――ℓ

ESSENTIAL PROPERTIES

peace, abundance, love, self-love, healing

Roman chamomile and German chamomile are the two most common varieties of this plant, and both work equally well. They have a sweet, apple-like scent and charming little yellow and white flowers, like tiny daisies.

MEDICINAL PROPERTIES

We all know the soothing, gentle benefits of a cup of hot chamomile tea. That sense of peace helps us to release and purify ourselves from whatever may be burdening us, from negative energy to the stresses of the everyday, to a headache or a cold. Chamomile is very good for the skin, relieving eczema and helping to clear any pimples or uneven skin tone. She aids in digestion, and can ease stomach cramps or menstrual pain.

MAGICAL PROPERTIES

If you take a bath in water sprinkled with dried chamomile, it will invite love into your life. In fact, if you make a chamomile tea and add it to your bath, you will experience a feeling of bliss. Working with chamomile is great for those struggling with stress and anxiety. She can alleviate overwhelming emotions, and you can hold dried chamomile in your hands as you recite affirmations or prayers to help ease the heart.

PLANT WISDOM

If you are able to grow chamomile, set your intentions before watering her, intending abundance in wealth, love, or whatever you desire, and then repeat those intentions as you gently pour the water over her.

Chamomile is so nurturing and loving that if you plant her next to a struggling plant, the chamomile will help nurse her back to health. Growing chamomile yourself and setting intentions of healing into her seeds will bring you together in a powerful way, for as you care for her, you are in turn caring for yourself. Place healing crystals near her in your garden to amplify her healing energies, and you can also place crystals such as quartz to amplify her energies for abundance.

Chamomile loves to show up in dreams, usually with memories of childhood, particularly for those who have suffered in life, had a traumatic childhood, and/or have trouble conceiving. She soothes the heart and sends healing love into the soul.

CHERRY BLOSSOM
Prunus serrulata

CHERRY BLOSSOM

ESSENTIAL PROPERTIES

opening the door between realms, new beginnings, banishing

The flowering Japanese cherry tree is one of the most peaceful, reverent plants I have ever known. Cherry blossoms herald the coming of spring, flowering in great bursts of color and abundance, and as their petals fall, they cover the newly thawed ground like snow.

MEDICINAL PROPERTIES

Enjoyed as a tea, cherry blossoms are high in antioxidants and essential fatty acids. They are good for the skin, and have antiaging properties. They are also an anti-inflammatory, and can reduce swelling or pain.

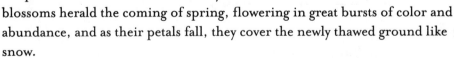

MAGICAL PROPERTIES

I collect fallen cherry blossoms and save them in a jar for any Magical workings. I set aside the stems for anytime I want to restart or reset myself, and keep the petals for when I want to banish something, like an old habit.

PLANT WISDOM

Cherry blossoms symbolize new beginnings and the fleeting nature of life. They visit us for such a short period of time, falling just two weeks after their beauty peaks. Spending this brief time with the tree will allow you to hear her guidance. I love to sit with her as I journal, meditate, or talk with her, so that I can receive as much of her wisdom as I can. Every time she blooms she brings a new insight—it's like visiting a tarot reader or a medium. She teaches that we always begin again, and evolve with every new start. Life is short, and we should never take the time we have for granted. If you have trouble slowing down or appreciating the sacred power of your time on this Earth, she will show you the way.

Dreaming of cherry blossoms brings peace to your heart. If you are mourning the death of someone you loved, or the death of a previous version of yourself, ask for her healing presence before you go to sleep.

CHICKWEED
Stellaria media

ESSENTIAL PROPERTIES

balance, amplification, love, strength

Chickweed is an extremely hardy plant. She's definitely considered a "weed," as she can be hard to get out of your garden, but honestly, why would you want to? She is sociable and strong-willed, so as long as you don't let her take over, she will give your garden energy and protection.

MEDICINAL PROPERTIES

Chickweed is edible and is traditionally consumed during the Japanese spring festival of Nanakusa-no-sekku. The leaf can relieve itching, constipation, and stomach and bowel problems, and can boost your iron and vitamin C if you're deficient. She can help with blood disorders and lung diseases as well.

MAGICAL PROPERTIES

Chickweed likes to grow in clumps, nestled with other plants. She can help you maintain your relationship with yourself as you work on your relationships with others. She's also very persistent, and can inspire your strength and endurance in difficult times. Chickweed will attract new love—or, to strengthen a healthy love, take a glass of cold water and place some chickweed in it, then keep it under your bed on your partner's side.

PLANT WISDOM

Chickweed's chief power lies in her ability to help you find balance, in all areas of your life, including love, healing, wealth, and relationships. She is the life coach of the plant kingdom. She lives everywhere, literally all around the world, and has seen and learned a lot from watching human behavior. Her wisdom is sacred, and I speak to her as if I were speaking to my elders. She talks about how important it is to see all different sides in any given situation, and how we so often suffer from blocked vision. She will help you learn to clear those blocks and amplify your inner guru presence. She does not show up in dreams, but if you meditate with her, she will take you far beyond this realm.

CHICORY
Cichorium intybus

CHICORY

ESSENTIAL PROPERTIES

unblocking, opening the door between realms, abundance

Chicory is a majestic-looking plant with mesmerizing bluish-purple flowers. She has been eaten by cultures all over the world for thousands of years, to add flavor, as a salad, or in coffee to enhance richness.

MEDICINAL PROPERTIES

A paste of chicory leaves applied directly to the skin is good for swelling and inflammation, and chicory can also treat high blood pressure and heart failure. In many Native American cultures, she is used to help with an upset stomach and constipation, and people all over the world work with her to treat liver and gallbladder disorders, and even cancer.

MAGICAL PROPERTIES

Chicory can help maintain frugality. If you're concerned about money, in addition to working with plants that invite prosperity, you should use chicory to help you save what money you have while you're working on your abundance. She can and will help you remove whatever obstacles are blocking your path, opening doors of opportunity in your life. It is said that her powers are at their strongest when she is gathered by moonlight, in silence.

Although chicory is a powerful plant to use for clearing blocked paths and opening new ones, she is also a great spirit communicator. When I work with chicory, she serves as a microphone for my ancestors. I often place a bowl of water next to her to amplify the whispers of the spirits she brings. You can ask chicory to visit you in dreams, but be warned, those dreams can be trippy! One moment you'll be flying, and another you'll be running through a spinning geometric tunnel. These dreams often bring a sense of fearlessness, reminding us of the inner power we all hold.

CHINABERRY
Melia azedarach

ESSENTIAL PROPERTIES
banishing, purification, energy clearing

Also known as paraiso, Persian lilac, and pride of India, chinaberry grows all over the world, from India to Africa to Hawaii. She is known for her timber, and her seeds are also used to make jewelry, especially rosaries.

MEDICINAL PROPERTIES

The fruit of chinaberry is poisonous to humans, but the leaves (which are also poisonous) can be stored with your produce to keep insects out. If used with care, an infusion of chinaberry leaves can calm Braxton-Hicks contractions.

MAGICAL PROPERTIES

Gather chinaberry leaves into a bundle and use it to sweep your home, clearing out evil spirits or stagnant energy. You can also perform this same ritual on yourself, brushing her leaves over your body, whisking away whatever may have latched on to you. Incorporate chinaberry into your banishing spells, or whenever you need to set some boundaries. Set your intentions while holding her in your hands, then bury her into the earth.

PLANT WISDOM

Chinaberry is a staple in many cultures and practices. She is great for banishing, purification, and setting boundaries, as she speaks of the importance of spiritual cleansing and keeping a healthy connection between yourself and the spirit world. Chinaberry is a little hard to get to know. She needs to trust that you are devoted to her, and so it takes a little work to establish your relationship. Start off with the techniques for connection from page 35, and do that for a few weeks before attempting to work with her. She needs to see that you are serious about your work, and not just using her. I meditate with her often, and work with her in my practice as often as possible. Chinaberry shows up in dreams only to those she has been working with for a long time, but those dreams are vivid and bring an abundance of wisdom.

CHINESE EVERGREEN
Aglaonema

ESSENTIAL PROPERTIES

luck, peace

Chinese evergreen has been cultivated in Asia for centuries, valued for her luck-giving properties. She can live in low-light conditions, which makes a wonderful houseplant. Her scientific name, *Aglaonema*, translates to "shining thread"—a fitting description given her distinctively marked leaves. She is sturdy and long-lasting, and so an ideal first plant for anyone looking to practice making their thumb a bit greener.

MEDICINAL PROPERTIES

This plant has no known medicinal properties.

MAGICAL PROPERTIES

Chinese evergreen's luck-giving properties are not just for one moment in time, but generally—she gives an overall sense of goodwill, good things, and good times. Placing her by your front door will bring in good-willed and kind people, and perhaps even lost strangers who will soon become friends. Place her by your north-facing window and she will bring happy energy into the home; place her in a south-facing window and she will attract fairies to protect your home.

PLANT WISDOM

Do you have a friend who is emotionally sensitive, who gets their feelings hurt easily, cries often, and can't stand to be around a lot of people? Like a super sensitive empath? This plant is for them. Chinese evergreen has a string-like energy that floats all around her, like a flowing spiderweb. I often stand next to her when I'm feeling oversensitive, or when my head and emotions are all over the place. Her web traps out-of-control emotions and beautifully and majestically ties them around your body to keep them grounded. Her language isn't like most other plants; where normally I can literally speak to plants, Chinese evergreen prefers energy communication, as she likes to keep her own headspace clear. She is not a plant to bring into your dreams, but I absolutely recommend having her in the home, especially by your bed at night to keep you peaceful and free of night terrors.

CINNAMON

Cinnamomum verum

ESSENTIAL PROPERTIES

success, love, abundance, spiritual development

The warm, spicy scent and flavor of cinnamon is obtained from the inner bark of the Ceylon cinnamon tree. Cinnamon was once so highly prized that it was thought to be reserved as a gift for either kings or gods, and the trees were protected by winged serpents. In ancient Egypt cinnamon was used to embalm mummies, but in the Western world the secret of her source was so valuable in the spice trade that no one knew where she came from. It was thought that cinnamon was fished up from the Nile, or perhaps from the nests of "cinnamon birds." Cinnamon trees are actually native to India, Sri Lanka, and Myanmar and can also be found in South America and the West Indies.

MEDICINAL PROPERTIES

Cinnamon is loaded with antioxidants, can calm inflammation, and is particularly helpful for people with blood sugar issues, as she can help reduce insulin resistance and help balance glucose uptake. Cinnamon may have beneficial effects on neurodegenerative diseases and may protect against cancer. She can also fight bacterial and fungal infections.

MAGICAL PROPERTIES

Cinnamon's warmth and vitality make her a powerful energizing plant, and adding cinnamon to any spell will amplify the vibrations of the other ingredients. Cinnamon is considered the spice of love, and has been used in love spells for centuries; and anointing a candle with cinnamon oil can be a powerful addition to success or money spells. Cinnamon can help you develop your psychic gifts and intuition. Burning cinnamon will raise spirit vibrations and assist you in developing your gifts.

PLANT WISDOM

The tree herself is where cinnamon's wisdom comes from, so sitting under a cinnamon tree and meditating will give you a sense of power, inspiring creativity. Taking a nap under the tree will send vibrations of love and healing throughout your entire being. Keeping her bark in your pillow will bring on vivid dreams or even visions if you're a seer.

CINQUEFOIL
Potentilla

────────────────────── ℯ

ESSENTIAL PROPERTIES

love, protection, wisdom, abundance, intuition

Cinquefoil is a common perennial herb native to eastern and Central America. She can be found growing in the most unusual of places, such as roadsides and waste areas. She has five leaflets and small yellow flowers with five slightly notched petals, giving her the name five-leaf or five-finger grass.

MEDICINAL PROPERTIES

Cinquefoil is an ingredient in mouthwashes, skin washes, diaper rash salves, and other cosmetics. She contains large amounts of tannins, and makes a good astringent. An infusion of cinquefoil tonic is good for diarrhea, fevers, toothache, dysentery, and jaundice. Cinquefoil mixed with honey alleviates a sore throat and is therapeutic for coughs.

MAGICAL PROPERTIES

In medieval times, cinquefoil was said to scare off Witches, which is interesting since she is a staple in many Witches' gardens, especially Witches of color. Work with her in health, money, protection, love, and power Magics. Cinquefoil is very protective, and can banish stubborn stagnant energies in your aura and bad vibrations from your home. She can also lift blocks interfering with your mind's eye. Placing a sachet of cinquefoil under your pillow will invite prophetic dreams.

PLANT WISDOM

I have to be honest, cinquefoil scares me a little! My mother has used five-finger grass for as long as I can remember, and each time she did my visions would take me to the craziest of places! But this was probably just because I was young and had no control over my gifts as a seer. Cinquefoil likes to speak in the lowest of tones, with a vibrating echo that sounds a bit

Cinquefoil's Incense Blend to Banish Negativity

There are many plants that can banish negativity, but cinquefoil's unique ability to help you see the unseen, with confidence in your inner wisdom, allows you to rid yourself of harmful energies you may not even be aware of.

YOU WILL NEED

- 1 teaspoon sandalwood powder
- 1 teaspoon dried cedar
- 1 tablespoon dried cinquefoil
- 1 small chunk of frankincense resin
- 1 teaspoon dried lavender
- Abalone shell or small dish

WHAT TO DO

- ✦ Start by opening all the windows in your home.
- ✦ Stir up all the ingredients into an incense blend.
- ✦ Light your incense and leave it to burn on an abalone shell or small dish.
- ✦ Carry it around your space, allowing the smoke to flow everywhere.
- ✦ Leave your windows open for at least 15 to 20 minutes after you've finished.

creepy—it's a little surprising since she is such a dainty and sweet-looking plant. But she means well, and all this intensity is because she wants so badly to help you see through all that is standing in your way. Her message is that of sight, inner sight. Working with her blossoms will help you see through the layers of your entire being, beyond the flesh. She does not visit dreams, but you can connect with her through meditation and by using her in your Magical workings.

CLOVE
Syzygium aromaticum

ESSENTIAL PROPERTIES

abundance, new beginnings, protection, love

This aromatic spice comes from the dried flower buds of the clove tree. This is an evergreen with flowers that turn from pale green to red when they are ready to harvest. Clove flower buds are harvested in their immature state and then dried, after which they are valued for cuisine, and medicinal and Magical purposes.

MEDICINAL PROPERTIES

Clove is a strong insect repellent, particularly against ants. Clove oil can soothe a sore tooth and also ease a toothache, reduce a fever, and prevent premature ejaculation. It is important to note that clove may cause adverse effects if taken orally by people with liver disease, blood clotting, and immune system disorders.

MAGICAL PROPERTIES

Clove is most commonly incorporated into love spells, perhaps because she has been known to increase libido. Ground cloves pressed into a candle can invite new love or strengthen a love that is already present. Clove is also a very protective being, and can be placed over your doors to keep out ill will, or over your bed to keep nightmares away. You can make a bracelet or necklace with cloves for your children to protect them from the evil eye, and you can put some clove oil on your forehead to keep other energies from intruding on your mind.

For protection spells, mix ground cloves with salt (it's best to grind them yourself with a mortar and pestle) and sprinkle the mixture as a barrier between you and whatever may be harmful, or simply all around your home. The bright, complex, and warm scent of clove can stimulate your mental processes, particularly your memory, and also open up your heart, making you more empathetic and present for others.

PLANT WISDOM

Clove brings a message of new beginnings. If you are lucky enough to have a clove tree or know where to find one, lie down and gaze between her branches into the sky, focusing on one spot. This is a form of divination, for what you see is what needs to be done in order for you to be reborn. Invite clove into your dreams by keeping her under your pillow. Your dreams will vary depending on what form of guidance clove believes you need, though primarily she works to remove any fear you may have about starting on a new path.

CLOVER
Trifolium

ESSENTIAL PROPERTIES

love, luck, success, protection

It's not only four-leaf clovers that are valuable and Magical! The most commonly found clover has three leaves, and her blossoms come in white or red. Clover, less commonly known as trefoil, has so many uses in Magic, as she has been part of a Plant Witch's practice for centuries. She is also well known as shamrock, a lucky symbol for the Irish.

MEDICINAL PROPERTIES

Red clover flower tops can treat respiratory issues such as asthma and severe cough. Clover may also be able to prevent cancer, to calm indigestion, to combat high cholesterol, skin disorders, and inflammatory conditions, and is great for general women's health issues.

MAGICAL PROPERTIES

The common three-leaf clover provides protection. You can keep a dried clover in your wallet or in your shoe, where she will journey with you and protect you from harm. A four-leaf clover doesn't just bring good luck, she strengthens psychic powers. You can work with her to amplify vibrations of luck, success, and love. White clover is best for protection and banishment spells. Keep clover plants in the home for happiness and luck, or gift this plant to those in need of an uplift, or to a new friend.

PLANT WISDOM

Clover is extremely helpful in our journey to self-discovery and awareness, particularly in the Witch community. Many of us have grown up in a society that looks down on Witches and gifted beings, leaving us scared and hidden for most of our lives. Clover can help us banish the programming we received in our childhood that makes us hide our gifts. Make sure to meditate with clover during the Full Moon to rid yourself of old programming and to help find your truth. The flowers are gentle beings who simply want to brighten up your day.

Dreaming of clover symbolizes good things coming your way, though if you dream of withering clover flowers, that indicates there is danger nearby.

COLTSFOOT
Tussilago farfara

COLTSFOOT

ESSENTIAL PROPERTIES
peace, psychic ability

Coltsfoot is a small cousin of dandelions and sunflowers. She got her name because her leaves look a bit like a horse's hoof—though she goes by many other names, too, including butterburr, coughwort, and clayweed. Indigenous people often used the fuzz that coats her young leaves for lighting fires.

MEDICINAL PROPERTIES

Coltsfood is an excellent curative for a cough, and drinking coltsfoot tea can help release mucus, though you don't want to have more than three cups a day. Her leaf is used to make medicine for bronchitis, asthma, and severe cough, as well as for a sore throat and hoarse voice.

MAGICAL PROPERTIES

In many Indigenous cultures, coltsfoot would be added to other herbs for smoking to induce visions. Burning coltsfoot will bring a sense of bliss and calm the mind, and if you burn her with lavender and orange peel, you'll feel like it's a sunny day even in the dead of winter. Her bright, cheery nature invites tranquility, and just having her around can give you a calm, happy feeling. Sprinkling dried coltsfoot around your altar or working with her in a divination spell will help you see more clearly, as coltsfoot is beaming with energies that will clear the fog blocking your mind's eye.

PLANT WISDOM

Coltsfoot brings you a message of freedom, of allowing yourself to be who you are, unapologetically. She is the plant to be around when you are going through a transition and need some loving support. Dreaming of coltsfoot is rare, but it does happen and usually means a spirit is coming through to speak to you—most likely a family member or close friend who has passed. Walk to her and slowly pluck her petals one by one, and the dream will end once you are done.

COMFREY
Symphytum

ESSENTIAL PROPERTIES

prevent thievery, abundance

Comfrey, also known as boneset, healing herb, and slippery root (among many other names) is a powerful healer. She produces beautiful bright flowers in purple, blue, and white, which look stunning against her deep green foliage.

MEDICINAL PROPERTIES

A poultice of comfrey can help heal a broken bone, and you can use a salve to heal a bruise or sprain. Comfrey contains allantoin, a compound found in breast milk, which stimulates the generation of new cells, though you should be careful not to consume too much comfrey as it can cause liver damage. Treat her as you would aspirin and use her sparingly—though she's perfectly safe when used topically.

MAGICAL PROPERTIES

Comfrey is a powerful protector. Keeping her roots in your car will prevent it from being stolen, and it's always a good idea to keep a little comfrey in your wallet or purse. Many people carry comfrey root in their luggage while traveling to keep it from being stolen or lost. Her ability to tie things together will bind your possessions to you. Her leaves are also used for abundance, especially in money, so keep dried leaves in your wallet, store register, and checkbook.

PLANT WISDOM

If you feel like you just can't forgive yourself for something you regret doing, bring some comfrey into your life. If you speak with her, she will gently exfoliate the guilt from your heart. Dreaming of comfrey symbolizes unresolved issues or situations, and when that comes up, I suggest journaling with comfrey near you, to find clarity on your next steps.

COPAL

Protium copal

ESSENTIAL PROPERTIES

purification, happiness

Copal is a resinous substance drawn from the *Protium copal* tree. Its consistency is somewhere between sap and a true hardened resin, as it's somewhat soft and sticky. Copal is sacred to the Indigenous peoples of Mexico and South and Central American countries, and has been for thousands of years. Mass amounts of copal were burned atop Aztec and Mayan pyramids as offerings to various gods and deities.

MEDICINAL PROPERTIES

Copal is known to be an antiseptic, and she also has potent tissue-repairing, anti-inflammatory, antibiotic, and antifungal properties. The oil can be applied to dry scalps, skin irritations, minor cuts, burns, boils, rashes, and acne. She can also treat insect bites, especially if you have an allergic reaction to the bite or sting.

MAGICAL PROPERTIES

Indigenous peoples still work with copal today, particularly in sacred sweat lodge or psychedelic substance ceremonies, and you can work with copal in a manner that is respectful of these cultures. Burning copal is a wonderful way to cleanse any ritual space, as it creates a pure and positive energetic environment. Allow the smoke from your incense to fill your room, taking the time to fan it into each and every corner. Remember to thank the copal after you're finished, and to always treat her with love.

PLANT WISDOM

Copal is a powerful being who can clear any demons lurking in your spirit. If you're ever in the presence of the tree herself, take a moment to give her a huge hug. While you're holding her, relax your body and mind. Take a deep breath and ask her to share her energy with you—this is especially helpful for those who suffer from depression and or anxiety. She purifies the spirit and mind, allowing you to feel joy, making room for light. Meditate with the resin in your hands, rocking back and forth, as this meditative motion amplifies copal's vibrations. Within a few minutes you will feel your body naturally sway on its own, possibly in circular motions, as you connect to copal's spirit. If you live on copal's lands, she may visit you in dreams and bring her healing to you there.

CORNFLOWER
Centauria cyanus

ESSENTIAL PROPERTIES

psychic ability, protection, happiness, love

Cornflowers are charming, bright-blue members of the daisy family. They grow in fields and even in the cracks of sidewalks in the middle of cities. Cornflower's bright blue can make a lovely ink, though it does fade fast. Cornflower petals are edible and often found in commercially available teas.

MEDICINAL PROPERTIES

My first experience with cornflower was when my mother made her into a tea that she used to clear out my eye, which was swollen and red after playing in the dirt. Cornflower can help reduce a fever and relieve menstrual cramps, as well as reduce water retention and inflammation. She is also taken as a tonic or a bitter for liver and gallbladder health, and is commonly known for treating vaginal yeast infections.

MAGICAL PROPERTIES

The cornflower has a tradition somewhat like the "he loves me, he loves me not" game—young men would wear cornflowers in their buttonholes (hence the nickname "bachelor's button") and if the flower lost its color too quickly, then their love was unrequited—but if the cornflower remained bright blue, it was returned. Keeping fresh or dried cornflowers strewn about your altar will enhance your psychic abilities, and if you ask her to, cornflower will also invite love into your life. You can also drink cornflower tea for the same purposes, or to enhance fertility.

PLANT WISDOM

If you look closely at the cornflower, you almost feel like she is trying to hypnotize you. That's because she latches on to your third eye and stimulates it, awakening a knowing and wisdom within you. You can work with her by drinking her tea, or by sitting with her and gazing into her flower, using her as a divination tool. She will take your eyes on a journey of geometric sacredness, tapping into your consciousness. With her, you can navigate truth and discover new ways to amplify your Magic. This journey is unique to each person, so keep your findings to yourself—they are sacred to you.

CROTON
Codiaeum variegatum

ESSENTIAL PROPERTIES
protection, banishing

This distinctive plant has variegated foliage that comes in red, green, yellow, and orange splotches—all the colors of fall, in one plant, all year round. She's a true beauty for those who love autumn! Handling this plant with care is important, as crotons emit a milky sap from their broken stems that can cause contact dermatitis. In fact, all parts of this plant are poisonous to people and pets.

MEDICINAL PROPERTIES

Despite serious safety concerns, croton seeds are used for emptying and cleansing the stomach and intestines, for gallbladder problems, and for malaria. They are also applied to the skin for muscle and joint pain. That said, I would not advise using croton for these issues, especially since there are other plants that can serve the same functions and are much safer.

MAGICAL PROPERTIES

If you are in need of a badass protector, this is your plant, Witches! She is most powerful when grown from a seed, as you can set intentions into the seed for who or what you want her to protect. If you can't grow croton from seed, she is readily available for purchase, and you can set your intentions as you water your plant. I grow a few in my home and garden, and I keep some in spots my cats can't get into, high up in the corners on shelves. I always keep a glass of water next to my croton plants to amplify the capture of negative energies and protection. Croton bounces back any ill will, evil eye, or curse that has been sent your way, as if it were marked "return to sender." You can use croton sap to anoint candles for protection, banishing, and hex-breaking spells—it will give those spells a huge boost, but be careful and make sure to wear gloves.

PLANT WISDOM

Croton is the protective mother of the plant kingdom, so don't mess with her babies! And never doubt that you are one of her children, for as a human you are a baby on this Earth, and she will protect you with all her might. Work with her for banishing and hexing or any other protective work. If you feel you're having a string of bad luck and might be cursed or hexed, invite croton into your dreams. She will bring clarity to what is really going on, and may even show you images of who has sent negativity your way.

DAFFODIL
Narcissus

ESSENTIAL PROPERTIES

luck, abundance, love

It is said that the appearance of wild daffodils is an indication of a sacred place. And so it may well be—daffodils, those bright, buttery flowers, are often the first heralds of spring, blooming right around the spring equinox.

MEDICINAL PROPERTIES

Daffodils are not to be eaten, as they contain the toxic chemical lycorine. But used externally, daffodil has astringent properties and can treat wounds, burns, or stiff and painful joints. Daffodil was the basis of an ancient ointment called Narcissimum.

DAFFODIL

MAGICAL PROPERTIES

Daffodil speaks of new life and new love, of luck and youthfulness. Working with her will bring high vibrations into your practice. Place her on your altar when you're doing spells for love, success, wealth, and abundance, and keep her with you for luck on tests, gambling, dates—really, for anything you want to make sure goes your way! Planting daffodils to greet you in springtime will bring you a year of abundance.

PLANT WISDOM

Daffodil teaches us to be youthful, both in mind and spirit. When we often get caught up with the stresses of life, we can forget how Magical the world can be—and how Magical we ourselves are. Nothing should ever bring down our spirit. Daffodil inspires us to be joyous and bright-eyed like children, with powerful imaginations that we can use to dream up the most enchanting of worlds . . . what we need to allow our inner Magic to blossom. Dreaming of daffodil may indicate that you are pregnant or will be soon, or perhaps that someone close to you may be expecting. But that pregnancy may not necessarily be literal—it may also mean the birth of a new direction in life or of the start of a new project.

DAISY
Bellis perennis

ESSENTIAL PROPERTIES
friendship, happiness

The English daisy, *Bellis perennis*, is the quintessential grows-in-a-field daisy, but any variety you find will have the same properties. Daisy, or "day's eye," closes at night and opens her bright face in the morning. Daisies grow wild and free and are most commonly seen in grasslands, meadows, and gardens. City Witches can tell you that they grow on lawns and even roadsides, so anyone can find a daisy to work with.

MEDICINAL PROPERTIES

Daisies are edible, and can help heal wounds. The juice can help disinfect bandages, speeding healing and preventing infection. In tea form, daisies can treat coughs, bronchitis, liver and kidney issues, and general inflammation.

MAGICAL PROPERTIES

The charming daisy is a flower of friendship, and a bouquet of daisies will brighten a friend's face—whether this is a new friend, an old friend, or anyone for whom you feel kinship. Daisy's most profound effect is to help you cultivate a childlike energy. Growing daisies, keeping a bouquet nearby, or even making and wearing a daisy chain crown can help you find your inner child, with all that childlike vibrant joy, sense of play, and emotional freedom. Bring happiness into your home by placing daisies by your front door, or hang a dried bundle in your children's rooms to bring them sweet and joyful dreams.

PLANT WISDOM

Daisy speaks of the kind of friendship that lasts forever, the friends who are there for you through thick and thin, who love and accept you just as you are. They support you and cheer you on. If you don't feel like you have friends like these, work with daisy to bring them into your life. You can also invite her into your dreams to help you determine if there's something keeping you from opening up and trusting the potential friends who come your way.

DAMIANA
Turnera diffusa

ESSENTIAL PROPERTIES
love, creativity

This low-growing plant with sweet yellow flowers is native to South Texas, as well as Central and South America and the Caribbean. The Indigenous cultures of these areas have always valued her as an aphrodisiac.

MEDICINAL PROPERTIES

Damiana's leaves stimulate the sexual organs, and she can be made into a tonic to boost virility. Damiana can also aid in combating depression, nervousness, headache, and digestion issues, and can boost mental and physical stamina.

Damiana Love Box

Creating a love box with damiana will enhance a love that is present or call back a love that has gone astray. If you are calling someone you have loved and lost, know that this will not make them love you if they no longer do, but if they do have some love for you, this box will help rekindle that relationship. You can also use this spell to awaken self-love.

WHAT YOU NEED

An empty box

A picture of you and your partner

Entwined strands of your hair

Anything else that symbolizes your relationship

A handful of dried rose petals

1 rose quartz

Affirmations or love poems to invoke the kind of relationship you want

Images from magazines of what you wish to manifest

A handful of dried damiana

Red candle

WHAT TO DO

+ Write a letter of intention for the love you will share, and place it in your box.

+ Add all the items except the damiana and candle to your box.

+ Sprinkle the damiana over everything.

+ Close the box and light your candle. Drip some red wax all over the top of the box. Sprinkle more damiana in the wax and allow it to harden.

+ Keep the box under your bed or in a safe place.

MAGICAL PROPERTIES

Damiana is the love and sex Magic queen! You can serve her as a tea, steep her in wine, or simply sprinkle dried damiana on a dish you have made for your partner—she will amp up both love and passion. But the best way to work with her is in a bath. I love a sensual and uplifting bath spell. Boil damiana for 10 to 15 minutes, then strain and add her to your bath, tossing in rose petals, rose quartz, and Himalayan pink salt. Light some incense or candles and climb in with your partner for a loving, sensual soak.

PLANT WISDOM

Damiana's hypnotizing flower pulls in the mind, and her deep green leaves have an alluring pattern that pulls in the spirit. She draws you in to give you her message of awakening, opening your eyes to your inner world, with the realization of the beauty that world has to offer. Her wisdom is intoxicating, blissful, and intimate—so much so that not everyone will be comfortable with how direct she is. When I first started to allow her in, through meditation and dream work, I felt uncomfortable. I was abused as a child, and she immediately sensed my trauma and left my body. She spoke to me from a distance about taking her in small doses, both energetically and physically, until I felt comfortable enough to fully dive in—and now we have a close and powerful relationship.

DANDELION

Taraxacum

ESSENTIAL PROPERTIES

wishes, opening the door between realms, resilience

Dandelion is very resilient—she will keep coming back even if you're trying to get rid of her! Dandelions have a signature brilliant yellow flower and a long taproot. Who hasn't blown at a puff of dandelion seeds and made a wish? It's one of childhood's greatest pleasures. And then there's the tradition of holding a dandelion flower under your chin and seeing if your face appears golden in its reflected light—if it does, you'll be rich someday. That particular game dates back to the Middle Ages.

MEDICINAL PROPERTIES

Dandelion is good for more than just wish fulfillment. According to Native American medicine, dandelion root can aid in treating stomach and liver conditions, as well as acne, eczema, high cholesterol, diabetes, and perhaps even cancer. Her sap can clear up warts, and her leaves are good for digestion and make a wonderful addition to a salad. They are highly nutritious and contain potent antioxidants, reducing inflammation and boosting your immune system.

MAGICAL PROPERTIES

When you want to use dandelion in a spell, think of the messages she gives: She is so resilient that she's able to grow and thrive anywhere. This makes her great for abundance work. Drinking a tea made from her leaves or roots before going to bed can give you prophetic dreams. Keeping a dandelion in a locket or pressed in your school books or planner will help in keeping you focused and productive.

PLANT WISDOM

If you have a pattern in your life you want to change, ask for dandelion's help. She is great for transformation, as she can help you stay resilient no matter what comes your way. She teaches us not to give up or give in. I am an Indigenous peoples' activist, a protector of the Earth—in my community, resilience is power, and dandelion feeds that power. I keep her with me to stay strong and to help those around me stay strong, and I know many other Indigenous activists who do the same.

Dreaming of dandelions symbolizes a breakthrough. When you meet her in dreams, know that she will comfort and support you when you're going through big life changes.

DATURA

Datura

ESSENTIAL PROPERTIES

peace, shadow work, opening the door between realms

Datura is known by many names, including Witch's thimble and devil's trumpet. She is in the nightshade family, as are her sisters belladonna and angel's trumpet—but unlike angel's trumpet, whose blossom points downward from heaven, datura sings from below (from "hell"). All datura plants contain alkaloids, especially in the seeds and flowers, that are toxic, narcotic, and hallucinogenic. The sap can cause irritation and rash, so it is vital that you wear protection when handling, and please educate yourself on this plant before working with her.

MEDICINAL PROPERTIES

Despite datura's toxicity, you can find her in ayahuasca brews and in smoking blends of datura and cannabis. Datura leaves are used to treat pain. In herbal medicine, especially in Ayurveda, she can treat asthma and help set a broken bone. The leaves of datura can relieve headache, rheumatic arthritis, and heart problems.

MAGICAL PROPERTIES

Trained shamans have worked with datura for spiritual journeys since Aztec times, but I don't recommend trying this on your own. Instead, take advantage of her powers safely, without ingesting her. Her presence alone will soothe you, helping you sleep and inviting prophetic dreams. If you let her, she can also help you explore the parts of yourself you don't necessarily want to face—your shadow self. She will guide you, keep you safe, and help you face your internal monsters so that you can see they aren't so monstrous after all. She will help you release them.

PLANT WISDOM

In many Indigenous cultures, including my own, poisonous plants are our most powerful allies in spiritual work. My mother has been growing datura—along with many other poisonous plants—since before I was born, so I am very close with this particular plant being. Datura spiritually cleanses the spirit and mind, purging the things that do not serve your well-being. She doesn't care whether you've acknowledged these things as toxic—she's getting rid of them whether you're ready or not! She's not gentle, either—she strikes like a serpent and shows the face of evil. Once you have worked with her, it will be hard to unsee what she has brought to the surface, and that can be painful. Make sure to spend some time on personal reflection, shadow work, and whatever other healing work you need to care for yourself.

Datura doesn't visit dreams, but if you meditate with her or keep some of her dried leaves in your pillow, she will send you gently into a vision or dream state.

DEVIL'S SHOESTRING
Viburnum alnifolium

ESSENTIAL PROPERTIES

protection, luck, awareness, banishing

Devil's shoestring refers to the dried roots of some types of viburnum—plants in the honeysuckle family native to eastern North America. The roots grow long and thin, like shoestrings, but they are firm yet flexible, like a vine. There are a number of devil's shoestring plants out there, but the species commonly included in Magical workings by Latinx and hoodoo cultures is the hobblebush (*Viburnum alnifolium*).

MEDICINAL PROPERTIES

The roots of devil's shoestring can serve as an antispasmodic, and you can also cut them up and make them into tea to reduce menstrual cramps or other aches.

MAGICAL PROPERTIES

You can keep out negative energies, evil eye, and other energetic attacks by tying a bundle of devil's shoestring above your door or burying it near your entryway. You can also grow these plants around your home, where their roots will spread and tangle together, forming a barrier in the earth. You can steep them in vodka or whiskey, making a tincture that you may either drink or rub on your pulse points to bring protection or good luck. Devil's shoestring is powerful in both protection and banishing spells.

PLANT WISDOM

Working with devil's shoestring is very intimate—she tells you, *Dear child, don't you worry about the shadows that try to creep.* She will show you the things you need to know, particularly spiritual attacks, but she will be there to protect you from them. She also brings luck by protecting you from losing, from failing, and from ignorance. Working with her will bring you the ultimate protection, as she also protects you from yourself—from distraction, procrastination, or self-sabotage. I always keep her in my pocket when I write, especially when a deadline is near. She is not a dreamworld plant, but will always be available to you through meditation.

DILL
Anethum graveolens

ESSENTIAL PROPERTIES

love, manifesting, protection, abundance

This aromatic, fern-like plant has a strong flavor, and you'll find it in lots of places besides dill pickles! Dill, also referred to as dill weed, was thought to defend against Witchcraft in the Middle Ages.

MEDICINAL PROPERTIES

Chewing dill leaves can make you more mentally alert, calm an upset stomach, and give you plenty of vitamins and minerals. Other uses for dill include treatment of fever, colds, cough, bronchitis, infections, nerve pain, menstrual cramps, and sleep disorders. Dill seed can also be applied to the mouth and throat to soothe a sore throat.

MAGICAL PROPERTIES

Dill is ideal for manifesting Magic, as she amplifies the energies of that which you desire. Placing dill by your windows or adding her to a crystal grid will bring in abundance, and you can dress a green candle with dill seeds for success and wealth. You can also use the seeds for protection by placing them on each side of your front door, around your back door if you have one, and by hanging a bunch of dill over your entryway. Dill is also good to work with for love—keep dill in your pocket or anoint your wrist with dill oil before going

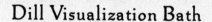

Dill Visualization Bath

This bath brings in all the powerhouse manifestation plants! It's extremely powerful, so think carefully about what it is you wish to manifest . . . and whether it's truly what you want.

WHAT YOU NEED

A handful of dill, fresh or dried

A handful of jasmine, fresh or dried

A handful of lemongrass, fresh or dried

The peel of 1 orange

1 aventurine crystal

1 cup kosher salt or table salt

A bucket

WHAT TO DO

+ Mix all the ingredients in a bucket of hot water and let it cool to room temperature.

+ Cup the water in your hands or in a small bowl and pour it over your body, working upward from your feet to your head. As you do so, visualize your dreams and desires at least 3 times before rinsing off in the shower.

on a date, when going out into town, and when meeting new people to lift your energies of happiness, love, and attraction.

PLANT WISDOM

Dill wants you to believe in all of your power and inner Magic, and know that you have no limitations. She can help release self-limiting beliefs, which will work against the intentions you are placing into your Magical workings. Dreaming of the scent of dill or of eating dill is a symbol of love and prosperity. When you dream of her, she is inviting you to place her in a special dish for your partner to rekindle love, or to work with her to fall into a new love. She senses when you have a lack of love in the heart space, and is always eager to fill it.

DOGBANE HEMP
Apocynum cannabinum

DOGBANE HEMP

ESSENTIAL PROPERTIES
awareness, clarity

Dogbane hemp is poisonous and, well, you wouldn't want your pets to eat her. *Apocynum* literally means "away, dog!" Although you'll see *cannabinum* as part of the name, dogbane hemp is not cannabis or actual hemp; she is so-named because her fibers can be twisted into a strong rope, much like hemp or flax.

MEDICINAL PROPERTIES

Dogbane hemp grows in North America, and her seeds are edible. You can squeeze latex from the plant to make a kind of chewing gum. But the roots, leaves, and stems can cause heart palpitations and nausea, so although Native American tribes work with dogbane hemp to relieve dyspepsia, fever, dropsy, and liver disorders, it's probably better not to ingest her.

MAGICAL PROPERTIES

Traditionally, Native American women tied knots in a rope of dogbane hemp fibers to mark important events in their lives. Knot magic has a long tradition; you can tie knots in dogbane hemp for the things you want to manifest, as this plant is great for bringing the unseen into reality. Placing dogbane hemp on your altar during the New Moon will bring visibility to the things that are hidden and need attention in your life. She is also powerful when the veil is thinnest, and can make the spirits walking the Earth visible.

PLANT WISDOM

Working with dogbane hemp is probably not for the easily offended, as the truth is sure to come out, even when we aren't ready for it. But if you feel you are prepared, and want clarity on what needs work, what needs healing, or what needs fine-tuning, then dogbane hemp is for you. In dreams, she symbolizes a coming out of sorts—a new you.

DRACAENA
Dracaena

ESSENTIAL PROPERTIES
abundance, feminine energy

Dracaena translates to "female dragon," perhaps because her stems are red like blood. Dracaenas make wonderful houseplants. They don't require much watering, but they like a humid environment, so placing pebbles around their base will help keep them happy.

MEDICINAL PROPERTIES

Dracaena produces a resin that was once used as toothpaste, for dyeing purposes, and as a cure for rheumatism and dysentery. Today, she's mostly used as a wood varnish, particularly for violins. Like many houseplants, she is a wonderful air purifier, and grown either indoors or outdoors she will reduce lead levels in particular.

MAGICAL PROPERTIES

Certain varieties of dracaena can grow into a large tree with branches growing wildly in all directions—much like a many-headed dragon. Incorporating dracaena into any spell, whether through using her leaves, resin, or bark, or by simply working with her energy, will help boost the power of your spell. Work with her for focus, drive, and confidence.

PLANT WISDOM

Dracaena is the perfect plant for the Boss Woman—she can support you in the running of your business . . . or the running of anything, really. Think of her as having a dragon for a partner—fierce, powerful, and unstoppable. She can help you rise and execute goals and plans, and will bring clarity to what you want to accomplish and how. You can build an empire with her; once you begin working closely with her, you can expect vivid dreams of your possible future.

Dragon's Blood
Daemonorops

ESSENTIAL PROPERTIES
protection, amplification, love

Dragon's blood actually refers to a resin, rather than to a specific plant. It can be obtained from croton, from dracaena, or from cinnamon. Today, most commercially available dragon's blood resin comes from one of several tropical palms of the genus *Daemonorops*. The resin is a bright blood red, and has been valued and used since ancient Rome.

MEDICINAL PROPERTIES

Dragon's blood has antiviral and wound-healing effects. Many natural beauty and care products have dragon's blood in their formulations for its antiaging, protective, and rejuvenating properties. Dragon's blood is also great for treating inflammation.

MAGICAL PROPERTIES

If you buy the hardened resin, you can break it up with a hammer and then grind it into powder using a mortar and pestle, making it easier to mix with water to create ink. With this ink you can write spells, intentions, even love letters to amp them up. Love letters can be to someone you love, to yourself, or to someone you are crushing on. You don't have to send them out but just the act of writing will bring those energies to you.

PLANT WISDOM

I simply had to include dragon's blood in this book, as it's such an amazing spell amplifier! And not only that, it also protects and purifies. You can burn dragon's blood to clear negative energies, or simply whenever you want to feel your Magical workings vibrating more powerfully. While its primary powers are love and money, dragon's blood can also be used for healing and protecting the home.

DUMB CANE
Dieffenbachia

ESSENTIAL PROPERTIES
protection, energy clearing

Like many houseplants, dumb cane contains oxalate crystals and shouldn't be eaten, and you want to stay away from her sap. Her name derives from her acrid and poisonous juices that numb the

DUMB CANE

tongue—leaving you speechless and "dumb." But she's a lovely little plant, with big, light-green leaves edged with dark green.

MEDICINAL PROPERTIES

In Brazil her leaves are made into a decoction that can be gargled to treat angina, and a tincture made from her roots can treat genital itching and gout. Indigenous peoples of the West Indies and the Caribbean chew a variety known as *Dieffenbachia seguine* to bring about temporary sterility in men, and in French Guiana the stems are used to treat ulcers. Arrows dipped in the sap are poisonous.

MAGICAL PROPERTIES

Dumb cane is your guard dog in the plant world, protecting you and your home from negative energies. She will "bark" an alarm by changing her color to yellowish green if there are bad entities or negative energies lurking nearby. I like to keep her near my front door, both outside the entryway and inside, so that she can detect negative energies within and without. It's also a good idea to keep her near you at work, keeping your co-workers' energy from invading your space, and to prevent any evil eye from entering your aura.

PLANT WISDOM

Dumb cane's wisdom comes in the form of speaking to you about greed. If you are someone who has a hard time not being selfish (which we all do from time to time), or trouble keeping a relationship balanced, then this is the plant for you. She will dig into the roots of the causes of this greed, bringing to light whatever is in your past that makes you hold tightly to what you have—and helping you overcome it. Invite her into your dreams if you are having night-mares, as she will go in and find the monsters that are haunting you.

ECHINACEA

Echinacea

ESSENTIAL PROPERTIES

healing, abundance, amplification

Also known as the purple coneflower, echinacea grows abundantly in both gardens and in the wild, though she is found in nature only in the prairies and woodlands of eastern and central North America.

MEDICINAL PROPERTIES

Echinacea's medicinal properties have been known for centuries, and you can find her in tincture, tablets, ointments, capsules, and extracts. During flu season, look for echinacea tea—it's a powerhouse for fighting off the flu, as echinacea has anti-inflammatory, antioxidant, and antiviral properties, and can help clear up a sore throat, headache, cold, bronchitis, and other upper respiratory infections.

MAGICAL PROPERTIES

Echinacea is one of several amplification plants that increase the effectiveness of spells in general, and of the other plants you may be working with. Including some echinacea in your Magical workings, or simply treating yourself to a cup of her tea, will boost your efforts, making them even more powerful. In a similar way, echinacea draws an increase of abundance at the same time that she protects you from poverty. This makes her a great choice for spells involving a desire for more success and opportunities. She is cheerful but soothing and can help with just about anything. Growing her out in your garden, or simply placing a bouquet in your home, will brighten up your energy and invite more wealth into your home.

PLANT WISDOM

Echinacea's message is so beautiful it makes me cry every time I hear her. She has always made me feel like her sister—to her, we are all family, connected, ONE. If you're a truth-seeker on a spiritual path seeking your purpose, she will bring a perspective no words can explain. She often visits those who work with her in dreams, particularly healers. A healer's energy is often chaotic and tired from their work with others, and echinacea comes to rejuvenate, reset, and clear your auric body.

ELDER
Sambucus nigra

ESSENTIAL PROPERTIES
opening the door between realms, healing, protection

Once thought to be a variety of honeysuckle, elder or elderberry is now known to be in the family Adoxaceae. The berry, bark, and flower of this large shrub-like tree are gifts to the world. The elder tree is sacred to a number of cultures' spiritual practices.

MEDICINAL PROPERTIES

Elderberries are powerful healers, and an elderberry syrup can soothe a sore throat, help cure a cold, and even relieve flu symptoms—she is taken in many homes around the world during the winter months to prevent illness. Make sure you're using *Sambucus nigra*, though, as other varieties are poisonous. Elderflower wine serves as another way of accessing elder's powers, as does her wood.

MAGICAL PROPERTIES

Elder has a dual nature—she is protective, but can also call evil spirits to you under certain circumstances. Elder is a gateway between realms and can be used to summon creatures of various kinds, most notably fairies. But elder is a great healer, and is sometimes called Elder Mother because of her potent healing magic. Smash some elder and rub it all over your hands, then place it over the parts of your body you wish to heal. You can also paint a circle of elder on your forehead and meditate to have her bring you into other realms. But please be careful, and make sure you have other plants there beside you who can protect you from evil spirits.

PLANT WISDOM

If you're not a fan of poetry, elder's message can be a little hard to interpret—she's very poetic and often speaks in rhyme. The best way to feel her message is by feeling her vibration—and knowing that there is so much wisdom to be found in learning to connect with those who are hard to understand. The language of vibrations and energies is universal and one we all must work on. Once you've formed a relationship with her, elder loves to visit you in dreams. If you travel all over in your dreams, she will come along and keep you company, reminding you that in real life you need to practice some grounding.

ELM

Ulmus

ESSENTIAL PROPERTIES

peace, balance, art Magic

Also known as the elven tree, elms are some of the most common trees in North America, with thousands populating New York City's Central Park—despite an attack by Dutch elm disease. It's not surprising that this tree is so precious to us, as her flexible wood can be made into just about anything.

MEDICINAL PROPERTIES

Elm bark can be used to soothe a cough, treat digestive disorders, or as an astringent. Elm bark can also clean open or festering wounds.

MAGICAL PROPERTIES

Elm provides a sense of peace and comfort, which is why so many of us feel at ease while resting under her branches. One of my favorite places to write and read is under an elm tree. She banishes negativity, and wakes the imagination, allowing me to dream without limits. She can bring out creative projects and even solutions to issues that may have been pestering you.

She sparks creativity, lending power to your art Magic. Yes, art is Magic, especially if you are the artist. Whatever your art form is, doing it under an elm tree brings your work to a higher frequency, imbuing it with healing energy that will lure people to your creations—and for good reason, since your work will be vibing with an energy we all need in our lives. If you set your intentions into what you are creating, elm will keep it locked in your art forever. If you can't work under an elm tree, just keep some bark near you while you work.

PLANT WISDOM

Work with elm to escape from real life and into your imagination, or simply to find peaceful, quiet solitude. If you have trouble with meditation, try working with elm and see how it becomes so much easier and more enjoyable. Dreaming of elm can mean a few different things: If you see branches falling off the elm, it means death is coming—either a literal death of someone you know, or a path in your life is dying, or a project, and so forth. If you are dreaming of climbing an elm tree, this means you need to leave something in your life—likely you are in a bad situation or toxic relationship, job, or environment. A dream of a peacefully swaying elm is a message from Mother Earth sending you love.

Enchanter's Nightshade

Circaea lutetiana

ENCHANTER'S NIGHTSHADE

ESSENTIAL PROPERTIES

new beginnings, balance, manifestation

This broad-leaved plant grows in shaded forest floors. The flowers are tiny, with two notched petals. Enchanter's nightshade received her botanical name from the Greek sorceress Circe, and also from Lutetia, the Latin name for Paris—not the city, but the man who stole Helen from her husband and started the Trojan War. Enchanter's nightshade is supposedly part of the potion Circe gave to Odysseus's men to turn them into pigs.

MEDICINAL PROPERTIES

In Austria, where this herb grows most profusely, it is made into a tea to treat rheumatism and gout, and to bring down a fever. However, she is considered a poison, so do your research and use with caution.

MAGICAL PROPERTIES

Enchanter's nightshade is a plant of transformation—but not the literal kind of turning a human into a pig. No, this sort of transformation is internal, and allows you the self-love and courage you need to become your true self. Working with her will help you shift, grow, develop, and find a new beginning. She will help you manifest the person you wish to be—from your health to your character, she can transform you into an entirely new person.

Enchanter's nightshade can assist you in finding an energetic balance between the light and the dark. This balance is one we all need to learn to work with and embrace—neither one is more powerful than the other, and if you can find this balance within yourself, your practice will transition into something that can truly impact the world. Dreaming of enchanter's nightshade symbolizes a hidden secret—this can be of a hidden part of yourself or a hidden gift you have yet to tap into. Ask her to help you bring what has been hidden into the light.

EUCALYPTUS
Eucalyptus

ESSENTIAL PROPERTIES

creativity, clarity, energy clearing, healing

The *Eucalyptus* genus has more than 400 different species, most of which are native to Australia. *Eucalyptus globulus*, also known as Tasmanian blue gum, is the main source of eucalyptus oil. Eucalyptus trees give off a strong, refreshing scent. They grow tall and fast, and some varieties store water so heavily that if you press on their bark, a stream runs down from your fingers.

MEDICINAL PROPERTIES

Eucalyptus has amazing antimicrobial properties; she can treat colds and respiratory problems, fungal infections, and wounds. She can support dental care, act as an insect repellent, alleviate pain, and stimulate the immune system.

MAGICAL PROPERTIES

I understand that not everyone can grow or have access to a eucalyptus tree, but you can have a beautiful relationship with her without that direct connection. You can work with her leaves, burning them to invite creativity and cleanse negativity. You can work with her oil, dressing blue candles for healing, or placing the oil on your wrists to deepen meditation. You can also add eucalyptus oil to water to use as a cleansing floor wash. I love to use her leaves to sweep my altar, leaving it vibrating with positive energy, energy that is great to work with for healing spells, creativity work, art, and even guarding against evil eye. I also religiously take a bunch of eucalyptus and hang it on my shower head, replacing it twice a year. This allows the steam of your shower to activate the eucalyptus, igniting her healing properties. The scent alone sends you into peace, calming both the mind and body.

PLANT WISDOM

Eucalyptus is possibly the sweetest soul I've ever met. Her wisdom speaks of keeping your body, mind, and spirit sacred and healthy. I grow my own trees, and the level of spiritual connection that happens when you care for her is unexplainable. She reflects back all that you give, and her gifts are simply life-changing. She is always chiming in when I'm having trouble making a decision, she nudges me when I need to do more spiritual healing, and she whispers when I need to cleanse my home or myself. She is a spiritual guide of sorts, and I would love for you to have that relationship with her. If eucalyptus visits you in your dreams, this means you may have a spiritual block. Listen closely to her wisdom, and put her advice to work to clear whatever may be blocking you.

EYEBRIGHT
Euphrasia

ESSENTIAL PROPERTIES
creativity, clarity, healing

Eyebright has been used for healing since ancient times. She received her name from her powerful healing properties for eye infections. Her flowers are the sweetest-looking things, with white, green, purple, and yellow colors dressing her petals.

MEDICINAL PROPERTIES

Eyebright can clear an eye infection, and can also strengthen your memory, either by using warm compresses made with the herb, or by drinking it as a tea, though you only want to drink it as needed, rather than over a long period of time. Eyebright is also great for allergies, colds, earaches, headaches, and sore throats.

MAGICAL PROPERTIES

Eyebright is an herb for clarity. She helps you to see the truth of people and situations, allowing you to view them without bias. She removes "cloudy" vision in those with delusions of grandeur or flights of fancy. Eyebright is also useful during divination or psychic work, especially for those who do not usually receive clear spiritual guidance; she can help you see the things that remain hidden, whether they are secrets you are keeping from yourself, or other ways of seeing the world and the universe that you may never have considered. She will also help you look at a situation objectively, without your emotions coloring your interpretations.

PLANT WISDOM

Work with her wisdom for seeing the unseen. She teaches us to be observers—patient, aware, and in tune with everything, not just in individual parts but as a whole. We often miss clues and lessons, or are unable to understand a person or situation because we have limited sight, both physically and spiritually. When she visits you in your dreams, it's a sign that abundance and healing are coming your way, so look forward to clearer skies and happier times.

Eyebright Third Eye-Opener Potion

This potion will bring you vivid dreams, messages, or visions, as eyebright shares with you whatever it is you most need to know at this moment. Begin this spell when you know you're going to go to bed soon, or if you've set aside time to meditate.

WHAT YOU NEED

2 cups water

1 tablespoon fresh or dried eyebright

1 teaspoon fresh or dried rosemary

1 teaspoon fresh or dried mugwort

1 teaspoon fresh or dried lavender

1 star anise

1 teaspoon salt

1 teaspoon grapeseed oil or oil of your choice

½ cup honey or maple syrup

WHAT TO DO

+ Bring the water to a boil and add all ingredients except for the honey or maple syrup.

+ Boil for 10 minutes, then lower the heat and cover, allowing the mixture to simmer for an additional 5 minutes.

+ Strain and mix 7 tablespoons of the tea with the honey or maple syrup.

+ When cool enough, lather this mixture into your hair and rub some on your forehead.

+ Let it sit for 3 minutes, then rinse.

FENNEL
Foeniculum vulgare

ESSENTIAL PROPERTIES

protection, courage, strength, purification

This aromatic plant is helpful in so many ways, and delicious too! Her seeds can be used as a spice, her thin, dill-like leaves used as an herb, and her bulb sliced and eaten raw, roasted, or sautéed.

MEDICINAL PROPERTIES

Fennel can relieve gas and cramping, and the seeds can relieve nausea. Fennel also has antioxidant, anti-inflammatory, and antibacterial effects.

MAGICAL PROPERTIES

In the way that fennel works so hard to protect your insides, she also tries to protect your spirit. She provides protection for the home and aura, and can help clear away negativity—and not just from outside forces, but from within yourself. Fennel gives you the strength to become who you truly are. She gives you the courage to follow your truth, and opens the throat chakra, allowing for better ease in communicating that truth. Fennel also supports those who are ready to see positive transformation or to release bad habits.

PLANT WISDOM

Work with fennel if you are seeking a new path or a new beginning. She empowers you to be who it is you see yourself to be. Meeting fennel in your dreams symbolizes a changing journey—not a subtle change but a completely different path. When you awake after dreaming with her, sit with her in the days after, working with her to feel within and clearly see where you should plant your next seeds.

FERN
Polypodiopsida

ESSENTIAL PROPERTIES

protection, self-awareness, intuition

Ferns grow easily both in the wild and indoors. Their light, airy fronds prefer warm, moist air—you can imagine them along the floors of rain forests or growing near a river. They love shade and can vary from the lightest of maidenhair ferns, growing in the cracks between rocks, to giant tree ferns, towering 20 feet high or more.

MEDICINAL PROPERTIES

The small, nearly open fronds—also known as fiddleheads—of many species of fern can be eaten, and taste something like a combination of asparagus and okra. The tubers of many ferns can also be eaten. Some varieties of fern, including maidenhair, Christmas, and bracken fern can be used to treat rheumatism and asthma.

MAGICAL PROPERTIES

While ferns do not reproduce through flowers, but instead through spores like fungi, there are still stories about fern blossoms and seeds. In Finland, it is believed that if anyone finds the seeds of a fern in bloom on the summer solstice, they will be guided by will-o'-the-wisps to hidden treasure—and they will be invisible as they travel. In the U.S. ferns are often tossed onto a fire to invite rain, and to ward off evil spirits. But ferns do not need to be set on fire in order to help you. Simply having ferns on your property will protect your land and home from negativity and those with ill intentions.

PLANT WISDOM

Place a fern frond in your pocket when you're going somewhere that has lots of energy, like a crowded space—she will protect you from energy vampires.

If you wear fern in your hair, she will protect you from those who want to intrude on your mind. She can also help keep you grounded—I have lots of ferns in my bedroom, as they help me calm down and get a good night's sleep. I also bring them into the bathroom when I want to take a calming, grounding bath. Work with her often, meditate with her, and lovingly care for her, and she will reflect that love back to you.

Fern sparks your senses—invite her into your dreams and she will help you develop your self-awareness and intuition, bringing them to a higher level.

FEVERFEW
Tanacetum parthenium

ESSENTIAL PROPERTIES

creativity, healing

Like chamomile, feverfew blossoms look like tiny daisies. This beautiful little darling is native to Eurasia, but these days she can be found growing all over the world.

MEDICINAL PROPERTIES

Feverfew can help relieve pain from menstrual symptoms, and may even soothe or prevent a migraine, though you wouldn't want to take her for too long as she can cause a rebound effect, inviting more headaches. She can also relieve dizziness and vertigo, and can treat rheumatoid arthritis, digestion issues, toothaches, insect bites, and infertility. And, obviously, feverfew can reduce a fever!

MAGICAL PROPERTIES

Feverfew has a way of bringing out ideas that inspire powerful creativity. Harvest feverfew when the Sun is highest, as this amplifies her energies. Take a bundle of feverfew and allow it to air dry. Once it's dry, hang it in your

Feverfew Hair Mask

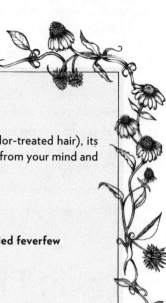

Not only is this mask great for hair health (and it is safe for color-treated hair), its Magical vibrations seep into your auric field, clearing out noise from your mind and helping you find both peace and clarity.

WHAT YOU NEED

½ tablespoon basil, fresh or dried

1 tablespoon feverfew, fresh or dried, plus 1 teaspoon dried feverfew

½ tablespoon rosemary, fresh or dried

½ tablespoon lemongrass, fresh or dried

½ avocado

1 egg

1 tablespoon olive oil

1 tablespoon honey

White candle

WHAT TO DO

+ Bring 2 cups of water to a boil in a small pot.

+ Add the basil, 1 tablespoon feverfew, rosemary, and lemongrass, and allow it to boil for 5 minutes.

+ Turn off the heat and let the mixture cool to room temperature, then drain, reserving the water.

+ Mash the avocado and add the egg, olive oil, and honey.

+ Mix in 2 tablespoons of the reserved herbal water.

+ Apply the mask to wet hair with your fingertips, starting at the ends and working your way up to the roots.

+ Leave the mask on for 10 or 20 minutes, and while you're waiting, light a white candle and brew a cup of tea with the remaining teaspoon of dried feverfew.

+ Relax in a quiet space, with no technology or television—just you and silence.

workspace. Or if you are able to, sit in a field of feverfew and take advantage of the passion she can send up from the ground, through your spine. Journal, draw, create, or meditate with feverfew, and you'll be full of inspiration, flowing with creativity. She is also a powerful healer, particularly of the mind. If you have a racing mind, full of noise, check out my Feverfew Hair Mask.

PLANT WISDOM

Feverfew reminds us that we are on an ever-changing journey, and helps us to appreciate the cycles of life as we work to birth beautiful things into the world. Your creative spirit has much wisdom and healing, and if you are having trouble remembering that, work closely with feverfew. Invite her into your dreams to help you release the limitations you have set for yourself.

FIDDLE–LEAF FIG
Ficus lyrata

FIDDLE-LEAF FIG

ESSENTIAL PROPERTIES
abundance, energy clearing, happiness

Fiddle-leaf fig is a tropical rain forest plant. She's become a popular houseplant, but she doesn't generally like being indoors. That said, you can keep her happy by making sure she has a humid environment (you may need a humidifier) and giving her plenty of care and attention. When grown indoors, she doesn't bear any fiddles, fruit, or flowers, but her leaves have a distinctive narrow middle with a broad top and bottom—you know, like a fiddle.

MEDICINAL PROPERTIES

This plant has no known medicinal properties.

MAGICAL PROPERTIES

Fiddle-leaf fig's specialty is abundance; she grows steadily and with confidence, and can help you do the same. Bring her to your altar when you're doing manifesting work, even if it is simply journaling, planning, or creating a vision board. If you have a more pressing concern and need good results right away, write it down on a piece of paper and place the paper in the dirt above her roots. Leave it there for three days, and then remove it. Please note, never ever place a curse or a hex, as no plant should ever be exposed to that energy—the idea here is to ask for her help, and maybe a little luck.

PLANT WISDOM

Fiddle-leaf fig is a gentle giant. She keeps to herself and emits positive energy, but if you don't take good care of her, her energy will turn turbulent, and she will fill your space with chaos. This isn't because she's vengeful or petty—she's trying to alert you that she needs help! But if you give her the care she needs and make sure her environment is supportive for her, she will fill your home with positive energies, as she sucks out the negativity and filters in the good. Dreaming of her brings an instant feeling of peace and love. She raises your mood and whisks away any negativity.

FOXGLOVE
Digitalis

ESSENTIAL PROPERTIES

protection, opening the door between realms

This classic cottage garden plant grows tall like a spire, with lovely bell-shaped flowers peering out. She goes by many fanciful names, including fairy thimbles, fairy petticoats, folk's glove, and Witch's bells. The tiny speckles within each flower are said to mark the spot where a fairy has rested within the blossom.

MEDICINAL PROPERTIES

Although foxglove is extremely poisonous, under careful monitoring she can be very helpful for heart conditions. A cardiologist may prescribe digitalis to help control heart rates, particularly if the patient has congestive heart failure.

MAGICAL PROPERTIES

You don't want to cross foxglove. Care for her well, because foxglove is the coven leader of the other realm—she is here to form a bridge to the other side. For those who want to create a bond with the fae, foxglove can do that for you, as she can connect to you to any creature, being, spirit, or entity, even gods and goddesses. She can detect ill will and bad intent, so don't try to work with her unless your intentions are good.

PLANT WISDOM

Grow her around your home for protection and safe passage—she will instantly turn your home into a Witchy and spiritual haven. Foxglove also is great at showing you the inner beauty within you and everything else—she knows that the inner world is even more beautiful than the outer, a concept that can be hard to grasp, especially when the outside world is so gorgeous. She brings to light that mighty power within, so we can fall in love with ourselves. Invite her into your dreams if you have never loved yourself or can't remember the last time you did. She uncovers your purity, allowing you to reconnect to your truest form.

GARLIC
Allium sativum

GARLIC

ESSENTIAL PROPERTIES

protection, clarity

We normally eat the cloves, but in fact all parts of garlic are edible and delicious. Garlic gets a bad reputation due to her strong scent, but I love it. I love "green garlic," the young shoots that form before the bulb fully matures, and "black garlic," full heads that have been heated very slowly over the course of weeks or months—they literally turn black, and have a sweet, syrupy, pungent flavor.

MEDICINAL PROPERTIES

Garlic has had medicinal uses for centuries. She can combat high cholesterol and hypertension, can ward off various forms of cancer, and is a powerful antibiotic (and so great to eat when you're sick). She can boost your immune system and give you more energy.

MAGICAL PROPERTIES

Garlic offers powerful protection, shielding you from evil energy, hexes, and gossip. She can also be used to ward off people who you no longer wish to have around, and so I suggest working with her to protect yourself or others from abusive relationships. Garlic helps to break things, whether it is a relationship or a curse, and is often used during exorcisms. Garlic also strengthens the energy field.

PLANT WISDOM

Garlic is the queen of truth-telling. Like garlic, we have protective layers we place around ourselves to keep us hidden, safe, unseen by the world around us. When we have a history of abuse, hurt, pain, or trauma, garlic will work with us to feel protected while at the same time uncovering the beautiful truths we have been hiding. She brings us out of the shadows and back into the light where we belong. Invite garlic into your dreams to reveal secrets and truths you may have kept from yourself—if you're not quite sure what your gifts are, garlic will help you find them.

GENTIAN
Gentiana

ESSENTIAL PROPERTIES

spiritual development

Gentian is named for Gentius, an Illyrian king who supposedly first discovered her useful properties . . . around two thousand years ago. She is still consumed frequently today, most often in bitters like Angostura or Peychaud's. She grows wild in grasslands and woods, and her flower is sometimes an intense, glorious blue.

MEDICINAL PROPERTIES

Gentian can treat liver function, improve digestion, detox the kidneys, and eliminate parasites. She can also improve circulation by increasing blood flow to the extremities. She may also treat anxiety and help with concentration. Used topically, she can speed wound-healing. That said, overuse can cause overstimulation, so take care and don't consume gentian for longer than two to three weeks.

MAGICAL PROPERTIES

Gentian isn't really someone you do spells with; she is more of a spiritual partner. She will bring to light the lessons you have learned in life, showing you that you have always been capable of getting through whatever troubles come your way. Gentian helps you cope with life's ups and downs.

PLANT WISDOM

If you are on a spiritual journey or simply want to develop your spiritual practice, create a relationship with gentian. She will help you seek the truth within. She is warmhearted and compassionate—you will find yourself basking in her serene energy. She encourages you to keep going, and fills you with the confidence to believe you will succeed, despite whatever setbacks, failures, and obstacles you may encounter. She teaches about the importance of having patience with ourselves and with life, reminding us to take things slowly and observe all that happens along the way. These obstacles that we encounter are not wasteful—they are tools for our life journey. If you are struggling with figuring out how to navigate through a difficult situation, invite gentian into your dreams. She will light your way.

GERANIUM
Pelargonium

ESSENTIAL PROPERTIES

happiness, abundance

This cheerful flower is so perfect hanging in baskets on a porch. Geraniums are easy to grow and some varieties have a fruity, generous scent. The leaves and petals are both edible, and varieties with a rose-like scent are valued for their uses in perfumes.

MEDICINAL PROPERTIES

Infusions made with geraniums can heal kidney concerns, lower a fever, and ease the discomfort of irritable bowel syndrome. A balm made with geranium can be applied externally to help draw out an infection, and her essential oil can be a powerful mood-booster.

MAGICAL PROPERTIES

Geraniums invite happiness and prosperity simply with their presence; place her outside your front door to bring these energies into your home. She also screeches at the sight of dark energy, and so is great to pair with rosemary, who will act on her warning and banish those dark energies. When combined with chamomile (see page 118) in a bath, you become instantly more aware of your body in a deeper sense, and you can feel where your body needs extra care and attention. If you're sick or unwell but you don't know where it's coming from, this is an excellent diagnostic tool. Geranium is also helpful for sympathetic Magic—so if you wish good things for someone else, you can use geranium to send your intentions outward. This works particularly well when your intention is to protect the Earth and all her children.

PLANT WISDOM

Geranium wishes for you to always be happy; she is kind and wonderful to people who live alone and or don't feel loved. She will tell tales of happy children, and teaches that we all still have that laughter beaming brightly within us. If you're feeling low, just stop to smell her scent—she will transport you back to those moments when you felt pure joy and bring it back into your heart space. Invite her into your dreams for peaceful nights.

GINGER
Zingiber officinale

ESSENTIAL PROPERTIES

self-awareness, unblocking, strength

The spicy, bright flavor of ginger root makes it a popular ingredient in cuisines all over the world. The stalks grow tall, with broad leaves, and some varieties (though not the edible ones) have fragrant, orchid-like blossoms.

MEDICINAL PROPERTIES

While many plants are good for easing an upset stomach, ginger is hands down the best. But she's also wonderful for a flu, as she can reduce inflammation, calm a cough or sore throat, and her warming qualities can soothe sore muscles. In Ayurvedic medicine, ginger has so many uses that she may well be the most valuable, despite being so widely available.

MAGICAL PROPERTIES

Ginger is great for all-around well-being. She gives energy, strength, and power that you can use in your spellwork, as well as in the body. Turn to ginger for both love and money work, particularly to overcome problems or deal with emotional stress. Keep ginger in your pillow for a better night's sleep that will be peaceful and uninterrupted. Use ginger to cleanse yourself by taking a root and, starting from the top of your head, touching your body with it, scanning all over and around. She will grab hold of any energies that have latched on to you, causing discomfort or aches. This is especially great for empaths. When you've finished, boil your ginger root for 10 to 15 minutes, evaporating the energies, before disposing of it—it's best to bury it.

PLANT WISDOM

Ginger will clear blocks, obstacles, and habits that keep you from moving forward. If you are seeking your truth or purpose, ginger will give you a push in the right direction, leading you to self-discovery. I find that she is particularly great for business owners, creatives, and entrepreneurs—she will help them keep building, rising, and expanding. When you invite ginger into your dreams, first set a clear intention for what it is you need her guidance on.

GINKGO
Ginkgo biloba

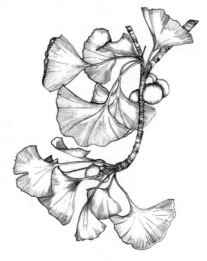

GINKGO

ESSENTIAL PROPERTIES

intuition, psychic ability

Ginkgo is also known as the maidenhair tree. Her leaves have a distinct fan
shape, and turn a vivid yellow in the fall.
She is a living fossil, having been around
for 270 million years. She is native to
China, where she was first valued for both
her nutritive and medicinal properties.
Ginkgo nuts do not smell good when they fall from their trees, but when
prepared properly they are delicious, and are served at celebrations of the
Chinese New Year.

MEDICINAL PROPERTIES

Ginkgo is widely appreciated for her ability to support memory function—she
has even been used to treat people with Alzheimer's disease. However, you
want to be careful not to consume too much, as the side effects of overuse can
include nausea, heart palpitations, and headaches.

MAGICAL PROPERTIES

The ginkgo tree can live for a thousand years, and helps us maintain our connection with our ancestors. Placing a fresh ginkgo branch on your altar when
doing ancestral work will allow you to see and hear the hidden world. She will
open your third eye, helping you tune in to the divine. She doesn't exactly
help you speak to your ancestors directly—rather, she helps you tap into the
lessons and teachings they have passed on to you.

To activate your psychic gifts, you can place a ginkgo nut in a glass of
water. Add a dash of pepper and one or two ginkgo leaves. Keep it in front

of you as you meditate. You can also carry ginkgo or drink a cup of ginkgo tea before working divination tools such as tarot or runes to awaken your intuition.

PLANT WISDOM

Ginkgo's wisdom is born of centuries of evolution and expansion. She knows that the knowledge we seek already lives with us, and so when she connects us with our ancestors, she is reminding us that they are there with us, running through our blood and bones. Dreaming of ginkgo is rare, but when it happens it means she has come to point out any blockages in your spirit that are preventing you from accessing your gifts.

GLADIOLUS

Gladiolus

ESSENTIAL PROPERTIES

protection, opening the door between realms

Also known as the sword lily, gladiolus is native to Asia, Africa, and the Mediterranean. Her leaves are narrow and firm, like tiny, slim swords. The flowers spike off the stems, and can range in color from white to a vivid red. They can be pollinated by bees, but are more often visited by moths. There is a legend that there was a maiden named Glad who was being held prisoner by an evil wizard. The prince Iolus went in search of her, and rescued her, but the wizard caught up with them and in his fury turned them into a flower—the gladiolus.

MEDICINAL PROPERTIES

Gladiolus can be used to treat digestive issues, to raise energy levels, and as a general tonic. If prepared properly, her corm can be eaten, and it can relieve painful menstruation and rheumatism.

MAGICAL PROPERTIES

A gladiolus's sword-like leaves are great for protection spells. I like to take several leaves and tie them together, then place them alongside my front door, points facing down. She will fend off any evil attempting to enter your home. Similarly, if you often travel in the dreamworld, or are visited by demons or evil spirits in your sleep, hang a bundle of her swords on the wall over your bed. She will guard you even in your dreams.

For a powerful ancestral or spirit communication practice, place a small bowl of water sprinkled with gladiolus petals, and lay her leaves over your altar. This will allow gladiolus to both open the door for you, and protect you from anything you don't want to have contact with.

PLANT WISDOM

I don't understand why everyone doesn't grow gladiolus—she's so darn gorgeous! Her flowers are so cheery and sweet . . . but they are deceptive, as gladiolus can be vicious if she needs to be! She is extremely protective, and will guard your home from any harm. She attracts spirits, but only if you specifically ask her to—otherwise, she will keep your Magical doors locked tight. If trouble is near, she will sound bells in your ears, and you can always count on her to be loyal and watch your back. When she comes to you in your dreams, she is passing along messages from your angels, spirit guides, or loved ones who have died.

GOLDENROD
Solidago

ESSENTIAL PROPERTIES
love, psychic ability

Goldenrod has a distinctive color, much like yellow mustard. She grows in fields, and her young leaves are edible. Goldenrod blossoms attract many kinds of pollinators, and honey made from them is nearly clear, with an almost spicy flavor. This wild plant reproduces through her roots, bulbs, and stems, as well as by seed.

MEDICINAL PROPERTIES

Goldenrod can counter bacterial infections and other causes of inflammation, especially kidney stones. If you are fasting, goldenrod can help clear out toxins. Some Native American tribes chew goldenrod leaves to soothe a sore throat, and the roots to ease a toothache. As a salve or tea, she is great at clearing up skin conditions.

MAGICAL PROPERTIES

Goldenrod is associated with the goddess Venus, and therefore with love. She is a wonderful addition to love potions, and it is said that giving goldenrod to a lover will seal your relationship. Use goldenrod in self-love baths and candle Magic to amplify love.

Goldenrod can also help with divination—sprinkle her on a table when doing psychic work. She is particularly good at awakening clairsentience, the ability to clearly sense emotions, vibrations, and energies. To build clairsentience, start by making yourself a cup of goldenrod and star anise tea, put goldenrod in your bath and allow the steam to fill your auric field, and finally light a yellow candle dressed in goldenrod. There! Now you have an entire ritual to awaken your clairsentience.

PLANT WISDOM

Goldenrod's message is loving and gentle. If you have a hard time growing up or are scared of old age, she is the best plant for you. She will change your perspective on aging, helping you see it for the beautiful thing it truly is, helping you to grow into the wise being you are meant to be. Invite her into your dreams if you suffer from anxiety attacks related to fears of death or aging. She can take that panic and dilute it so that you can clearly see the true cause of your fears.

GRAPE
Vitis

ESSENTIAL PROPERTIES

creativity, new beginnings, abundance, amplification, wishes

The grape has been a part of cultures all over the world for centuries. This woody vine's berry has been used to make wine, grapeseed oil, and vinegar, and can be eaten fresh or dried. She grows easily and her fruit can be crimson, black, orange, blue, pink, green, or even white.

MEDICINAL PROPERTIES

Grapes—especially red grapes—contain resveratrol, which can lower cholesterol and treat heart disease in general, as well as boost the immune system and cognitive function. Grapes can also treat diabetes and allergies. Cutting a grape in half and rubbing it on your face is an effective astringent that can clear up skin conditions such as acne. In particular, grapeseed oil can improve circulation, bone strength, mental resilience, and kidney function, and may reduce your risk of cancer.

MAGICAL PROPERTIES

You can work with grapes in so many different ways, such as mixing purified water and halved grapes in a spray bottle to purify and cleanse your home. To work with grapes for manifestation or wishes, make a wish or set an intention for each grape as you work your way through a cluster. You can also hang grape vines on a vision board or an outline for a creative project, or place them in your planner to help your dreams manifest. Indeed, grape vines are particularly powerful and can take your spellwork to the next level. Try cutting a length of grape vine into small pieces, and use them to amplify whatever spells you're working on.

In my culture, grapes are transformative. They help with manifesting a new path in life, and as such they are sacred. Grapes are wonderful for fertility and abundance work, and their energy is so loving that simply leaving a bowl of grapes out on the table blesses the home. I would suggest setting out a bowl of grapes every day—this ritual act will allow her energy to create a sacred environment. I always keep a bowl of grapes on my altar.

HAWTHORN
Crataegus

ESSENTIAL PROPERTIES

healing, love

The hawthorn tree, also called thorn apple among other names, has for centuries been sacred to many Indigenous peoples all around the world. Hawthorn has small, tart berries and beautiful white or pink flowers surrounded by thorns. She features as a Magical tree in a variety of folklore and fairy stories.

MEDICINAL PROPERTIES

Hawthorn's tasty, edible berries, along with her flowers and leaves, are a medicinal heart tonic. As a nutritive herb, she can restore damaged heart tissue, strengthen the heartbeat, and regulate blood pressure. Hawthorn can support joints, veins, tendons, and ligaments. She also helps with circulation, improving blood flow to the extremities. Hawthorn's medicine is gentle, so a tea or tincture made from her can be taken as a long-term heart and circulatory tonic.

Hawthorn Meditation Tincture

You can adapt this recipe to use with any edible plant in this book. Take a dose of 10 milliliters, or approximately 2 teaspoons. In this case, hawthorn will bring forth that which you have held on to, hiding from the world, and even from yourself.

WHAT YOU NEED

> 1 cup dried hawthorn berries
>
> Glass jar with a lid
>
> 1 pint 80-plus proof rum or vodka *(you can also use apple cider vinegar or food-grade vegetable glycerine)*
>
> 1 tablespoon honey or maple syrup *(optional)*

WHAT TO DO

+ Pour the berries into the jar, and cover the berries with the alcohol, vinegar, or glycerin. Secure the jar tightly with the lid.

+ Date and label your jar so you remember what it is and when it was made. Store in a cool, dark place for at least 3 to 4 weeks, and shake it a little bit every day to release the juice from the berries.

+ When it's ready, strain the hawthorn tincture. You can either keep it in the same jar or use a dark tincture bottle. If you used apple cider vinegar, you'll need to store your tincture in the refrigerator.

+ When you would like to meditate with hawthorn, find a quiet and comfortable place to sit.

+ Before taking the tincture, speak to her. Let her know you are ready to heal your heart, and thank her for the medicine journey she is about to guide you through.

+ Place a drop of tincture on your tongue and be still. Allow your senses to take over. Pay attention to any emotions, thoughts, visions, or images that come to you. She works with your healing waters, so don't hold back any tears that come. Let them flow and fall as they please.

MAGICAL PROPERTIES

Hawthorn is one of the most powerful beings for heart healing and heart opening. She can heal your heart physically as well as spiritually, and can remove emotional blockages. You may create a relationship with hawthorn through meditation or just by being in her presence, but the following remedy can help you foster that connection.

PLANT WISDOM

Hawthorn is one of our great elders, and like all elders shares her wisdom and love with depth and purpose. Her love is somehow tough and gentle at the same time—she brings forth what you need to heal, but helps you purge the pain, never leaving you to deal with it on your own. She is very thorough, so expect to have a powerful heart-healing journey when you work with her.

HAZEL
Corylus

ESSENTIAL PROPERTIES
wisdom, psychic ability

The hazel tree was sacred to Irish cultures—so much so that cutting one down could be punishable by death. There is a story that nine hazel trees grew around a sacred pool, and their fallen nuts were eaten by the salmon living there, who absorbed the hazel trees' wisdom. A druid and his student made camp by the pool, and the student was instructed to catch and clean the fish. He had been ordered not to eat it, but he cut himself, and when he licked his finger clean, he absorbed some of the fish's blood with his own, thereby gaining all its knowledge. The student was Fionn Mac Cumhaill, a legendary Irish hero.

MEDICINAL PROPERTIES

Hazelnuts are delicious and packed with nutrients, vitamins, minerals, anti-oxidants, and healthy fats. They are known for improving blood sugar levels, regulating blood pressure, and reducing inflammation. Pliny the Elder recommended using the bark to cure a cough, and a poultice made from the nuts and shells may ease rheumatism.

MAGICAL PROPERTIES

Hazelnuts are sacred and powerful, but like all nuts, they are often overlooked. But nut Magic should be a part of every Plant Witch's practice—they amplify your work and increase the vibrations of your spells. If you want to awaken the gifts you carry within, hazel will help you.

PLANT WISDOM

Hazel teaches us that all we need is already within us. Work with hazel to access your inner wisdom, learning how to use yourself as a tool for divination. If you dream of hazel, that means good news is on its way. If you can't find a tree to sit with, simply hold hazelnuts in your hands while meditating, or keep them on your altar or in your sacred space. I keep them in my pocket while hiking or walking in nature, for they can connect us to nature spirits.

HEATHER
Calluna vulgaris

ESSENTIAL PROPERTIES

protection, weather manipulation

Heather is a low-growing shrub, and can cover a vast area, such as the moors of Scotland, Ireland, and England. Heather can be used for dyeing, and is an important food source for sheep and deer. She is wonderful for making besoms, or small handmade brooms.

MEDICINAL PROPERTIES

Heather can soothe a migraine, and can also relieve stress and negative think-ing. Steep the flowers and then add them to a bath to help strengthen and tone muscles. You can also make heather tea to treat kidney issues, arthritis, sleep disorders, and coughs or colds.

MAGICAL PROPERTIES

Heather is extremely protective, particularly in cases of violence against women. She keeps intruders out—intruders of the mind, body, and spirit. She believes in the sacredness of our vessels, and helps us remember that no one should have access to us without our permission. Work with her in spells that deal with repelling a person and/or energy.

Burning heather is said to bring the rain, but before you do, I need for you to understand that this should be done only if the rain is truly needed. We do not burn the members of our plant family without good reason. Remember, we don't use plants, we work with them . . . and in fact, plant Magic will not work if your intentions aren't pure.

PLANT WISDOM

I was abused as a child, sexually, mentally, and spiritually, and because of this I have had a difficult time with relationships for much of my life. I had trouble letting people in, or being fully present. But in my late teens, I began working with heather, and she told me stories of the power we all carry. She taught me that this power is never taken away from us, and that even when we are abused or traumatized, that power is never lost—it is simply hidden in the spaces we hid within to cope with that abuse or trauma. Heather can help you uncover that power, reminding you not to fear it—just because someone has used their power to hurt you doesn't mean using your power will do the same. Heather will help you reclaim your power, and understand the sacredness of its pure roots. Dreaming of heather symbolizes freedom, peacefulness, and resilience.

HELLEBORE
Helleborus

HELLEBORE

ESSENTIAL PROPERTIES

healing, protection, peace

Hellebore is one of the earliest flowers to bloom in the spring, and it will brighten dark corners of your garden. They look somewhat like roses, but are actually members of the buttercup family. *Hellebore* translates from Greek to "injurious food"—and the flowers are quite poisonous. There is a story in Christian traditions that says the first hellebore bloomed from a tear dropped by a girl who had no gift for the infant Jesus.

MEDICINAL PROPERTIES

Hellebore was once used in ancient Greece to cure insanity, but it is so poisonous it's best not to touch without gloves. It is theorized that Alexander the Great was killed by hellebore.

MAGICAL PROPERTIES

Are you an introvert? I am. Those of us who have trouble in crowded spaces need to have hellebore around—she will bring down those energies so they won't affect us. Keeping her on you when you go out to a gathering creates a bubble-like cloak, hiding your energy field so that all that energy surrounding you can't interact with you and you become energetically invisible. This is also useful for empaths, who need some protection from the emotions of others. In fact, hellebore is great for invisibility spells in general—dusting dried hellebore over someone while setting your intentions can keep them from being seen.

Hellebore's calm and compassionate nature can help to soothe mental and emotional pain and struggle. Just her presence alone sends healing to these spaces. I would suggest keeping her where you work, to help you focus. I place her next to my work table, and I also keep her in my bathroom—so I can enjoy my baths and showers without a running mind—and in my sacred space while I do yoga, breath work, and other body-spirit practices. If you are a healer and work with people who need quieter minds and hearts, keep her with you and she will support your efforts. Dreaming of hellebore symbolizes a need to set healthy boundaries.

HIBISCUS

Hibiscus

ESSENTIAL PROPERTIES

love, peace, healing

Hibiscus plants are known for their large, colorful flowers—they bring so much color into your garden or home—and they have many uses. You can crush the blossoms until they release a sticky substance, which you can then use to blow bubbles. Hibiscus tea is valued all over the world, and being high in vitamin C, it is quite tart and delicious. Hibiscus comes in beautiful vibrant hues, including red, yellow, peach, or white. In Hindu traditions, the red hibiscus symbolizes the goddess Kali. Tahitian and Hawaiian women often wear hibiscus in their hair.

MEDICINAL PROPERTIES

Hibiscus teas and liquid extracts can help treat a variety of conditions. In Ayurvedic medicine, hibiscus promotes hair growth, and can prevent your hair from going gray. It can help balance your hormones and keep your body temperature cool. Hibiscus is also good for the skin, and can relieve acne.

Healing Hibiscus Waters Ritual

This powerful but gentle spell offers a soothing vibration, one that evaporates from the water and into the air all around you, permeating your energy field.

WHAT YOU NEED

Clear glass bowl

5 to 7 fresh hibiscus blossoms

Rose quartz

Rose essential oil

WHAT TO DO

+ Fill your glass bowl with cold water.

+ Place the hibiscus blossoms in the water, letting them float.

+ Add the rose quartz and let it sit at the bottom of the bowl, and then add 1 to 2 drops of rose essential oil.

+ Place the bowl in the room that needs the most harmony and love—you can put it in the living room to bring everyone together and ease tension, or keep it in the bedroom to rekindle and fire up passion. You can also just place it next to you to heal your heart, and sit with your bowl while you journal, writing for self-love.

MAGICAL PROPERTIES

Hibiscus has an affinity for love and passion. She works on the sacral chakra to help you to rediscover your zest for life. Though commonly worked with to promote intimate love, hibiscus paves the way for love of all kinds, including discovering your purpose in life. Hibiscus teaches you to flow with life rather than against it, and to find harmony in all that you do.

PLANT WISDOM

Hibiscus brings harmony to us all. Place bouquets of fresh hibiscus all around your home during the spring and summer, leaving your windows open to circulate her balancing energies and loving flow. Dreaming of hibiscus means that you have been drowning in self-pity and self-hate; she has come to help you swim back to the top. She brings new breath into your life.

HICKORY
Carya

ESSENTIAL PROPERTIES

strength, healing, spiritual development

Hickory trees are very slow growing, and their wood is extremely hard. There are harder woods, but hickory combines strength, toughness, and resistance, making it an exceptionally valuable wood, especially for crafting tools. It has been used for bows, wheel spokes, and paddles, among many other useful objects. Hickory bark can also be made into a syrup, rather like a dark and smoky version of maple syrup. Some hickory nuts are edible, while other varieties are overly bitter.

MEDICINAL PROPERTIES

Native American tribes have used hickory bark for a variety of purposes, including easing arthritis pain and headaches.

MAGICAL PROPERTIES

For healing spells or spells pertaining to strength, work with hickory bark. You can carry it with you on days when you feel you need to be more present or patient. Keep the bark close to your heart center, perhaps on a necklace or in a pocket. After my father passed away, my mom used to tape hickory bark on my chest.

Hickory Strength Syrup

This syrup will bring you strength during tough times. You can add it to hickory tea to double its healing properties, or to any foods or Magical workings. If you can collect the bark yourself, make sure to use bark from fallen branches. Do not pull the bark from the tree, unless it is already loose. And make sure to clean your bark— scrub each piece on both sides, preferably under running water, and remove any insects or lichen. After you're done, place the bark aside to dry or pat with a towel.

WHAT YOU NEED

> **1 large piece of clean hickory bark, approximately 12 inches**
>
> **4 cups water**
>
> **4 cups cane sugar**

WHAT TO DO

+ Preheat the oven to 325°F.

+ Break the bark into small pieces—about 4 inches long is fine.

+ Spread a layer of bark onto a cookie sheet.

+ Toast the bark for 25 to 35 minutes, by which point you should be able to smell hickory's enchanting scent.

+ Place your toasted bark into a large pot and cover it with filtered water.

+ Bring to a boil, and immediately lower the heat. Simmer 20 to 30 minutes, then strain out the liquid. Add 1 cup of cane sugar for each cup of hickory tea. Stir well, and then return to a boil. Allow the liquid to reduce to your desired syrupy consistency.

+ Pour into a glass jar with a strong lip.

Hickory can inspire us with her strength, and with her patience. Hickory grows slowly, but into such a majestic and purposeful tree. She teaches us to slow down and take our journey one day at a time—her message is of mindfulness and being present in the moment. To work with her is to work on the inner self, on self-growth, and spiritual development.

Invite hickory into your dreams to help you communicate with a passed loved one, or to navigate through whatever is troubling you—she will bring peace and clarity. Try drinking hickory tea before bedtime; she will soothe the heart and bring you a peaceful sleep.

HIGH JOHN THE CONQUEROR
Ipomoea jalapa

ESSENTIAL PROPERTIES
abundance, new beginnings, unblocking, luck

When dried, the root of *Ipomoea jalapa*—a flowering plant related to the morning glory and also known as *Ipomoea purga*—is called High John the Conquerer. High John's pleasant, earthy scent grounds you instantly. It has been a staple in Magical practices for centuries, especially in hoodoo. According to legend, it is named for an African prince who was enslaved but never gave up hope.

MEDICINAL PROPERTIES

The tuber is used medicinally; it can be taken to treat constipation, colic, and intestinal parasites.

MAGICAL PROPERTIES

What can't High John the Conqueror do? This root is invaluable in luck or success spells, and can amplify any of your other Magic work. But for me, his most profound influence is over renewal and in the burning away of obstacles.

A High John the Conqueror floor wash can clear way just about anything that has been blocking you and give you a sense of rebirth, so that you are ready to begin afresh. Do this wash during spring cleaning to amplify its energies with the spring's wisdom. Place the root in your pocket or keep it close to you to overcome anxiety and fear, and to keep you from procrastinating, so you can get work done. With High John the Conqueror, you are sure to command a work meeting with confidence, knowing your energy will grab everyone's attention.

PLANT WISDOM

High John the Conqueror is associated with success and overcoming obstacles. It's a great plant to keep around because it is able to provide solutions to even the most challenging problems. It is also associated with happiness, thanks to the legend that John the Conqueror escaped the clutches of the devil to find happiness with his love. Invite High John into your dreams to work on finding your inner power, especially when you are facing new beginnings and transitions.

HOLLY
Ilex

ESSENTIAL PROPERTIES

protection, shadow work, new beginnings, resilience

Ilex is a genus of more than 400 species of flowering plants, and is the only living genus in that Aquifoliaceae family. Holly is such a beauty—most people think of the holidays whenever they see her. Holly also has a lot of symbolism in Christianity—the spiky leaves are said to represent the thorns of Jesus's crown, and the red berries are meant to be drops of blood.

MEDICINAL PROPERTIES

While most holly is inedible, a few varieties can be used to make tea—for example, from the leaves of *Ilex paraguariensis*, or yerba maté (see page 331). These leaves will reduce a fever partly by inducing sweating, are an expectorant, and a good general tonic.

MAGICAL PROPERTIES

Turn to holly when you are doing shadow work, or when you are seeking more resilience. Keep holly in your home, particularly during the winter months, and she will protect you from the shadows roaming the Earth. You can hang her over doors that aren't opened very often to keep them from building up stagnant energy. And if you are going through a transition in life, work with holly—she will help you let go of your old life, to be reborn into your new one.

PLANT WISDOM

Holly will pull you to your best self even if you go kicking and screaming. She doesn't want to hear your excuses—and that can be a good thing! Some of us need tough love in order to see that even if we are comfortable where we are, that isn't good enough. We are evolving and ever-expanding beings, and holly makes sure we know it. Work with her when you practice self-development, and be ready for the ride of a lifetime. If you dream of holly, that means you are probably someone who gets back up whenever they are knocked down. Holly honors your resilience, and wants to make your journey a little less painful—she will get you to a place where you can finally experience some peace.

HOLLYHOCK
Alcea

ESSENTIAL PROPERTIES

creativity, abundance, new beginnings

The name *Alcea* is derived from the Greek word for "healing," but hollyhocks have an unusual kind of healing. They are associated with the cycle of life, and have been for time immemorial: An excavation in Iraq, which uncovered nine Neanderthal skeletons around 60,000 to 80,000 years old, indicated some kind of elaborate funeral ceremony—and the pollen from hollyhock was present. Ancient Egyptians also made wreaths of hollyhock and buried them with their mummified dead.

MEDICINAL PROPERTIES

Hollyhock can ease the pains of labor, if used in moderation, and a salve made from the blossoms is good for the skin. Her roots are rich in sugars, and may be eaten or made into a syrup. Her flower is used to make a medicinal tea that can be good for treating breathing disorders and digestive tract problems. Some people apply hollyhock directly to the skin to treat ulcers and painful swelling (inflammation).

MAGICAL PROPERTIES

Hollyhocks are bridges to the other side and assist you in crossing over safely. They stand tall, reaching unapologetically for the heavens, guiding lost souls still roaming the Earth onward to the next journey. Those of us who are able to see and communicate with spirits are drawn to hollyhocks, and I recommend growing them in your front garden to invite visiting spirits. You can also create a wreath of hollyhock and hang it on your front door from October through November, when the veil between worlds is thin—this will keep unwanted spirits from entering the home, instead encouraging them to cross over. When I was a little girl, my mother would place hollyhock in my sock or in my hair to keep me safe while I roamed the cemetery that was my playground.

Work with hollyhock for abundance and fertility. If you are trying to conceive, or are working sympathetic Magic for someone who is, hollyhocks can help you with that energy. Similarly, she can invite monetary abundance, allowing you to grow within yourself and within your life more of whatever it is you wish.

PLANT WISDOM

Hollyhock brings perspective to the importance of love and of those around you—she reminds you not to take life for granted, and to spend more time with your family. She visits those who feel alone and have no extended family. For this reason, I often bring hollyhock to local homeless shelters, where she can share her energy of love and belonging.

HONESTY
Lunaria annua

HONESTY

ESSENTIAL PROPERTIES
Moon Magic, clarity

Honesty's Latin name comes from the shape of her seedpods, which are silver and round, shining just like the Full Moon. Honesty is highly regarded for her fragrant flowers, and her papery seedpods are often used in dried flower arrangements.

MEDICINAL PROPERTIES

Honesty's roots and seeds are edible. The seeds can be used to make a spice or paste much like mustard: Grind up her seeds, add them to cold water, and let them rest for 10 to 15 minutes; they will develop a strong flavor. Then mix them with hot water or vinegar and add some salt.

MAGICAL PROPERTIES

Honesty's seedpods are like thin paper, you can pretty much see through them. This quality of transparency indicates her ability to reveal the truth, and to reflect yourself back to you. Work with her when you need to find clarity. Placing her in your home brings transparency between you and your loved ones. You can keep her on the table or in the room when you're having a family meeting or a difficult conversation with a partner; she will help bring out true feelings and thoughts while still keeping the peace. I love to hold a dried bundle when I need to ask myself hard questions—honesty helps me see behind my own self-deceptions. She will help you check yourself, and own your thoughts and actions.

PLANT WISDOM

Honesty can also support any Full Moon intentions or Magical workings. If you have trouble reaching other worlds, spirits, or your higher self, invite honesty into your life. She will bring light to the unseen. I often ask her to visit my dreams to help me navigate through a tough habit I want to let go of. She brings clarity to the underlying reasons I keep returning to thoughts and behaviors I know aren't good for me.

Honesty Self-Reflection Scan

I do this self-reflection scan at least once a month. It helps me see beyond the surface of my intentions, taking me straight to the source of my actions, feelings, and thoughts. No one is perfect, and we all have underlying issues we need to work out. Honesty will help you check yourself, and make sure you are aligned with your higher purpose. Do this scan whenever you start to feel a little off, or simply make a habit of performing it once a month, just to keep on top of things.

WHAT YOU NEED

Mirror

Bowl of water

Honesty flower petals

White candle

Bundle of dried honesty seedpods

WHAT TO DO

+ Sit in front of your mirror, making sure you're in a private, quiet space.

+ Set the bowl of water in front of you and add a few honesty petals to float in the water.

+ Light the white candle and place it next to the bowl.

+ Take the bundle of seedpods and swipe it down your body, starting at your head and working your way down to the ground.

+ Make a whooshing or swiping sound as you envision sweeping dark clouds away from your body.

+ Do this 3 times, and when you've finished, sit still while holding your bundle of honesty pods.

+ Look into your eyes in the mirror and take 7 to 10 deep breaths. This can be intense, so breathe deeply, calming your mind.

+ Have a conversation with your reflection. Ask a question in your mind, and allow your reflection to answer. Your higher self will speak through the mirror.

HONEYSUCKLE

Lonicera

ESSENTIAL PROPERTIES

banishing, protection, psychic ability

The honeysuckle gets her name from the practice of picking the blossom and sucking on the end to drink its nectar—though of course this can be done with a variety of pollinator-friendly flowers. However, the berries shouldn't be eaten, as they are toxic.

MEDICINAL PROPERTIES

Honeysuckle's flowers, seeds, and leaves can be used to treat digestive disorders, upper respiratory tract infections, bacterial infections, swelling of the brain, fever, urinary disorders, headaches, and more. Honeysuckle blossoms steeped in honey can be used to treat a sore throat or a cough. Honeysuckle is sometimes applied to the skin for inflammation, itching, and to kill germs, but as with all herbs, please do a patch test as she can sometimes cause irritation on the skin.

MAGICAL PROPERTIES

Honeysuckle loves peace and freedom, and she protects what she loves—I use honeysuckle to protect my family, the Earth, and all of our Mother's children. Add her nectar to your protection candles, workings, or intentions to amplify their vibrations.

PLANT WISDOM

Honeysuckle's wisdom lives within the spirit of awareness of your surroundings and inner self. She keeps your spiritual antenna aligned so that it may protect you. If you dream of honeysuckle, you may fear losing someone close to you or something you cherish. If you suck on her nectar in your dream, she will tell you what it is.

Honeysuckle Banishing Steam

Meditate with honeysuckle before attempting this spell, for in order for it to work she needs to trust you on a spiritual level. Ask her for her help, and pluck her flowers yourself to amplify your spell.

WHAT YOU NEED

4 to 5 honeysuckle blossoms

Cup

2 cups water

WHAT TO DO

+ Suck the nectar from the honeysuckle blossoms. Don't swallow—just let the nectar mix with your saliva, and then spit it into a cup.

+ Bring 2 cups of water to a boil, add the flowers, and turn off the heat.

+ Pour the boiled water into your cup of nectar and saliva, cover, and allow the mixture to steep for 3 minutes.

+ While this is steeping, write on a piece of paper what it is you wish to banish. Remember, you should never banish a person, though you can ask for protection from someone.

+ When you're ready, remove the lid and hold your paper over the steam, allowing the moisture to seep into the words of your spell; 1 minute per side is long enough.

+ When you've finished, roll up the piece of paper and bury it.

HOPS
Humulus lupulus

ESSENTIAL PROPERTIES

peace, animal Magic

Hops are the green, conical flowers of a climbing vine. They have been used to make beer since the 9th century, today tasted most clearly in a strong IPA. Hops can also be found in teas and soft drinks. The vine itself is edible and can be prepared much like asparagus.

MEDICINAL PROPERTIES

Even if hops aren't fermented, they can assist with a good night's sleep, much like valerian root. They have a sedative effect, and can calm anxiety. Their bitter flavor is also good for digestion, and they are a powerful antibacterial agent.

MAGICAL PROPERTIES

The hops plant is associated with sleep and calming the mind. She is a mild sedative, and can help with lucid dreaming, as well as to ward off nightmares. If you find yourself having trouble remembering your dreams or even sleeping, hops will help. Add her to your collection of plants you work with for visions or vivid dreams, or even meditation. She quiets your mind while you meditate, so you can stay in that state of mind for longer periods of time.

PLANT WISDOM

Hops is associated with animal magic, particularly wolf magic. Take her with you out into nature and pay attention to how you feel and where you are pulled to go—she will lead you to animals that have messages for you. Wisdom from the animal kingdom is powerful, and hops will be your guide. Hops is also a guide in the dreamworld; she can calm your running mind and allow you to see clearly. She is a kind and genuine being that wants to serve and help—we can all take her wisdom into our own lives, and serve and help others in this world.

HOYA

Hoya

ESSENTIAL PROPERTIES

protection, psychic ability, intuition

This waxy flowering vine is native to Asia. The flowers bloom in a bulb, with dozens of tiny flowers forming one large umbrella. Her scent is sweet and delicate, and grows stronger at night. Hoyas grow well indoors and can tolerate low light, but if you want your hoya to bloom, make sure you're giving her some bright sunshine.

MEDICINAL PROPERTIES

This plant has no known medicinal properties.

MAGICAL PROPERTIES

Hoya's flowers are star-shaped, and some say they look like pentagrams. She expands outward, symbolizing divinity. The flowers can help amplify your intuition and psychic abilities, though always ask her permission and set your intentions before you pluck.

Hoya's vine is best for protection Magic. You can incorporate her into any spellwork, or simply ask for her help, being specific about what it is you want protection from. Most often, I ask her to protect me *and* my creative work. Unfortunately, as you will discover, being a successful Witch means you need to protect everything you put out into the world from those who may be jealous or want to take your work for their own.

Hoya will keep negative entities away from your home and form a protective field in any room she is in. Placing her on a porch or next to the front door will create a boundary against intruders, ill-willed spirits, and lost souls. Dreaming of hoya is rare—I have only had a handful of dreams with her in my entire life. Each time, she has visited me right after I've gone through an expansion, awakening, or some kind of spiritual attunement. She helped my physical body align with my shifted spirit. The more you work with her, the more you will feel her presence, as she opens your mind and allows you to feel more deeply.

HYDRANGEA
Hydrangea

ESSENTIAL PROPERTIES
healing

Hydrangea was first cultivated in Japan and is often referred to as Ajisai. Her name stems from the Greek words *hydros* (water) and *angos* (jar) because of the shape of her bunches of flowers. Her blooms are frequently white, but can also be pink, purple, or blue. Amacha, the Japanese sweet tea made from hydrangea, is part of a Buddhist cleansing ritual.

MEDICINAL PROPERTIES

The root and underground stem of the hydrangea can be used to help clear up bladder infections, to relieve hay fever and other allergies, and to calm an enlarged prostate. Native Americans use hydrangea root as a diuretic, and her bark to treat muscle pains and burns.

MAGICAL PROPERTIES

Hydrangea carries a message of forgiveness—she knows that to forgive is to be set free. Work with her to help find forgiveness, both for yourself and for others. If you are having difficulty forgiving a trauma, invite hydrangea into your dreams, where she will gently and lovingly help you find release.

PLANT WISDOM

Hydrangea is a friendly and caring plant. She is compassionate, understanding, and forgiving, and I know that I want her energy around me as much as possible. When we work with hydrangea, we learn to embody her qualities—and when we do, we can ignite our fullest potential, both Magically and spiritually. As Witches we have to be compassionate, for without compassion, our ability to connect to different energies is severely hindered. Compassion comes from the heart and spirit, and it allows us to help others, to understand exactly what they need, whether it is guidance, healing, or Magical works. Compassion is a language that allows us to understand different energies.

Hyssop
Hyssopus officinalis

ESSENTIAL PROPERTIES

purification, protection, healing, clarity

Hyssop is a meadow wildflower that grows tall with blue or purple blossoms. Her scent is very inviting, sweet and uplifting, warming to the heart. Long ago, she warded off the plague, and is mentioned in the Bible for both purification and spiritual cleansing.

MEDICINAL PROPERTIES

Hyssop is a strong disinfectant, hence her reputation as a purifier. She's also an expectorant, so is good for a cold or cough, and she makes a good mouthwash. As a tea, she is great for stomach issues like gas, bloat, and inflammation. She can also heal bruising and scarring.

MAGICAL PROPERTIES

Hyssop has a long, rich history of Magical work. She clears negative energy of all kinds, from stagnant energy after an argument, to malicious spirits who won't leave. Hyssop is a tool for clarity in difficult situations, as she helps you to stay calm when things are falling apart or becoming overwhelming. You can work with hyssop to clear out stagnant energy from the home by burning her, walking around your home while wafting her smoke, making sure to let it glide over all furniture and objects to get that stubborn energy moving.

Another way to work with hyssop is to sweep with her. Simply bunch up some fresh or dried hyssop and move your hand as you would move a broom—but don't let it touch the ground. Instead, sweep the air close the ground, brushing that energy out your front door. Discard that bunch and place a new bunch of hyssop over your front door to prevent all that stagnant energy from coming back in.

PLANT WISDOM

Hyssop's message is that of healing, something we all need in our lives. She can move any stagnant energy you may be carrying within you—which is fantastic, but can be quite intense and emotional. Expect some waterworks when working with her, but just sit and burn some hyssop and listen to her calming voice as she moves through you. She will shake your inner world, allowing old energy that is stuck to move out of your body—stay calm and let her do her work. For even more intense healing work of the heart and mind, invite her into your dreams.

IRIS

Iris

IRIS

ESSENTIAL PROPERTIES

self-awareness, intuition, spiritual development

This distinctive flower has three drooping sepals, often called "falls." In the traditional fleur-de-lis often featured on coats of arms, each of these stand for faith, wisdom, and valor. Iris is named for the Greek goddess who traveled via rainbow—and for the rainbow itself. While it is more often the roots that are used (see orris root, page 251), the flower also flavors gin and enhances certain perfumes.

MEDICINAL PROPERTIES

This plant has no known medicinal properties.

MAGICAL PROPERTIES

I love talking about iris! She has helped me find myself, trust in myself, and become a better being. She can connect you to your higher self, that divine wisdom flowing within, and she does this in a way that leaves you feeling unstoppable. Just looking at her array of colors, patterns, and presence brings the spirit inward and reminds you of the beauty this world has to offer. When you get to those moments when life hits you hard and you need a reminder of Magic, keep her by your side.

PLANT WISDOM

Many of us go through life-changing events that cause us to grow spiritually, and we often need to get to know the new person we have become. Iris will keep you safe until you feel whole again, helping you to find a new identity. If iris visits you in a dream, know that you have an important mission on this Earth: She comes to remind you to keep going, keep rising, and keep expanding.

IVY

Hedera

ESSENTIAL PROPERTIES

new beginnings

The reason you frequently see ivy featured in the sign above a pub is because it was once believed to relieve drunkenness . . . which it does not do. On the contrary, a brew made with ivy was consumed by the followers of Dionysus, the Greek god of revelry and, well, drunkenness.

MEDICINAL PROPERTIES

Ivy can be used to treat whooping cough, as she has a mild antispasmodic effect. For that reason, she may also help with bronchitis, and a poultice made of her leaves may bring down swelling. Be careful with her, though, as some people have a bad reaction to ivy, whether used internally or externally.

MAGICAL PROPERTIES

Ivy is considered a pest by some because of her ability to grow on literally anything—upward or sideways. But she sets an example for us in this way, and inspires us to persevere and to try, even when we think a situation is impossible. She reminds us of the things we have been through—all the falls, fails, and obstacles we have experienced—and that we not only survived, but that we became stronger and better able to face whatever comes our way.

PLANT WISDOM

Ivy teaches us that change isn't always a bad thing. Change can mean changing paths, habits, relationships . . . anything, really. She wants you to know that change is nothing to fear, as you are always guided by your ancestors. If you are feeling unsafe when going through a transition, ivy can bring you peace of mind. She is the queen of journeying, as she climbs, twirls, reaches—basically, she goes wherever her spirit leads her! This trust in the universe is something we should all bring into our lives.

Jack–in–the–Pulpit
Arisaema triphyllum

ESSENTIAL PROPERTIES

balance, protection

Jack-in-the-pulpit is an unusual flower—she can change her sex. Her flower looks a little phallic, but although these plants are typically male when young, as they get older, they become female or hermaphroditic. A single plant can change sex several times over the course of its life.

MEDICINAL PROPERTIES

Fittingly enough, jack-in-the-pulpit can both enhance fertility in men and act as a contraceptive for women. Her bitter and warm properties are used in Chinese medicine to treat respiratory disfunction. But remember to cook this plant carefully before you consume—jack-in-the-pulpit contains calcium oxalate crystals, making her poisonous when she is raw.

Jack-in-the-Pulpit Protection Jar

This protection jar allows you to be very specific—what is it that you want protection from? Jack-in-the-pulpit will help you.

YOU WILL NEED

Incense *(I recommend cedar, copal, frankincense, myrrh, or lavender)*

1 tablespoon black pepper

Lemon peel of 1 lemon

1 strand of your hair

1 clear jar

3 to 6 jack-in-the-pulpit seeds

Olive oil or other oil of your choice

WHAT TO DO

+ Start by burning some incense to clear your space and tools.

+ When you're ready, place all the ingredients except the seeds and the oil into the jar.

+ Add your seeds 1 at a time, and as you do, set an intention for protection for each area of your life, using a different intention for each seed—for instance, "protection from judgment" or "protection for the heart," and so forth.

+ Finally, pour the oil all the way up to the top of the jar.

+ Seal the jar tightly and place it by your windowsill for 30 days.

+ After the 30th day, take the jar outdoors and bury it in the earth.

MAGICAL PROPERTIES

The dual nature of jack-in-the-pulpit can serve as an inspiration for us. We all have opposing forces within us, and jack-in-the-pulpit can teach us how to hold both possibilities at the same time. Perhaps when you are in a fight with someone, jack-in-the-pulpit can help you see both sides more clearly. I myself am bisexual, and have found that jack-in-the-pulpit accepts me entirely as I am. Jack-in-the-pulpit heals those who are similar in spirit, and when I work with clients from the LGBT community, I bring jack-in-the-pulpit in to give the warm embrace they have been longing for, offering an acceptance of some kind to the spirit itself. Keep jack-in-the-pulpit in your sacred space for all prayer and healing work.

PLANT WISDOM

When jack-in-the-pulpit shows up in your dreams, she is bringing a message that is unique to the dreamer. For example, jack-in-the-pulpit deals with a lot of the hidden aspects of the self, things no one else knows but you. She will teach you to embrace all the sides and shades of who you are. Keep jack-in-the-pulpit in the wild, outdoors, where her balancing energy can create a beautiful, safe sphere around your home.

JADE
Crassula ovata

ESSENTIAL PROPERTIES

abundance, friendship, luck

Jade is a popular houseplant with fleshy, oval-shaped leaves. If properly cared for, she will produce white, softly fragranced flowers in late winter. Jade plants can last for decades, while never growing very big, making them ideal bonsai plants.

MEDICINAL PROPERTIES

In folk remedies, jade is good for removing warts, and in Africa, where jade originates, she is used to treat epilepsy and diarrhea.

MAGICAL PROPERTIES

In feng shui, jade is known as the "money plant," as she activates financial energies in the home. But you can't just plunk her in a pot and expect the money to roll in. Amp up her energies by surrounding her with citrine, pyrite, green jade, and green aventurine, and bring her into your sacred space or place her on your altar when working on abundance. I like to place money under her pot, add the crystals, and burn cinnamon incense for three days after doing any abundance work, to keep those energies lifted.

PLANT WISDOM

Along these same lines, jade is a lucky plant, and you can use her luck to bring any kind of abundance you desire—not just financial. Jade is also known as the friendship tree, and she looks after you in every way, like a good friend should. At the same time, she reminds you to show up for yourself as well as for others, as that is the most important gift in life. When you make a new friend, grow that relationship by giving them a jade plant. She can also help you rejuvenate a longstanding friendship that may have grown a little distant—jade can touch the heart and open it to forgiveness, if need be. Dreaming of jade symbolizes good fortune and miracles headed your way.

JASMINE
Jasminum officinale

JASMINE

ESSENTIAL PROPERTIES

love, creativity, feminine energy

Jasmine derives from the Persian word for "fragrance," and no wonder—this plant is renowned for her sensual, bewitching scent. In India, she is known as the Queen of the Night, for her delicate white blossoms bloom in the evening and invite a restful sense of peace.

MEDICINAL PROPERTIES

Jasmine-infused green tea can help improve your mood, and may also relieve symptoms of cirrhosis (liver disease). Jasmine can also bring relaxation, heighten sexual desire (she's a renowned aphrodisiac), and has been studied for uses in treating cancer.

MAGICAL PROPERTIES

If you practice fertility Magic, jasmine will amplify your spellwork, particularly when you are working to birth new creative ideas, projects, wealth, and, of course, pregnancy. You can brew up some jasmine tea to drink and to pour in your bath—do both, and allow her to take you deep within your heart space, a place we are often too scared to dive into too deeply. But heart space energy may be one of the most powerful energies in the world—for what is more powerful than love? Heart space energy is the bridge between life and death.

Wearing jasmine will draw true love to you—those with pure hearts, who will be faithful to you and love you dearly. Placing jasmine in your bedroom is also a great way to lift those romantic energies and attract heartfelt conversations.

Jasmine will help you tap into the Divine Feminine. She will give you the confidence to stand in your own femininity, with all the beauty, vulnerability, intuition, and wisdom that entails. Plant her in your garden by your front door to attract good company and abundance to your home. If jasmine visits you in your dreams, an abundance of love is on its way to you.

JUNIPER BERRY
Juniperus communis

ESSENTIAL PROPERTIES

protection, opening the door between realms, purification

Juniper berries are used today to flavor many foods, particularly in Europe—their piney flavor seasons pork, cabbage, and sauerkraut, though most of us recognize it mainly as a key aromatic in gin. They are very easy to grow—you can probably find them in parks or as shrubbery—but if you want to forage for them make sure you are seeking out *Juniperus communis*, as other varieties are too bitter to eat. Juniper berries can also be toxic if overused.

MEDICINAL PROPERTIES

Juniper berries were once used as a form of birth control, though these days they are more often used to treat arthritis, and to cleanse the digestive tract. Juniper is energizing, and can be used in a sickroom to ward off illness. Juniper also wards off insects!

MAGICAL PROPERTIES

Juniper is one of the best purification plants available. She offers protection from low vibrations, hexes, and psychic attacks. She is a common ingredient in spells intended to fight black or dark Magic, as well as malicious spirits. Juniper can also help you solve problems, especially those caused by strong emotions or toxic energy.

Juniper Berry Dirt to Ward Off Evil

This dirt harnesses the power of the Earth, infusing it with juniper's protective energies.

WHAT YOU NEED

5 to 10 juniper berries

1 teaspoon rue, fresh or dried

1 cup of dirt (*not cemetery dirt, as that would not be right for this purpose—but if possible, collect your dirt from near a river*)

2 tablespoons salt

1 teaspoon witch hazel

WHAT TO DO

+ While setting intentions for protection from evil and negative energy, grind all the ingredients together with a mortar and pestle, or by using a bowl and wooden spoon to smash and mix them.

+ When you've finished, sprinkle your dirt in each corner of your front door, or of any door you wish to ward.

+ You can also write your name on a piece of paper and cover it with your dirt, burying it in the ground—this will keep you protected.

Burning juniper during the Full Moon, or lighting a black candle dressed in juniper, will create a bridge to other realms—and the beauty of juniper is that she will protect you by not taking you to realms she feels you cannot handle.

PLANT WISDOM

The more you work with juniper, the more she builds your spirit and mind to help you travel like a boss. You will quickly become more aware and intuitive, able to see and hear the signs and messages these realms have in store for you. If you dream of juniper, take heed—she is bringing you a warning of unfortunate events to come. Pay attention, as she will offer clues for how to avoid coming disaster.

LAVENDER
Lavandula

ESSENTIAL PROPERTIES

peace, intuition, healing, awareness

Also known as elf leaf, lavender may be the most soothing of all herbs in a Plant Witch's garden. Her distinctive sweet-yet-spicy scent has made her the most popular of all calming herbs—think about how often you see people using lavender essential oil! In the Middle Ages, lavender was used to launder clothing (hence the similarity between the words *lavender* and *launder*), and washing women were known as "lavenders."

MEDICINAL PROPERTIES

Lavender can calm anxiety, invite a restful sleep, and relieve headaches, and has been used for these purposes for centuries. She is also an effective insect repellent, and is delicious as either a spice or as a tea.

MAGICAL PROPERTIES

Work with lavender in spells that deal with self-love and healing, as she will make them more intimate and more impactful. Lavender oil in a diffuser can spread her energies into the home; in oil form her energies are more uplifting, which is better than burning dried lavender. Dried lavender definitely has its uses, though—keeping dried lavender in your pillow allows you not only to sleep better, but brings in peace to your dreams, pushing night terrors away. A glass of cold water with lavender sprinkled in it and placed under or next to your bed evaporates throughout the night, creating a mist of peace and protection from night spirits.

Lavender's ability to increase awareness is unmatched. She works on the spirit directly, helping you foster deeper intuition and overall communication. Lavender renews health as well as relationships, restoring peace. Dreaming of lavender symbolizes the wild spirit we so often trap within us—she is telling you that your spirit needs freedom for expression and creativity.

LEMON BALM
Melissa officinalis

ESSENTIAL PROPERTIES
happiness, abundance

Lemon balm, being a member of the mint family, smells exactly like that—lemon mint. She is also called Sweet Melissa because of her ability to attract bees (*mélissa* is Greek for "honeybee"). She attracts people, too, leading to her use in perfumes and aromatherapy.

MEDICINAL PROPERTIES

Lemon balm is the main ingredient in Carmelite water, an alcoholic extract developed in medieval Germany to relieve headaches and anxiety, and to be used as a perfume since bathing wasn't always an option. Carmelite water is still available today. Lemon balm is praised for her ability to counteract depression, to balance the emotions, and to bring a good night's sleep.

MAGICAL PROPERTIES

Lemon balm is excellent for emotional wellness. She supports you at the beginning of relationships by attracting love and friendship, but she can also comfort you at the end of a relationship by bringing peace, helping you find closure. She will do the same for you across all of your life experiences, supporting you during any challenges or shifts. She is perfect for any self-directed Magical workings, as she will boost your spiritual growth.

Lemon balm is a powerful abundance plant because of her high, happy, and healing vibration. Add her to any abundance spell to lift that energy right up. Keep her next to you while you pray, meditate, or do any spiritual work, and she will help you raise the energy within in the room, and within yourself. Sprinkling lemon balm in your bath will lift negative energies off your auric body, pulling them into the water.

PLANT WISDOM

Lemon balm is soft-spoken with a gentle message, so you must be very quiet and still when listening to her, or you may miss her words of wisdom. She urges you to do more, to go for your dreams. When you dream of lemon balm, you are considering taking a leap—you may often see her at the edge of a cliff in dreams, or as you fall from an endless sky, gaining the courage to fly.

LEMONGRASS
Cymbopogon citratus

ESSENTIAL PROPERTIES
psychic ability, amplification

Lemongrass has a bright, spicy flavor reminiscent of both ginger and citrus. It is used for culinary purposes in many East Asian cultures. Lemongrass is easy to grow, and forms tall, whiplike strands of grass, which must be chopped up small or pureed into a paste. Alternatively, you could use chunks of it to flavor a sauce, as you would with ginger.

MEDICINAL PROPERTIES

Lemongrass invites a fresh burst of energy, and can be used as both an aphrodisiac and to calm anxiety, bringing a new frame of mind to a situation. She is also an effective insect repellent, and is delicious as either a spice or a tea. Planting lemongrass at the edge of your property will keep snakes out.

MAGICAL PROPERTIES

Lemongrass is useful for all things having to do with psychic work, and has a particular affinity for clairvoyance. She opens the third eye, making it easier for messages and spiritual guidance to be received. Work with her during the New Moon to open your third eye chakra. Take 4 to 5 cups of water and 2 tablespoons of chopped lemongrass and boil for 10 to 15 minutes. Let cool, and use this water to mop your floors and clean your sacred space. You can also pour some in your bath while you sip lemongrass tea and have lemongrass oil running in your diffuser or burn. Focusing your entire mood and energy solely around her will bring her in deeper and stronger, so prepare for all your senses to expand and wake. This is a great opportunity to sit in silence and journal. Write all that you feel, especially any visions or messages you receive.

PLANT WISDOM

Lemongrass is bright and happy, associated with radiance and vitality. Invite lemongrass into your dreams to help you travel into your own present life, becoming an observer of the self—this different perspective will help you take in intuitive lessons as life-changing wisdom.

LILAC
Syringa

ESSENTIAL PROPERTIES

wisdom, psychic ability, spiritual development

The heavenly scent of lilac feels delicate and as though it could disappear in an instant, but it actually lasts for quite a long time—and the flowers are so hardy they can withstand being covered in hot water. Lilac blooms in late spring, like a final gift before the heat of summer. The flowers can vary from white to a deep purple, with all the shades in between.

MEDICINAL PROPERTIES

Lilac is edible, and lilac blossoms with honey make a wonderful, fragrant treat. Lilac was once used to treat kidney disease, but it is likely more useful these days as an astringent. If you steep the flowers in distilled water, you can use it as a toner to cleanse the skin.

MAGICAL PROPERTIES

There are some who believe lilacs are bad luck, but I have never found this to be true. Having lilacs growing in or around your home will bring in positive vibes and joyful energies.

Lilac Finding Answers Spell

The scent of lilac alone is pure Magic, and it can help you quickly receive answers to any questions you may have.

WHAT YOU NEED

A bouquet of lilac blossoms

WHAT TO DO

+ Take a deep breath and begin to hum, choosing a note as high as you can go. Keep your mouth closed—remember, you are humming, not singing.
+ Hold the note for the length of your breath, and then inhale, breathing in her scent through your nose.
+ Repeat this twice more for a total of 3 breaths, and on the third breath close your eyes and ask her your question. She will give you an image with her answer.

Lilac is Magically potent with positive energy, but her high frequency can be too much for those who haven't done much inner work—they may feel weary, or even like she's a "bad" plant. But if you've been practicing self-love and growth Magic for a while, you will find that lilac is smart, witty, and carries divine wisdom. Dreaming of lilacs symbolizes new beginnings, especially in relationships. She has come to let you know that you made the right decision, or to push you to take the necessary steps to get out of a toxic relationship.

LIPSTICK PLANT

Aeschynanthus radicans

LIPSTICK PLANT

ESSENTIAL PROPERTIES

creativity, abundance, happiness

Lipstick plant is an epiphyte, which means she grows on other plants or in midair. This evergreen vine got her name because of her flowers, which really do look like cylinders of red lipstick, as the red blossom peeks out of a dark tube. (Some may say she looks like something else, but let's keep it PG, shall we?) She has shiny foliage, and grows well in a hanging pot. Give her plenty of sunlight so you can enjoy her flowers.

MEDICINAL PROPERTIES

This plant has no known medicinal properties.

Lipstick Plant Movement Spell

This spell not only harnesses the power of lipstick plant, it uses your physical body to generate creative, energetic motion to bring you whatever it is you want to manifest.

WHAT YOU NEED

Sunlight

Cinnamon incense

Drumming music

A glass of water with a pinch of salt

1 green candle

3 lipstick plant petals

WHAT TO DO

+ It's a good idea to perform this spell outdoors, but if that's not possible, find a space to move near a window where the sunlight can reach you.

+ Light your cinnamon incense and put on your drumming music. Before you start to move, think carefully as you set your intentions for what you want to manifest.

+ Begin to sway with the rhythm of the drumming. If this feels awkward at first, lean into it. Feel the Earth beneath your feet. Let loose! Relax your mind and just let your body move.

+ Keep focused on your intention, and pick up the pace, moving until you feel sweat dripping.

+ Brush your sweat with your finger and drop it into your glass of water and salt.

+ Take the glass and hold it up to the Sun. Speak your intentions out loud.

+ Take a sip, but don't swallow. Hold it in your mouth for a second and then blow it out to the north. Take another sip, and blow it out to the east. Repeat until you have blown your intention in each direction.

+ Keep moving with the drums, and keep envisioning your intentions until you have ignited a fire within your core.

+ Finally, sit with your candle and light it. Take 3 deep breaths.

+ Hold a lipstick plant petal against your womb, allowing it to feel your fire. Light the petal on fire and set it aside.

+ Repeat this spell with the remaining petals, then sit quietly, allowing your breath to come back to normal, and your fire to subside, for now.

MAGICAL PROPERTIES

Lipstick plant's powers lie in the interconnected fields of creativity and abundance. If you want to physically create a being and increase your fertility, you can keep her in your bedroom, as long as it has plenty of natural light. Keeping her in your workspace or place of business will bring abundance in money, customers, and success.

Don't cut or pluck her leaves or flowers for spellwork—this makes her very unhappy, understandably! Instead, collect her leaves and flowers when they fall and store them in a jar until you are ready to use them. If you have several lipstick plants, like I do, you can set a specific intention for each one. Make sure you keep the leaves and flowers from each plant separate, as they will have different meanings.

PLANT WISDOM

Lipstick plant is so joyous she will make the deepest frown turn into a smile. I think of her like a little kitten, because that's the kind of energy she radiates. Bringing her into your home will create a beautiful flow and invite an abundance of love, good health, and happiness. As long as you keep her happy with plenty of sunlight, she will recycle any negativity in the air, replacing it with positive energy. If lipstick plant appears in your dreams, she has come to tell you that you're about to create something—perhaps you've got a baby on the way, or a new career opportunity is about to open up.

LIVERWORT
Hepatica

ESSENTIAL PROPERTIES
protection, clarity, healing

These tiny, woodland-loving flowers are so named because their leaves vaguely resemble the liver, with its three lobes. Liverwort grows in well-drained, fertile, and shaded soil all over the world.

MEDICINAL PROPERTIES

Liverwort was once thought to be good for liver function, although there seems to be no reason for this theory beyond the shape of its leaves. But the leaves are an astringent, and so are good for the skin, or for drawing out wounds. Liverwort is also an expectorant, and has anti-inflammatory uses as well. Don't consume the leaves directly as they can severely irritate the stomach—instead create an infusion.

MAGICAL PROPERTIES

Caution! Liverwort is only for those who are truly ready to find their purpose. This herb brings suppressed emotions and truths to the surface, allowing you to confront and move past them. In this way, liverwort can help with sleep, because she eliminates the deep-rooted stresses that can keep you awake without understanding why. Liverwort is also a powerful protective plant and will stand between you and those wishing to do you harm.

PLANT WISDOM

Liverwort is your path finder, lighting the way so you can start on your true journey. The beauty of this plant is that she brings your present purpose to light—she shows you what you need to do *right now*. This is important! We often worry about our final destination, but the truth is that the journey itself is our purpose. She is especially helpful for those who have trouble listening to their intuition, doing what they *think* they should be doing rather than what they *feel* is right. If you work closely with liverwort, she will begin to show up in your dreams—I love seeing her there, for in dreams she lights up, glowing like an enchanted forest in a movie, lighting a path for me to follow.

LOVAGE
Levisticum officinale

ESSENTIAL PROPERTIES

love, self-love

This plant's name is said to come from the medieval "love-ache," which sounds unpleasant until you learn *ache* simply meant "parsley" back then. In truth, lovage a very positive plant. All parts are edible—her flower, seeds, leaves, and roots—and she is quite delicious. Her flavor is like a very intense parsley, and her seeds make a useful spice, much like fennel seeds.

MEDICINAL PROPERTIES

Lovage is an aquaretic, meaning that she is much like a diuretic—causing you to urinate—but without the accompanying loss of electrolytes. This quality makes her fantastic for purification and detoxing—she can help clear out a urinary tract infection and prevent kidney stones. She can also regulate menstruation, ward off a migraine headache, and calm indigestion.

MAGICAL PROPERTIES

The assumption in the Magical community is often that lovage's primary function is to bring you love—but her true richness lies in helping you to love yourself. Lovage is associated with all things self-love and self-care. She is both a beauty and a love herb, healing the spirit by clearing heart-centered wounds and raising your self-confidence. As your love for your inner being grows, you will begin to attract love from the entirety of the universe.

PLANT WISDOM

Self-love is your innate right, gift, and power. But it isn't an easy journey. I know how hard it is to love yourself in a world that highlights your "flaws" and claims to know what "real" beauty should be or look like. And it certainly doesn't help if we've experienced a trauma. But here is the thing: Self-love is healing work, and it's about getting back in touch with the sacredness of your existence, the beauty of your unique self, and your truth. Lovage will latch on to your heart and never let go, gently helping you navigate the twists and turns of your life with unconditional love. Invite lovage into your dreams, and she will be gentle and intuitive in her healing heart work for your subconscious. She is truly the queen of hearts.

LUNGWORT
Pulmonaria

ESSENTIAL PROPERTIES

healing, courage

Lungwort has a charming variety of alternate names, including cowslip, bloody butcher, spilt milk, and spotted dog. I'm not certain where "bloody butcher" came from, but the leaves are speckled with white—looking just like someone splashed milk on them. Slugs go after lungwort, so you could use this easily grown plant as a border to protect your other plants.

MEDICINAL PROPERTIES

The mucilage (a gummy substance, like you find in okra) contained in lungwort leaves is very effective in combating bronchitis, and can calm a sore throat. Lungwort can also help wounds heal, and stop bleeding. Lungwort doesn't have much flavor, and the leaves are a little hairy and slimy from the mucilage, but cooked they make a nice side dish, much like cooked baby spinach.

MAGICAL PROPERTIES

Lungwort nurtures the connection between the outer self and the inner being—she helps us to slow down and take time for self-healing. She calms the spirit and eases the stress of daily life, so that you have the space to listen to your inner truth.

My *abuela* would tell me this all the time—the reason so many people don't succeed is because they are afraid of their own power. Lungwort can help you embrace your power and allow you to find your true self and understand what you are truly capable of. We all lose ourselves from time to time, but lungwort will bring you the courage to find your way back to yourself. Remember, getting lost isn't a bad thing—it's a healing thing—for in that lost space we have nowhere to turn but inward. Dreaming of lungwort symbolizes a return, a return back to your true self.

MAGNOLIA
Magnolia

ESSENTIAL PROPERTIES
purity, feminine energy

These splendid, fragrant trees with their showy, abundant blossoms herald the arrival of spring. They are ancient, having evolved before bees, and so are pollinated primarily by beetles. The flowers are thick and tough, yet soft.

MEDICINAL PROPERTIES

Most species of magnolia have edible flowers, which are either pickled or used to make tea. The young leaves and flower buds can be cooked and eaten as well. Magnolia has long been a part of Chinese medicine, where the bark is used to calm anxiety and promote restful sleep. There have also been studies suggesting that one of the compounds in magnolia may ward off cancer, particularly leukemia and colon cancer.

MAGICAL PROPERTIES

One way to work with magnolia is to tap into the sacred source of your feminine power: Mash magnolia petals with your menstrual blood and place the mixture next to you while you do any ritual Magic, including dancing or even prayer. If you can't use menstrual blood, saliva will work just as well—both men and women can access this power. Magnolia will bring you confidence, abundance, healing, and connection to the Earth and your higher self.

PLANT WISDOM

The strength and grace of magnolia give her an energy very much in keeping with the Divine Feminine. She has a maternal nature, and can help you tap into your own feminine power. Work with her to bring out the goddess within you. She supports you and tells you to shine—and she certainly sets a good example! She loves to chat, but be careful not to speak ill about other women—she won't stand for that! She wants to lift us all. As always, I suggest growing your plants yourself, but if that isn't available to you, you can use her petals in your Magical workings and during meditation.

When you dream of magnolia, she is awakening the sleeping giant within you, the powers you have that you don't even realize. You are capable of so much, and magnolia will help you access your untapped potential.

MANDRAKE
Mandragora

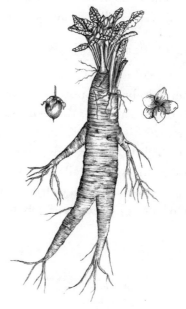

ESSENTIAL PROPERTIES
protection, abundance

Mandrake refers specifically to the root of the plant, which is thick, upright, and somewhat hairy. The base of the root branches out into a fork, so that it looks much like a torso with legs. Mandrake is a hallucinogenic, and can cause vomiting or diarrhea. You may remember folk stories

MANDRAKE

around mandrakes screaming when they are uprooted—screaming mandrake babies were featured in *Harry Potter*.

MEDICINAL PROPERTIES

Mandrake is a narcotic. In ancient times mandrake was used to relieve pain or to knock out patients before surgery, but these days you're better off not consuming it. It was also considered a powerful aid to fertility—the story of Rachel and Leah in the Bible tells that mandrake reversed Rachel's infertility.

MAGICAL PROPERTIES

Mandrake has a long and deep-rooted Magical history. She is often used for sympathetic magic, but not necessarily always with the best of intentions. Mandrake's resemblance to the human body has led to her being used much like a voodoo doll, where what is visited upon the mandrake root happens to the person the mandrake is meant to represent. This is not the kind of Magic the mandrake wants to be a part of, unless the intentions are to protect or heal. Mandrake is often overlooked for her true properties: She is a powerful protector, and helps with manifestation and abundance work. Write down something you want to come true, then stick your paper in the dirt near where mandrake is growing; she will root that wish and send its energies out into the universe.

PLANT WISDOM

Because of my work, I often have spirits visiting, and I have been attacked energetically by demons. Mandrake is one of the most important beings in my life, as she keeps that evil away. Place mandrake anywhere you need her protection—over the front door, in the bedroom over your head, or under your bed. I keep a mandrake in each of my children's bookbags, in my car, and I carry one with me all the time. Working with mandrake teaches us to go for what we want and not to fear anything. Invite mandrake into your dreams to help with confidence and self-love.

MAPLE

Acer

ESSENTIAL PROPERTIES

protection, creativity, abundance, wisdom, balance

The glorious maple tree looks so astonishingly beautiful during fall, my favorite time of year. Her signature branching leaves turn so many different colors, through all shades of yellow, orange, and red. While maple wood is used for many things, including furniture, she's also a tonewood, meaning she carries sound. This makes her particularly good for crafting a variety of instruments, including violins, cellos, and basses. She is also used to create paper.

MEDICINAL PROPERTIES

We all know and love maple syrup, and it can be very soothing to a sore throat. But the bark from a sugar maple can also be used to make a tea that will calm a cough. Molasses, also made from maple sap, is wonderful to use in cooking, and in horticulture as well—stirring molasses into water mixed with compost makes a hearty drink for your plants.

MAGICAL PROPERTIES

Some Native American tribes, particularly the Algonquins, believe the graceful maple tree represents balance. Her practical and useful nature is offset by her sweetness, and by her beauty. We all need to encompass both pleasure and hard work, and maple is here to help with that. Maple has so much wisdom, particularly when she speaks about the necessity of balancing the heart and the spirit. She wants us to learn who we are and work to balance our truth with "real life." This is so hard for so many of us, but maple shows us that it is not impossible.

Are you living your best life? Are you living your life with purpose? For a purpose? Have you figured out the whys to your questions? Maple can help you navigate these important concerns and queries, and when you work directly with her, her wisdom will flow into you. You can sit beneath her branches, or take some of her bark or even maple syrup. If you burn the bark as incense, sit in quiet meditation and allow her to take you exploring. You can also pour maple syrup into your bath (make sure it's the real stuff, and not the fake pancake syrup), add some bark, and drink maple tea—this bath session will provide a powerful spiritual opening. Keep some of her bark over your front door—or any door for that matter—to repel evil, and if you grow a maple, she will prevent demons and other evil entities from roaming your land. Dreaming of a maple tree symbolizes fertility and abundance, which of course go hand in hand—you can expect abundance in whatever it is you are working to create.

MARJORAM
Origanum majorana

ESSENTIAL PROPERTIES

love, healing

Marjoram tastes a bit like lemony oregano, though her essential oil smells more like camphor. Aphrodite—goddess of love and beauty—is said to have grown marjoram, and so marjoram has absorbed much of her sensual nature.

MEDICINAL PROPERTIES

The ancient Greeks worked with marjoram for medicinal purposes, believing she could help people heal from poison, convulsions, and edema. You can use both leaves and flowers when working with marjoram. She can dry up a runny nose, calm mood swings (particularly hormonal ones), and settle nerves. She is also good for circulation, and will help the flow of breast milk.

MAGICAL PROPERTIES

Keep marjoram with you when going on dates, meeting new people, or even just when socializing online—she will keep away those who don't have the best intentions. If you wish to know if someone you are starting to like or love is good for your heart, work with marjoram along with your divination tools, such as tarot. For an intensive heart healing and opening spell, draw a heart and place dried marjoram over it. Keep it on your altar next to a blue candle.

PLANT WISDOM

Marjoram is particularly effective when working with grief. If you've been sad for a long time because you have lost someone, experienced broken love, or endured a trauma in your life, it's time to bring marjoram into your Magical workings. Marjoram acts as a barrier against sadness, giving you the space to breathe and find happiness again. Dreaming of marjoram symbolizes history repeating itself, so make sure to pay attention to the dream itself; she will show you how you may be close to repeating a mistake, particularly around heartbreak.

MINT
Mentha

ESSENTIAL PROPERTIES

opening the door between realms, psychic ability

There are so many varieties of mint, but here I'm talking about "regular" mint, the mint we use to make mint tea, to cook with, and that grows so easily in an herb garden. Mint is a wonderful companion plant, as she repels harmful insects and attracts beneficial ones—but be careful, because mint tends to spread, and you don't want her crowding her neighbors.

MEDICINAL PROPERTIES

Mint can calm an upset stomach, relieve a headache, and is being researched for her effectiveness in treating irritable bowel syndrome. And of course, mint has wide applications in aromatherapy, particularly to promote energy and clarity.

MAGICAL PROPERTIES

Mint strengthens psychic skill and divination. She helps you communicate with the divine, with your higher self, and with loved ones who have passed— all of which is critical to finding clarity and purpose. Mint connects you with the ancestors who have walked this Earth before you and have illuminating messages to help guide you. Perhaps that is why mint grows so wildly—because your ancestors are always present around you. Mint helps you to understand that you are never alone, and that you can speak your truth knowing you are being guided by the highest of powers.

PLANT WISDOM

Mint has a protective side, and won't allow ill-willed spirits to come in contact with you while you are working with her. She brings wisdom that is deeply rooted into the Earth, giving you access to divine medicine for the soul. Dreaming of mint symbolizes harmony and balance coming your way, so keep up whatever you are doing! She clearly approves.

MONSTERA
Monstera deliciosa

MONSTERA

ESSENTIAL PROPERTIES

creativity, abundance, love

Also known as the Swiss cheese plant, for the holes in her leaves, her name derives from the Latin word for "monster." This is because she can grow to an enormous size, and not just her individual leaves, which are indeed quite large; this creeping vine is able to cover an entire cliffside. Not many people know that she can flower, as it's rare for her to flower indoors—but when she does, she produces large fruit, which tastes like a cross between a jackfruit and a pineapple. Like a pineapple she grows scales, so after you pick the fruit, let it sit for a few days, and she will let go of her scales an inch or so a day, eventually revealing the edible fruit. You will know she is ripe by her strong, fruity fragrance—but don't eat her before then, or her oxalate crystals will irritate your throat.

MEDICINAL PROPERTIES

This plant has no known medicinal properties.

MAGICAL PROPERTIES

Place monstera by your windows where there's indirect light and she will grow abundantly, bringing you abundance as well. Like any good friend, she's also great to work with when you're trying to have a baby, or for any creativity Magic.

PLANT WISDOM

Monstera emits so much love, and she always wants to chat—even to gossip! She's wonderful to have around, particularly if you live alone or feel alone. I chat with her daily, though in truth she sometimes makes it hard to focus! She is so demanding, she nags me for attention almost like a little sister, whistling and singing until I talk to her. My family often hears me yelling out, "Not now, please!" and they know I'm just talking to monstera! But this amazingly strong bond that she can form with you will help you manifest what you desire, bringing abundance into your home. You don't necessarily cast spells with her—instead, just talk with her. Tell her your stories, how you feel, what you want to manifest, and so on. She will make sure to grow with those intentions so that they become a reality. She is not a dreamworld plant, but instead prefers to connect with you in "real" life.

MOONWORT
Botrychium lunaria

ESSENTIAL PROPERTIES
Moon Magic, feminine energy, spiritual development

There is quite a story about this little fern: As far back as the 16th century, moonwort was believed to be an extraordinarily powerful plant. Her power? She could control iron. She could open a door locked with iron and could literally pull iron shoes off horses hooves. It was said that the Earl of Essex in Devonshire, England, put his horses out to pasture in a field covered in moonwort and they lost all their shoes as a result.

MEDICINAL PROPERTIES

You can pack moonwort around a fresh wound to speed healing, and some varieties can be eaten.

MAGICAL PROPERTIES

Unsurprisingly, moonwort is a powerful plant for Moon Magic! She helps particularly with intuition, death and rebirth, and spiritual development. Her feminine power sings so loudly that it vibrates into the depths of anyone who works with her. Moonwort can help you navigate your journey to awakening your own feminine power and reclaiming your sacredness. Work with moonwort to bring Moon energy into your spellwork; even if it's daytime, you can use moonwort to harness the energy of the Moon and bring it into you work. Add rose of Jericho (see page 277) to truly explode with Moon energy.

PLANT WISDOM

Moonwort brings light to who we are: We are not one thing: We are not titles, we are not our jobs, and we are not our life choices. We are expansive beings, colored in a variety of different shades. So often we get stuck in this notion that we need to embody only one thing—if we are Witches, we can only do "Witchy" things and if we want to "look like Witches," we can only wear or love dark and black things. This is of course ridiculous—the commercialized idea of a Witch—you can love pink and listen to heavy metal. Moonwort helps you to remember to be *you*, to be unique and not get stuck by limiting yourself to other people's vision of you. When moonwort appears in your dreams, she is working with you as you would work with clay, molding your energies to a more harmonious balance.

MORNING GLORY
Ipomoea

ESSENTIAL PROPERTIES
new beginnings, energy clearing

The blossoms of the morning glory vine are delicate but stunning—their colors can vary from a deep purple-blue to a sweet pink. As her name indicates, she blooms with morning sunshine, and closes up again after only a few hours. If you choose to grow morning glory, you will be blessed by her presence; but keep an eye on her, as she likes to take over.

MEDICINAL PROPERTIES

The latex from certain species of morning glory can be used to make rubber, and some seeds can serve as a laxative. Some varieties may be eaten (they are known as "water spinach") while others are hallucinogenic.

MAGICAL PROPERTIES

Morning glory can inspire you with her daily process of renewal and resetting. If you want to let go of something and begin again, morning glory will help. Adding her to your bath will bring in energies that help reset your auric field—this is particularly important for those of us who are empaths and intuitive. Let morning glory clear off the junk and leave you with a clean, vibrant auric body. I suggest treating yourself to a footbath with her petals, rather than soaking in a full bath—she can drain from the feet particularly well, since that is where she pulls in energy from the Sun. Placing her where you do any spellwork will help you reset your space while still leaving the spell itself in place. You can also place a dried bundle of morning glory in your window to bring in light, happiness, and general good vibes.

PLANT WISDOM

If you need help figuring out the best way to approach a situation, conversation, and/or issue, work with morning glory. She'd rather chat with you in person—she doesn't generally prefer to connect in the dreamworld. That said, she will show up if she feels she needs to—and if you are besties, know that she will visit you in your dreams when you are sick.

Morning Glory Cleansing Footbath

This footbath will draw out any negativity you may be carrying, and infuse you with a renewed sense of positive energy.

WHAT YOU NEED

A large bowl or pot

A handful of morning glory petals

1 cup sea salt

1 teaspoon agrimony, fresh or dried

3 bay leaves

Cleansing incense

Candles

WHAT TO DO

+ Make sure your bowl or pot is big enough to fit both your feet in, allowing them to be fully submerged. Fill the bowl with warm to hot water (whatever temperature is most comfortable for you) and add all the ingredients except the incense and candles.

+ As you do so, set intentions for love and peace. Ask each ingredient to cleanse you of negative energy.

+ When you're ready, burn some cleansing incense or light some candles to set the scene.

+ Rest your feet in the bath for a minimum of 15 minutes. Close your eyes and relax, remaining quiet and calm.

MOTHERWORT
Leonurus cardiaca

ESSENTIAL PROPERTIES
protection, intuition

Motherwort is part of the mint family. She's been cultivated since ancient times, and can be found in the most peculiar of places, anywhere from roadsides to burial grounds. There's a legend concerning a village that got all its water from a spring that ran through a patch of motherwort. Every day, the villagers drank from that spring . . . and all of them lived to be more than a hundred years old.

MEDICINAL PROPERTIES

The parts of this plant that grow above ground are used for healing. Motherwort can calm anxiety, and also regulate menstruation and help expel afterbirth. Motherwort may also treat heart conditions like arrhythmia or a fast heartbeat.

MAGICAL PROPERTIES

Motherwort will support any protection spell, and you can also add her to any spell you want to last for a long time—she will extend its energies. This is a particularly good idea for money, success, and health spells. Motherwort will also help you in your own internal wisdom, and you can amplify your intuition by growing motherwort yourself, rather than just purchasing her dried. As you care for her, imagine your auric field expanding and your third eye opening, and she will make it so.

PLANT WISDOM

To be honest, motherwort isn't very mothering. In fact, this extremely protective plant is also known as lion's-ear or lion's-tail, and she is indeed ferocious when she needs to be. She is the protectress of mothers and children.

If you are a single mother, bring her into your life and she will help you in tough times. If your child is being bullied, feels like they don't belong or fit in, suffers from depression, or just likes to be alone a lot and has difficulty letting people in, motherwort will help. She can bring perspective and a sense of belonging. You can have your child meditate with her, care for her, and talk with her, or you can simply sprinkle some motherwort in your child's pockets before sending him or her off to school. Invite motherwort into your dreams to discover a hidden talent or gift that you never knew you had!

MUGWORT
Artemisia vulgaris

ESSENTIAL PROPERTIES

protection, psychic ability

Mugwort is probably one of the most valuable—and easily accessible—herbs in a Plant Witch's garden. She grows very easily (some unknowing people consider her a weed), and is available dried in most natural food or herbalist stores.

MEDICINAL PROPERTIES

Mugwort derives most of her medicinal power from thujone, a chemical that does induce a sense of being "high." For this reason, some people consider her to be dangerous; but she is used in cuisines all over the world, especially in Asian dishes, as well as in drinks, tinctures, and teas. She can help you find a restful night's sleep, repel insects (especially moths), and assist with difficult childbirths.

MAGICAL PROPERTIES

Work with mugwort to develop your psychic gifts, as she is very intuitive when it comes to finding the fog clouding your abilities. She will help you to receive messages through dreams, and deepen a psychic practice.

PLANT WISDOM

Mugwort is associated with all things of the night. She is a soft, pillowy herb whose physical characteristics are mirrored in her spiritual qualities. Her energy aligns with the Moon, feminine wellness, the psychic eye, and dream messages. Mugwort helps women move through the various cycles of life with ease and grace, and she can also open pathways to the divine. She wants nothing more than to connect with you—because a connection with her allows a connection with the self, and with the universe. She often stands back as an observer. Like a wise elder watching over her family, she is mostly silent . . . but don't let that fool you! Her intentions speak for themselves, swiftly mapping out the best route for you to take as you expand and evolve.

MULBERRY
Morus

ESSENTIAL PROPERTIES

self-awareness

Mulberry, particularly white mulberry, is cultivated for both its medicinal uses and to feed silkworms. She grows very quickly, and so can be planted and used very soon thereafter! While white mulberries aren't quite as tasty as black or red ones, they are still flavorful and nutritious.

MEDICINAL PROPERTIES

The phytochemicals of white mulberry specifically lower blood sugar, which can combat diabetes as well as high cholesterol or high blood pressure. White mulberry can also treat the common cold, arthritis, dizziness, and tinnitus, as well as work to prevent hair loss and prematurely graying hair.

MAGICAL PROPERTIES

The Magical properties of the mulberry tree can be found in how she blooms. She turns inward during the winter season, but as soon as the frost has passed, she explodes—seemingly overnight—with vibrant leaves and luscious berries. Mulberry helps you expand into your fullest potential, as though you have the entire energy of the universe present within you. Each leaf and berry of this tree represents a little morsel of cosmic wisdom.

PLANT WISDOM

Mulberry teaches us to honor the seasons and cycles of life. When we are in need of rest, we should slow down. When we are in need of healing, we should let go. And when we are in need of expanding, mulberry encourages us to bloom. Mulberry helps us listen to both body and spirit in order to create a balance that nurtures all parts of us. If mulberry visits you in your dreams, she's telling you it's time to declutter, to let go of what no longer serves you, and to sort your seeds. Which seeds do you want to grow?

MULLEIN
Verbascum

ESSENTIAL PROPERTIES
protection, shadow work

This woolly little plant with sweet yellow flowers has been used for both Magic and medicine for thousands of years. Roman legionnaires would dip mullein stems in wax to use as candles at funerals, a practice that continued through the Middle Ages. According to lore, the sorceress Circe often used mullein in her spells—and Odysseus used mullein to protect himself from Circe! This

certainly indicates mullein's wide variety of uses.

MEDICINAL PROPERTIES

These days, we work with mullein
most often to soothe a cough, particularly those dry, tickly coughs that
just won't go away. Mullein leaves
soften the membranes of the lungs,
opening the chest and allowing you to
breathe clearly and easily at last. You
can also rub a balm or tincture made
from mullein flowers around the base
of the ear to draw out any infection.
Mullein root makes an excellent tonic
for pain, particularly nerve pain from
headaches or spinal issues, though it
can also soothe arthritis and broken
bones.

MULLEIN

MAGICAL PROPERTIES

Mullein stands at the veil between
worlds, making her an excellent
choice for both protection and assis-
tance in reaching out to spirit. We naturally open our auras during sleep
or divination work, but doing so can leave us vulnerable to darker forces.
Mullein will surround you in a cloak of invisibility, allowing you to travel the
spiritual realms without worry, making her ideal for both astral projection
and shadow work.

PLANT WISDOM

Working in the shadows is sacred, for there is wisdom and growth to be had
in the dark places. A Plant Witch knows this: Spirit may bloom in light, but
seeds and roots thrive in the darkness. We are both, and we can't fully be
without one or the other. I used to struggle with this concept of light and love,

as I found I couldn't really be my true self—I simply was not a being made up only of love and light. As I came to fully accept myself, I understood that light cannot exist without the darkness—both are sacred, and both are necessary for Magic, healing, and expansion. Working with mullein will help you navigate the realms of light and dark and all the shades of gray in between. This is so important if you are seeking truth, identity, and power in your practice.

If you dream of mullein, you should take pride in being a powerful Witch! Mullein visits those she feels are gifted in the ability to journey, travel in spirit, and navigate the unseen. Allow mullein to take you to places you've never been before, and you'll come back with wisdom from the depths of the hidden worlds.

MYRTLE
Myrtus communis

ESSENTIAL PROPERTIES
love, psychic ability

This fragrant, evergreen shrub has tiny star-shaped flowers, usually white. She has been around for thousands of years, and featured heavily in Greek mythology: When the nymph Daphne was trying to escape the unwelcome attentions of Apollo, she turned into a myrtle tree. In Greece and its surrounding areas, myrtle is frequently used in cooking. Her leaves are steeped in olive oil to give it flavor, her berries are used to make liqueurs, and when they are dried they can be used as a substitute for pepper.

MEDICINAL PROPERTIES

Like willow, myrtle bark contains salicylic acid, a natural form of aspirin, and so she is a powerful pain reliever and fever reducer. She can also clear up a sinus infection. The leaves are rich in essential oil.

MAGICAL PROPERTIES

Work with myrtle to open your third eye and develop your psychic gifts. Although there are quite a few plants who can do the same for you, myrtle is gentler than most. She is careful not to spring open anything that you cannot handle, offering just a little at a time, so I recommend her to beginners and to those who have a bit of fear or hesitation about opening up to higher divinity.

PLANT WISDOM

Myrtle is sacred to Aphrodite, and on the first of April, Greek maidens would bathe in waters steeped in myrtle to honor the goddess of love. But myrtle's loving nature has been recognized all over the world. In many Indigenous cultures, bathing with myrtle brings abundance in love; especially for those who have suffered trauma, myrtle is a gentle but powerful healer of the heart. Myrtle's primary message is that of compassion—and all of us need to be more compassionate. We often *think* we are, but without realizing it our words can be more hurtful than healing. Invite myrtle into your dreams to learn more about what compassion truly means and how to embody it fully.

NEVER–NEVER PLANT
Ctenanthe oppenheimiana

ESSENTIAL PROPERTIES
self-love, secrets

This variegated plant has narrow, tricolor, oval-shape leaves. She's mildly poisonous, so it's best not to consume her or to let your pets do so. This ever-green perennial is native to Central and South America.

MEDICINAL PROPERTIES

This plant has no known medicinal properties.

MAGICAL PROPERTIES

Never-never plant has the ability to take a secret and keep it hidden for you. She disguises truth with all of her beautiful patterns and color, almost like camouflage. If there is something you truly don't want anyone to know, this is your plant! You can grow her from seed and whisper your secret—as she grows, your secret will be more and more hidden by her roots. If you purchase her as a fully grown plant instead, carefully lift her out of her pot, whisper your secret to her roots, and then repot her, asking her to take this secret and hide it away forever.

PLANT WISDOM

While she is great at hiding deep, dark secrets, never-never plant is also wise and shares the message of self-worth and ambition. She thinks highly of herself—as she should!—and she loves to be around that same energy. She will amplify confident and ambitious vibes, so if you feel like this is something you need in life, place never-never plant near your north-facing window. Within a few days you'll feel changes in the wind, bringing power into your bones. Keeping her at your workspace will do the same; place a quartz crystal in her pot to amplify her energies. She doesn't intrude without permission, but if you invite her into your dreams, she will have you dreaming of the life you want, which will help you in your manifesting work.

NUTMEG
Myristica fragrans

ESSENTIAL PROPERTIES
clarity, strength

This essential spice for baking pumpkin pie comes from an evergreen tree, *Myristica fragrans*, which is actually the source of two common spices: Nutmeg comes from her seed, and mace comes the seed's outer covering. Although perfectly safe when consumed in the quantities we usually enjoy as a spice, when eaten in excess, nutmeg is a psychoactive and should be used with caution.

MEDICINAL PROPERTIES

Nutmeg is very calming and can help you sleep. Brew yourself a cup of warm milk before bed, then sweeten it with honey and sprinkle with some nutmeg to find a good night's rest. Nutmeg can also aid in digestion and boost appetite.

MAGICAL PROPERTIES

Nutmeg brings clarity, purpose, and focus to your Magical craft. She works to increase your personal power and to open your psychic eye. When you are present in your power and that power is backed by clear intention, you will find there is nothing you cannot accomplish. Over time, nutmeg will strengthen your energy, leading to increased abundance, creativity, love, and overall good luck.

PLANT WISDOM

Nutmeg knows how important it is to be confident in your life, work, and spirit. She quiets the noise around you so you can better listen to your intuition, helping you to see clearly what is working for you, and what is working against you. With that insight, she gives you the confidence to move forward, knowing what you're doing is right. Invite nutmeg into your dreams as a means of divination—she will listen to your request through either prayer or intention, and will meet you in your dreams, answering any questions you may have for her.

OAK
Quercus alba

ESSENTIAL PROPERTIES

protection, banishing, opening the door between realms, strength, wisdom

Oak is known as King of the Grove, for this holy tree is the master of truth. All parts of the tree are valuable and useful, from the leaves to the acorn to the bark to the wood. The oak has been a symbol of strength and endurance for thousands of years, and is sacred in a wide variety of religious and spiritual beliefs, from Christianity to Greek and Norse mythology to druidism and Witchcraft.

MEDICINAL PROPERTIES

Oak bark is an astringent and antiseptic, and when combined with chamomile can calm a fever. When you've been ill with the stomach flu and are dehydrated, make a decoction of oak bark to help calm your stomach down so you can retain fluids. This decoction will also soothe a sore throat. Acorns are edible, but they're bitter unless boiled first; they can relieve bad breath and constipation, and may be used to treat alcoholism.

MAGICAL PROPERTIES

Oak is deeply protective, and she will spread her branches over you and your home, sheltering you. If you carry an oak leaf near your heart, no one will be able to lie to you, and bathing with oak leaves will cleanse your spirit and give you the strength to face whatever comes. Work with oak to amplify your banishing and reversal spellwork, as she is a believer in sending back what isn't yours, especially something sent your way with bad intentions.

PLANT WISDOM

The oak has been here since before humankind, more than 65 million years ago. She is an elder god in the plant kingdom. All of our ancestors have befriended an oak tree, leaving traces of wisdom and enlightenment within their roots. Sitting under an oak tree and meditating, taking a nap, or simply resting in silence will connect you to ancestral wisdom. Keep one question in your mind, repeating it over and over until you feel energy rising from the roots into your body—and then be still—body, mind, and spirit—and await your answer. To journey with oak in your visions or dreams, you must visit an oak 13 times within 13 days, then wait patiently for her spirit to visit you in the dreamworld.

ORANGE
Citrus sinensis

ESSENTIAL PROPERTIES

creativity, purification, truth

The orange tree originated in ancient China—mentions of her can be found in Chinese literature as far back as 314 B.C. Every part of the delicious orange is useful and valuable. Her flowers give off an amazing fragrance, and her wood is used for smoking and seasoning meats. Orange leaves can be used to make tea—and of course her peel and fruit are used in cooking!

MEDICINAL PROPERTIES

We all know oranges contain a ton of vitamin C, which not only improves immune system function, but can also prevent cellular oxidation, lower cholesterol and blood pressure, and improve eyesight.

MAGICAL PROPERTIES

Orange is a truth-teller, unveiling hidden lies. Use her peel in your truth spells to uncover what is being kept from you. You can also add her peel or juice to creativity spells—she will give them energy and passion. In addition,

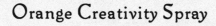

Orange Creativity Spray

This spray is great to use in your workspace, or anywhere you are seeking some inspiration. It will spark your imagination, allowing your creativity to flow.

YOU WILL NEED

Peels from 2 oranges

2 to 3 sprigs rosemary

5 to 6 drops orange essential oil

2 to 3 drops lavender essential oil

2 to 3 fresh mint leaves

WHAT TO DO

+ Place all the ingredients in a jar and fill with purified water.

+ Allow the mixture to steep for 1 to 2 hours, then strain and place in a spray bottle.

+ Make this spray fresh, as it doesn't keep for long, and use it within 1 to 2 days.

orange is great for cleansing and purifying spells; you can add her to floor washes, baths, sprays, or any other Magical workings.

PLANT WISDOM

Connecting with orange is a deeply intimate experience. You don't have to have an orange tree to do this—in fact, the best way to form a relationship with orange is to eat her in an intentional way. Hold her in your hands and gently turn her around, being mindful of her texture, color, and shape. As you begin to peel her, do it slowly and gently. How does it feel when the peel comes off the fruit? What scents can you detect? Can you feel her spray on your cheek? Before taking your first bite, thank her for her medicine. Take your time, eating each segment slowly. Allow the segment to sit on your tongue, and then bite, releasing her juices into your mouth. How does she make you feel? What energy does she ignite within you? Sounds pretty intimate, doesn't it? Connecting to nature is an intimate experience, and should be felt fully, deeply, and mindfully, with all your senses.

If orange appears in your dreams, she comes bearing a message of abundance. Expect some good news!

ORCHID
Orchidaceae

ORCHID

ESSENTIAL PROPERTIES

love, protection

This widespread family of flowers can vary so much in appearance, and yet they are always recognizable. In Greek mythology, Orchis is the son of a satyr and a nymph—and like many Greek gods, he wasn't a particularly good guy. During Bacchus celebration, he attempted to rape a priestess and was sentenced to death. His father prayed for his release, and Orchis was reprieved, sort of: He was granted eternal life as the orchid root.

MEDICINAL PROPERTIES

In Chinese medicine, the dendrobium orchid is used to strengthen the immune system and improve eyesight. In Turkey, the roots of salep orchids are made into a drink that can cure a sore throat and calm digestion. And orchids in general, but vanilla in particular, can serve as an aphrodisiac. They can also reduce fever and stress.

MAGICAL PROPERTIES

Don't let orchids fool you; they are beautiful but mighty beings. They protect the home from other realms, and they screech at the sight of imposters. If you look closely at the orchid, you will notice her gentle beauty, but also her fierce little face in the center—that tiny face wards off evil. Orchids are great to place in the center of the home, perhaps in the living room. They will direct all the protective energy, flowing it throughout the home. But be careful, because they expect love in return. You need to know how to care for them and keep them happy and thriving in order for them to do their thing.

I often work with orchids when I'm channeling to keep me safe from ill-willed spirits. You can place them on an altar during thunderstorms to bring that energy into your spellwork that day, amplifying your power. And you may want to have orchids in your sacred space, or even where you work out—they will keep you present in your body, motivating you to finish your workout or your practice.

PLANT WISDOM

Orchids bring a message of willpower and fierceness. They are mighty coaches who motivate your spirit and push your negative mind out of the way so that you can get things done. Dreaming of orchids symbolizes an internal battle, so if you meet an orchid in the dreamworld, make an effort to get out more often, meditate, and generally work to heal the mind.

OREGANO

Origanum vulgare

ESSENTIAL PROPERTIES

purification, protection, energy clearing

In Greek, *oregano* means "joy of the mountains." In ancient Greece it was believed that if oregano grew on the grave of a deceased loved one, that person would be happy in the afterlife, and newly married couples wore wreaths of oregano to ensure marital bliss.

MEDICINAL PROPERTIES

Oregano can boost the immune system as she is a powerful antibiotic and antifungal. She calms an upset stomach and can help regulate the menstrual cycle. Rubbing oregano oil on your gums can relieve a toothache, and adding oregano to a massage oil can calm sore muscles.

MAGICAL PROPERTIES

Oregano is a strong herb as far as flavor goes, and has some pretty strong Magic, too. She is incredibly purifying and protecting—she clears negative energy, comforts during times of distress and grief, and protects you from black magic and hexes. She is the perfect defense against all things in the lower vibrations; she cuts them off entirely, allowing you the freedom to chase peace of mind and happiness.

PLANT WISDOM

Oregano speaks of the purity of the heart and soul. She preaches a kind of "kill them with kindness" wisdom, raising your energy until you are vibrating with light. Work with her if you want a deeper experience with your spiritual practice—whether it's meditation, yoga, or anything that elevates the spirit, ask oregano to join you. Dreaming of oregano in food symbolizes an awakening of the spirit, but if you dream of her in her live plant form that may indicate a need to free your spirit.

ORRIS ROOT
Iris

ESSENTIAL PROPERTIES

love, protection

Orris root, also known as Queen Elizabeth root, comes from the underground stem—or rhizome—of irises. She has a powerful, heady, violet-like fragrance, making her a frequent addition to perfumes. She is also a common ingredient in gin and is said to taste like a raspberry.

MEDICINAL PROPERTIES

Orris root can purify the blood and increase kidney activity, aiding in digestion. She can also relieve headaches, toothaches, and joint pain. Orris root contains compounds that act as an expectorant, so you may take her to help treat a cough or cold.

MAGICAL PROPERTIES

Orris root is one of the best-known herbs for love magic—she's even more powerful than rose. Although most commonly sought out by women looking to attract a new love, she is powerful in any type of love work. Orris increases beauty, making you appear more attractive to potential lovers. Finally, orris root calls in spiritual support, to surround you in loving protection.

PLANT WISDOM

Orris' wisdom is so pure, so poetic, that you simply can't misunderstand her. The way she speaks on the powerful essence of love and on Magic is so inspiring and impactful. If you need a new perspective on love, or want to truly feel love in its purest form, please treat yourself to the pleasures of working with orris root. She will visit you in dreams, but you should invite her only if you are seeking her advice regarding a current relationship.

OXALIS

Oxalis

ESSENTIAL PROPERTIES

love, psychic ability, opening the door between realms

Also known as wood sorrel or sour grass, oxalis grows all over the world, particularly in Central America and South Africa. The leaves form into little branching clusters much like clovers, for which they are often mistaken. But their flowers are very different, as they bloom in delicately veined bells. She blooms early in the woodlands, making her a herald of spring.

MEDICINAL PROPERTIES

Oxalis has served as a food source for millennia, and traditionally, various Native American tribes treated mouth ulcers, cramps, fevers, and nausea with her leaves and tubers.

MAGICAL PROPERTIES

Oxalis brings on visions and can help you develop your psychic gifts. If you are able to grow her in your garden, make a space where you can lie on the grass surrounded by her, so that you can meditate or dream in her presence. I wouldn't suggest snipping her leaves, but if she blooms, you can work with her flowers (asking her permission first!) in spells for truth, love, psychic protection, and amplification. You don't have to work with them right away—her flowers are so powerful that you can save them in a small jar to use during Full Moon ceremonies, rituals, or spells. She will help you harness that powerful Moon energy, bringing it into your work tenfold.

PLANT WISDOM

When I first started working with oxalis, I was in my teens. Her beautiful wisdom is so penetrating that it came as something of a surprise to me—she is able to tickle the psyche so profoundly that the moment I was in her presence, I went right into a vision. It was incredible. Keeping oxalis in your garden and/or home brings loving energies—not of passion or intimate love, but childlike, joyous love, lighthearted and carefree. It feels like the type of love you experience in the very beginning of a relationship, when you have butter-flies fluttering within you.

Invite her into your dreams if you wish to work with the fae—like several other plants, she attracts fairies while also creating a safe boundary for you. Not all the fae are good, so we need to be careful. Oxalis will help you see through to their true intentions.

PARSLEY
Petroselinum crispum

ESSENTIAL PROPERTIES

opening the door between realms, protection, strength

Parsley has long been associated with death—in ancient Greece she was used in funeral ceremonies and to decorate tombs. She was never ever eaten, lest she bring death with her, but nowadays parsley's sharp, bitter flavor makes her a common ingredient in cuisines all over the world.

MEDICINAL PROPERTIES

You can use parsley oil to repel lice, or in an infusion as a hair rinse. Drinking parsley tea can treat urinary tract infections. You can also make a poultice of parsley to treat insect bites or to reduce swelling. Placing parsley on a plate as garnish dates back to ancient Rome, where it was used to keep

Parsley Spirit Communication Chocolate Cake

If there is a certain spirit guide, ancestor, or angel you want to contact, this cake will serve as an offering, inviting them to speak with you.

WHAT YOU NEED

1 box chocolate cake mix and related ingredients

1 teaspoon dried parsley

1 teaspoon dried mugwort

½ star anise, ground into powder

Orange or vanilla frosting

1 teaspoon dried basil *(optional)*

WHAT TO DO

+ Bake your cake according to the instructions on the box, adding the parsley, mugwort, and star anise when you add the eggs.

+ As you mix the cake batter together, set your intentions for communicating with your guides, or with a specific spirit or angel.

+ When the cake has cooled, frost it with either orange or vanilla frosting. For vanilla, mix in the basil, if using, before frosting the cake.

+ Carve the name of your spirit into the frosting.

+ Cut a slice of cake and place it on your altar as an offering, and have a slice yourself. With each bite, ask your angel or guide to come through.

food from being contaminated, and to sweeten the breath when the meal had ended.

MAGICAL PROPERTIES

This common kitchen herb is associated with the afterlife and communing with loved ones who have passed on. Parsley can also represent symbolic funerals, such as a breakup or a need to release bad habits. In that way, she represents both endings and new beginnings. Parsley is often used to honor the dead and to send them safely to the next world. Parsley also supports you during difficult times, providing the strength to move on after sudden and unexpected change.

PLANT WISDOM

Parsley's favorite phrase is, *All will be all right, dear child.* Parsley brings so much healing—she helps us to let go, and to see that nothing is ever truly lost or gone. Invite her into your dreams to bring you closer to your angels and spirit guides.

PASSIONFLOWER
Passiflora

PASSIONFLOWER

ESSENTIAL PROPERTIES

love, new beginnings, creativity

You might assume passionflower is named for romance (and indeed she is often used for that purpose), but in fact her name comes from "the passion of Christ"—her shape was thought to be a physical representation of the crucifixion. Her three stigmata represent the nails on the cross, her filaments the crown of thorns, her five stamens the wounds, and her 10 sepals the 10 loyal disciples (Judas and Peter didn't make the cut).

MEDICINAL PROPERTIES

Passionflower tea cools the body and calms the mind. Drink her when you're stressed and she will give you a sense of relaxation. She's as safe as chamomile, and can be given even to small children or the elderly. The pulp from the fruit of *Passiflora edulis* (called purple granadilla) is tart and extremely flavorful, and used to make juices and jams; it can also help regulate the thyroid.

MAGICAL PROPERTIES

Passionflower can bring harmony, love, and passion back into any relationship, and also help you make new connections or reinvigorate old relationships and projects. Work with passionflower if you are looking to awaken your relationship with your creativity. She will bring new ideas and inspiration as you begin a project, whether it's something as simple as trying a new path or as profound as a complete reinvention of the self. Her guidance comes from a pure state, not a material one, so you can count on her to inspire you to follow your heart, not your wallet.

PLANT WISDOM

Passionflower—either her blossom or her vine—vibrates with a nurturing and clinging kind of energy, similar to how she grows. She extends out, surrounding you in a loving embrace and soothing you in her healing grasp. She teaches you to explore without fear.

PAU D'ARCO
Tabebuia avellanadae

ESSENTIAL PROPERTIES
healing, purification, happiness

Pau d'arco, also known as taheebo or lapacho, refers to the inner bark of the Tabebuia tree. This tree grows in South America and in the American tropics, and flowers in tiny trumpets—giving the nickname "trumpet tree." Have you seen her? She's gorgeous beyond belief!

MEDICINAL PROPERTIES

Pau d'arco is available in supplementary form, or can be brewed as a tea. She contains a number of protective compounds, and so she is an antiparasitic, antiviral, antibacterial, antifungal, anti-inflammatory, and antioxidant plant! She gives a powerful boost to the immune system, and may be helpful in treating cancer.

MAGICAL PROPERTIES

Several Indigenous cultures value pau d'arco not only for her medicinal uses, but for her spiritual and Magical uses as well. She is prized for her protective nature, her positivity, and her qualities of purification. Work with her to connect to your roots and your divine being. She fills you with a sense of belonging, of being in the right place at the right time. She purifies the mind, removing all negative self-talk.

You can add pau d'arco to spells dealing with bringing luck, wealth, and prosperity, or whenever you're sending those intentions out into the world. If you want to bring laughter into your home, sprinkle some pau d'arco in the corners of your main space, like the living room. Drinking a cup of pau d'arco while journaling brings inspiration—she will draw out of you whatever you're struggling to express, and fill that space with healing. Burn pau d'arco to purify your home, tools, altar space, crystals—anything her sacred smoke touches will instantly shift energetically.

PLANT WISDOM

The wisdom of pau d'arco brings peace to those who need guidance in life, those who feel stuck, lost, or have no idea what their place is in this world. She teaches that everyone and everything is important, and each of us has a purpose. She will clear the way for you to find what you are meant to do in this life. When you dream of pau d'arco, you are being visited from the other side—oftentimes an elder or ancestor is bringing you a message.

PEACE LILY
Spathiphyllum

ESSENTIAL PROPERTIES

self-love, peace, healing, reflection

Peace lilies are among the best plants to work with for self-love and inner healing. They are named for their white blooms, which resemble flags of peace or surrender. If you need a guide to help you dive within, release what no longer serves you, and help you make yourself a priority, then the peace lily is for you. She's gentle but powerful, and knows how to navigate your spirit carefully so as not to trigger anything that may stir chaos within. Peace lilies teach us to reflect on what's really standing in the way of loving ourselves, to learn to voice our truth, and to heal.

MEDICINAL PROPERTIES

Indoors, the peace lily filters out dangerous common air pollutants and also prevents mildew formation. A peace lily can be placed just about any-where in the home. She will help create moisture and keep your other plants healthy and happy. I've seen her healing work on plants I was trying to revive—she can pull them out of their sadness and inspire them to rise. Keep her by your bed at night to help you sleep soundly, quieting anxiety, stress, and a running mind. If you've become ill or are trying to heal, she will be your plant nurse.

MAGICAL PROPERTIES

Peace lilies fail when they're in need of water, and stop growth when the environment isn't to their liking. This alone teaches us to set boundaries and adjust our surroundings to better suit our growth, instead of trying to fix ourselves—for we are not broken.

If you find yourself drawn to peace lilies, know that you're a natural seeker who yearns for purpose and inner healing. When dreaming of a peace lily, if she has drooping leaves and fallen flowers, that signifies an imbalance with your body, mind, and spirit. A dream of someone gifting you a peace lily symbolizes your need of love and connection. If in your dreams you are able to smell her flower, that means there's a message for you; a guide or a passed loved one is trying to reach your spirit. If you don't find the message in the dream itself, meditating with the peace lily after you wake will bring clarity.

PENNYROYAL
Mentha pulegium

ESSENTIAL PROPERTIES
protection, amplification, secrets

Pennyroyal has been used for herbal medicine for thousands of years, mainly to either assist with childbirth or to serve as an abortifacient. A medical text on gynecology written by a female Greek physician named Metrodora described mixing pennyroyal with wine to either bring on menstruation or abortion. Unsurprisingly, pennyroyal is poisonous if consumed in excessive quantities. She is also known as pudding grass, lurk in the ditch, and organ broth. She is a member of the mint family, and creeps along as a ground cover with small clusters of purple flowers.

MEDICINAL PROPERTIES

Drinking pennyroyal tea is not only good for inducing menstruation, it is also helpful for regulating blood sugar; however, it should not be used in excessive quantities or for an extended period of time. Please do your research before consuming pennyroyal.

MAGICAL PROPERTIES

When working with Magic, we need to draw in energy from somewhere. We can of course use our own energy, but this can be extremely draining, and even the most experienced Witches try to avoid it. Pennyroyal can give your workings a needed boost. Take a bath with pennyroyal to clear your auric body and fill it with energy before and after doing spellwork.

Pennyroyal can help with anything you need. You can place her on a picture of yourself or of a loved one to repel evil, or to bring good health, love, luck, and so forth. You can also hang dried pennyroyal above your mirror; make sure to wipe it down with pennyroyal tea once a year to turn your mirror into a reflective protector. When you stand in front of it, ask pennyroyal to reflect back her protection onto you, envisioning her bright light shining over you.

PLANT WISDOM

Pennyroyal teaches us to rise above, to reach for the stars, and to keep going. Ask her to visit you in your dreams to chat about things that cannot be said in this realm—you can protect your deepest secrets by discussing them with her in the dreamworld. She will keep them safe.

PEONY
Paeonia

ESSENTIAL PROPERTIES

*protection, abundance,
opening the door between realms*

These incredible puffball flowers are so packed with petals they seem to be bursting. It is thought that the peony's name comes from Paeon, the Greek physician

PEONY

of the gods, who healed Ares and Hades with his herbal remedies. There is a superstition that says that you must be careful while picking peony fruits, or a woodpecker might peck out your eyes.

MEDICINAL PROPERTIES

While the leaves and flowers of the peony aren't typically eaten as they can cause nausea, the roots were frequently used in Asian cooking, so much so that Confucius supposedly said, "I eat nothing without its sauce." The roots of the peony are prized in Chinese medicine for their wound-healing qualities. Peony root is also calming, making it a good treatment for cough, nerve pain, and headaches. Peony can also be used to treat menstrual pain, and may be given to ensure a healthy pregnancy—but be careful and do your research, as dosages can be tricky.

MAGICAL PROPERTIES

Peony is truly special. When cared for properly, she will grow for a hundred years or more, making her a powerful support for any spellwork dealing with longevity. You can also incorporate her into any kind of spell you want to make sure will last for a long time. For this kind of Magic, use the root or seeds.

Peony is also great for stability, grounding, and protection spells. She wants us to work smarter, not harder. When you need to slow down and get organized, peony is your gal. I especially love to add the root and flower to my baths whenever I feel I need to ground myself—when mixed with the water, they fill me with a calm, blissful feeling. For protection, take peony seeds and place them on each side of your front door, or in the corners of the room—I often place peony seeds in the corners of my kids' bedrooms.

PLANT WISDOM

Peony wants to help you connect with your ancestors, as she understands the importance of knowledge passed down over time. You can make a tea of peony by bringing some water to a boil and steeping the petals and root for 10 to 15 minutes. Place this tea on your altar as an offering and a gateway—she will invite them in, creating a safe space for communication. If peony appears in your dreams, that means good fortune is on its way.

PINE

Pinus

―――――――――――――――――――――――――――――e

ESSENTIAL PROPERTIES

abundance, healing, opening the door between realms, wisdom

I've never met a single person who did not enjoy the smell of a pine—his dreamy scent is due to chemical compounds called terpenes. *Pinus* is the largest genus of the Pinaceae family, which evolved around 153 million years ago, making it one of the oldest and largest conifer families. Pine seeds are carried in pine cones, and pine trees carry both male and female cones on the same tree.

MEDICINAL PROPERTIES

Pine oil can help loosen a cough and relieve other respiratory issues or sinus conditions. Pine nuts from within pine cones are hard to get at, but are delicious. The resin can be easily harvested for incense, and the white inner bark is edible and nutritious. You can also make an energizing tea from pine needles.

MAGICAL PROPERTIES

Pine can bring you abundance in life, so consider working with him for spells on money, health, love, success and so on, as he will amplify those vibrations. There are several ways you can do this: At the beginning of spring, add pine to your floor wash and mop your floors to help the seeds of your intentions blossom. You can also place an intention in a single pine needle and burn it with a green candle to release that intention into the universe. Keep going with as many intentions and pine needles as you like. In addition, keeping a fresh wreath of pine on your door during winter keeps the people in your home protected, healthy, and blessed.

Pine has been around so long he has seen and felt everything. As our elder, he should be protected, respected, and honored. Pine is also deeply wise, and has an immortal presence that whispers to us down to our bones. If you are lucky enough to have access to a pine tree, spend time with him, meditate beneath him so that you can grab hold of the wisdom that flows out of him like rivers. You can use pine needles to do the same—just place the needles in a singing bowl filled with water. When you ring it, its vibrations will fill you with wisdom and healing. If pine doesn't show up in your dreams on his own, invite him in—dreaming of pine brings you closer to angels, as pine's essence serves as a spiritual bridge to the realm of angels.

PIPSISSEWA
Chimaphila umbellata

ESSENTIAL PROPERTIES
manifesting, banishing

Pipsissewa (what a charming name is that!) is a small plant with pink or white flowers that bloom in a bell shape. She can be found throughout the Northern Hemisphere, primarily in arid woodlands. She gets her name from the Cree, a native tribe of Canada, who called her *pipsisikweu*, which means "it breaks into small pieces." She is also known as prince's pine or umbellate wintergreen, among other names. She is sometimes used to flavor root beer.

MEDICINAL PROPERTIES
Native Americans traditionally treated a variety of ailments with pipsissewa, including kidney stones, blisters, and backaches. She's a diuretic, and helped early European settlers treat both kidney issues and rheumatism. You can chew her leaves, or brew her leaves, stems, and roots for tea. In Mexico, she is an ingredient in *navaitai*, an alcoholic drink produced from sprouted maize.

Pipsissewa Repelling Potion

Use this potion to keep away the people, situations, or beliefs you no longer need.

WHAT YOU NEED

Leaves, stems, and petals of pipsissewa

1 sprig of rosemary

1 teaspoon feverfew, fresh or dried

1 teaspoon wormwood, fresh or dried

2 to 3 eucalyptus leaves, fresh or dried

1 teaspoon salt

WHAT TO DO

+ Bring a pot of water to a boil. Lower the heat and add all the ingredients except the salt. Cover and simmer for 10 minutes, then remove the pot from the heat.

+ Add the salt, and then hold your hands open and close to your mouth. Blow a hot breath into your palms 3 times, and then whisper what it is you wish to repel.

+ Envision your brew bursting into flames, burning up what it is you want to be rid of.

+ Keep your palms close to your mouth for 11 deep breaths, and then dispose of the potion however you like—down the drain, into the toilet, whatever. Rinse your hands when you're done.

MAGICAL PROPERTIES

When I'm working with clients who are creating a new beginning or a new life, I suggest pipsissewa because she can help them see what they need to achieve their desires—and what they need to let go of to make space for something new. If you're having trouble manifesting or releasing, pipsissewa works like an antenna, tuning in to your inner world while at the same time tracking what's going on externally. She can zero in on exactly what you need to attract, and what you need to repel.

However, keeping her in your home can create a bit of chaos, as she will tune in to everyone who lives there and shake them up! This is a good thing of course, but it can be a lot all at once. I would suggest keeping her outdoors if you want to grow pipsissewa, and ask her to focus only on you, or whomever it is you want her to help. You can help maintain this by placing a picture of yourself next to her, so she remains focused on you. This will keep the spells and intentions you have set with her going long after they have begun. You can also work with her petals, leaves, and stems for attracting and repelling.

PLANT WISDOM

Pipsissewa is a dual spirit that knows what she wants, and knows what she doesn't need. Her wisdom is simple, and yet so many overlook it: In order to bring in something new, you must let something else go, to make room for what it is you want. She is not one to visit dreams; instead, connect with her in the plant meditation suggested at the beginning of this book (page 40).

POINSETTIA
Euphorbia pulcherrima

ESSENTIAL PROPERTIES
faith, wishes

Poinsettias are Indigenous to Central America, and can particularly be found in an area of southern Mexico known as Taxco del Alarcón, where they flower during the winter months. Ancient Aztecs called them *cuetlaxochitl*, but of course we associate them with the Christmas season, when poinsettias can be found in every grocery, florist, and garden store. And for good reason: The poinsettia symbolizes the return of the Sun after the winter solstice, and the promise of the coming of spring and new life.

MEDICINAL PROPERTIES

Contrary to popular belief, while mildly toxic, poinsettias are not, in fact, lethal to animals and humans. However, to consume them will frequently bring on nausea, vomiting, and diarrhea, so best not to. That said, sometimes the plant's latex (her sap) is taken to kill bacteria and pain, and some work with the whole plant to treat fever and stimulate breast milk production.

MAGICAL PROPERTIES

Do you believe in wishes? I do. Take one of poinsettia's petals and make a wish, then place it in the snow. If it doesn't snow where you live, you can bury the petal in the winter ground. Your wish will grow to blossom in the spring.

PLANT WISDOM

Poinsettia has a rich history with a variety of religions and cultures—which makes sense, as she is the embodiment of faith, prayer, and devotion. I often feel that we lack devotion—we get so caught up in our daily lives that spiritual work gets pushed to the side. Poinsettia teaches that even our daily lives can be spiritual, as long as we are mindful and present. She is a guide, a spiritual counselor of sorts; work with her during the winter months particularly, when we turn inward and the world casts shadows. She is able to thin the veil between you and the spirit world, allowing you to tap into it and be heard, while still remaining safe. When you feel you have lost faith in yourself or the world, when you feel your prayers aren't being answered, when you feel like Magic isn't what you thought it was, or whether you're not sure whether Magic is even real—and yes, we all go through this from time to time—poinsettia will clear the fog of doubt.

Dreaming of poinsettia can mean that angels are speaking to you, offering a divine message—so pay attention!

Ponytail Palm
Beaucarnea recurvata

ESSENTIAL PROPERTIES

balance, psychic ability, happiness

Ponytail palms, also sometimes called elephant's-foot, are native to several parts of eastern Mexico. They are easy to care for and nontoxic (though your cat will probably want to chew on their leaves). Despite her name and appearance, the ponytail palm is not a true palm. She makes a wonderful houseplant, and will remain small indoors; but in the wild she can grow to 30 feet tall and can live for centuries. Her leaves grow in a rosette out of the top of her trunk or the ends of her branches, cascading beautifully, like a willow tree or a fountain.

MEDICINAL PROPERTIES

This plant has no known medicinal properties.

MAGICAL PROPERTIES

Ponytail palm plants are feng shui favorites for good reason—they represent an inner balance of yin and yang energy. Balance is something we all strive for in our lives, and she will be your guide. You can grow your ponytail palm outdoors during the summer, and then bring her indoors for winter, and she will thrive. She knows how to survive in both the light and the shadow, and this makes her powerful. I love to keep her on my worktable, in my sacred space— really in all the places I want to ensure a balanced energy flow.

PLANT WISDOM

However, when I'm doing serious work with a deadline, I take her off my work desk. Ponytail palm also taps into your free spirit, and when I'm tapped into my free spirit, I'm not worried about anything—I'm stress-free and happy to move at a slower pace. Which is great . . . except when you're on a deadline!

So it's best to keep her in places like the living room to help the family wind down at the end of the day. If you're having trouble releasing stress and just want to feel free and wild, work with ponytail palm. She brings out the wild child, the free spirit within us all—and with that comes joy, a cheerful energy that we all deserve to have in our lives. Work with her for a few weeks before inviting her into your dreams, but once she comes she will help open your psychic capabilities.

POTHOS
Epipremnum aureum

POTHOS

ESSENTIAL PROPERTIES

success, prosperity, spiritual development

Pothos is also known as devil's ivy because she is very difficult to remove from your garden once she takes over! Incredibly, even when grown in the dark, her leaves stay green. It's amazing that she can reproduce, as she rarely flowers. Because she doesn't need much light, she makes a terrific houseplant, particularly hanging from a basket; she can also be grown in aquariums or ponds, with her roots dangling into the water. She does have oxalate crystals, so be sure to keep her out of reach of pets.

MEDICINAL PROPERTIES

This plant has no known medicinal properties.

MAGICAL PROPERTIES

Pothos is good to keep at home. Her ability to stay awake and rested through the day and night means she's always watching, observing, and keeping an eye out for you. I particularly love when she sways at the sign of negative energy, alerting me to cleanse my space and be careful with whom I surround myself. Pothos plants are extremely powerful spiritual beings—they help us understand how to grow both in the light and in the shadows.

PLANT WISDOM

Pothos's message is that of learning, thriving, and expanding. She teaches us how to use our hard or even traumatic experiences as fuel for growth. Work with pothos to ignite inner expansion, to dive deep within and heal from the roots up—you will grow, having been watered by the tears you have shed. Her resilience spreads energies of success, making her a great plant to work with for drawing in what you desire. I recommend placing her at your work desk to inspire big boss energy, keeping you focused, determined, and productive. That is her natural essence, after all. Pothos visits those who are most connected with her. Take good care of her and work with her often, and she will bring dreams with messages from your ancestors.

PRAYER PLANT
Maranta leuconeura

ESSENTIAL PROPERTIES

healing, wisdom, opening the door between realms, faith

Prayer plant is also called praying hands, so named because at night her leaves fold in half to close, like hands held in prayer. She also raises her leaves, stretching toward the night sky—and her circadian rhythms mean that she will do this when grown indoors as well as out in the wild.

MEDICINAL PROPERTIES

This plant has no known medicinal properties.

MAGICAL PROPERTIES

If you work actively with your ancestors, place prayer plant on your ancestral altar and she will keep your connection strong. During times of the year when the veil is thin, like Samhain or Día de Muertos, harness the power of prayer plant to open your communication with the spirit world. Placing crystals in any plant is always a good idea, and for prayer plant I would suggest using angelite, lepidolite, clear quartz, or rainbow moonstone to amplify her energies.

PLANT WISDOM

Prayer plant needs no mysterious explanation, as her physical presence speaks for itself. She is devoted to faith—faith in the Earth, the Sun, and the Moon. She prays for us all, sending healing out into the world. She will fill your space with healing energy, and so is particularly helpful for someone who is ill, or when you've got a lot of chaotic energy going on. I love to keep her in my bedroom, as she brings me peaceful dreams, helping me set aside any worries or anxiety. I also have a prayer plant designated for each member of my family, so that they have someone carrying my prayers for them always. Invite prayer plant into your dreams if you need help letting go of a loved one you have lost. She can help heal the devastation.

PRIMROSE
Primula vulgaris

ESSENTIAL PROPERTIES

opening the door between realms

This cottage garden staple is such a charming little flower, as evidenced by the translation of her German name, "little keys to heaven." Primrose grows low on the ground, and has sweet, fragrant flowers. The flavor of her leaves and blossoms can be anything from lettuce-like to quite bitter, and are delicious in salads.

MEDICINAL PROPERTIES

The leaves and roots of the primrose can relieve pain, as well as stop muscle spasms and act as an expectorant. She can treat rheumatism and gout, and a tincture made from her leaves and roots will calm anxiety and insomnia.

MAGICAL PROPERTIES

Primrose is also known as fairy flower, so if you work with fairies you should absolutely grow primrose in your garden! In fact, she can help you contact all forms of nature spirits, as she acts as a wonderful bridge between our normal daily lives and the powerful Magic that is happening on Mother Earth at every moment. When you are caught up in work or other responsibilities, primrose will help you reconnect with nature.

PLANT WISDOM

Primrose is a chatty little being! Don't whisper your secrets to her—before long, the whole plant kingdom will know. But I don't hold this against her; it's simply because she is so connected to all the other plant spirits in the world, as she learns and exchanges wisdom with them. She is essentially a school of knowledge, and can quickly get you whatever information you need. This makes her a great partner for herbalists or healers or anyone who actively works with natural remedies, potions, and spells. If you're not sure of an ingredient or are simply not able to get it easily, primrose will suggest a good substitute. Simply meditate with her while asking for her advice. At first the answer will come as an intuitive knowing, then it will grow into a nudge, until before you know it she's chatting your ear off! Dreaming of primrose symbolizes fertility and abundance.

QUEEN ANNE'S LACE
Daucus carota

———————————————————————— ⟲

ESSENTIAL PROPERTIES

new beginnings, opening the door between realms

Queen Anne's lace grows wild in fields and on roadsides all over North America. Her distinctive flat, umbrella-shaped flower curls up into a tumbleweed to disperse her seeds. She's actually a wild carrot, and is edible—you can eat the root when it's young, and fry up the flowers. However, her leaves are very similar to the poisonous hemlock, so make sure you know which plant you're working with. She received her name because of her lacy flowers, and for the Queen of England in the 1700s.

MEDICINAL PROPERTIES

Queen Anne's lace has been a staple in medicine for centuries, mostly to treat digestive disorders, as well as kidney and bladder diseases.

MAGICAL PROPERTIES

When you are feeling lost and in need of her hopeful Magic, keep Queen Anne's lace with you or on you, particularly her petals. You can also drink her tea before meditating, as she will bring visions of manifesting what it is you are hoping for, filling you with the energy you need to make that hope a reality.

Queen Anne's Lace Spirit Bath

Queen Anne's lace can whisper messages from spirits into your soul. This bath spell will boost your connection with past loved ones, making their messages ring loud and clear.

WHAT YOU NEED

½ cup milk

3 tablespoons honey

2 tablespoons lavender, fresh or dried

3 drops rosewood essential oil

Frankincense incense

1 cup Himalayan pink salt

3 bay leaves

1 cup Queen Anne's lace, fresh or dried

White candle

WHAT TO DO

+ Heat the milk and honey in a pot on the stove, stirring continuously while keeping your mind quiet.

+ Run a bath and add the lavender, rosewood oil, and salt.

+ Pour the milk and honey into the bath, and as you do so, set your intentions for the spirit you want to communicate with.

+ Add the bay leaves, and then speak the spirit's name aloud as you add the Queen Anne's lace to the bath.

+ Light your candle and your incense, then relax quietly and listen.

PLANT WISDOM

Don't be fooled by the delicate appearance of Queen Anne's lace—this beauty is strong, hardworking, and a true spiritual being. She comes with the message of hope and transformation, offering missives from passed loved ones. Transformation energy lives strong within her—butterflies are attracted to Queen Anne's lace, and she is intertwined with a butterfly's energy of rebirth and transformation. Work with her to help you transition, transform, and/or change any part of yourself or your life. I recommend interacting with her out in nature where the Magic happens naturally, but you can also bring her fresh or dried flowers inside where you do your Magical workings. If you feel you are not the person you are supposed to be, whether physically, emotionally, mentally, or spiritually, she will guide you through a journey of transformation and fill you with hope and peace of mind that you are not alone in this— she is watching over you. Invite her into your dreams if the transformation you wish to go through is one that is extremely hard, or perhaps a little scary.

RASPBERRY
Rubus strigosus

ESSENTIAL PROPERTIES
feminine energy, love, protection

Though there are numerous types of raspberries in a variety of colors, the most easily found is red raspberry, *Rubus strigosus*. Her berries can be used as a dye as well as a medicine, and her leaves are used in teas by both herbal and traditional healers.

MEDICINAL PROPERTIES

Red raspberry's fruit and leaf have a variety of purposes. Women sometimes take red raspberry leaf orally in order to ease labor and delivery. The leaves also purportedly aid in stopping diarrhea, are good for bronchial issues, and may help with heart problems and protect against age-related mental decline.

MAGICAL PROPERTIES

Raspberry has a mothering, nurturing quality. She eases the various stages of the feminine Moon cycle, helping you through menstrual periods, childbirth, and menopause. Fertility can be quite a challenge when the sacral chakra is under distress, and raspberry eases any trauma and pain you may be carrying there, healing you and bringing you to better reproductive health. Raspberry also facilitates self-trust, as well as trust in relationships.

PLANT WISDOM

Raspberry's wisdom is powerful, and her healing embrace is even more so. Work with her if you want to heal your womb, particularly if you have been sexually abused or are having a hard time conceiving. Her message is unique to each person, and she will show up in dreams only if she needs to show you something that will propel your healing or your intentions forward.

ROSE
Rosa

ESSENTIAL PROPERTIES
protection, love, intuition

According to fossil evidence, the rose is 35 million years old. There are several hundred species of roses, and beyond the obvious ornamental function, there's a long history of using various parts of the rose in food, drink, and medicine. Roses have been cultivated for the past 5,000 years, and are associated with love and friendship.

MEDICINAL PROPERTIES

Rose hips (the base of the flower after the blossom has dropped off) are used to make an oil that is widely used in skin care and makeup products. Roses are a source of vitamin C—which is excellent for the skin! Certain varieties of roses are used in Chinese medicine to move stagnant energy, ease pain, and improve digestion.

MAGICAL PROPERTIES

If you grow your own roses, you will create a Magical shield of protection for life, or at least that is what my *abuela* says. Roses are fierce and are often underestimated when it comes to their protection ability. You'll find rosebushes around the homes of many Witches, especially Indigenous *brujas* who have grown roses for this purpose for centuries.

When you grow your own roses, you can create a purpose for each rosebush you have—one for protection Magic, another for love Magic, another for opening the third eye, another for creativity, and so on. Snip a rose off the bush that holds the relevant intention so you can use it in Magical workings— the power it will give your spell will be so noticeable you'll feel bone-deep vibrations. But you can still work with rose even if you're unable to grow her— buy freshly cut roses and place them in a glass vase. As you fill it with water, pour your intentions into the water. You can also separate the roses and place them in single vases for different intentions. Wearing rose perfume (making sure it contains actual roses!) or sprinkling rosewater on your clothes will protect you throughout the day, or you can anoint your forehead with rose oil to amplify intuition.

PLANT WISDOM

Roses are queens. They are luxurious and sophisticated, and hold so many different meanings for so many different cultures. I could write an entire book just on the rose! She teaches us to open our eyes to the beauty of the world—the beauty of all things and all people. Dreams of roses can mean different things, depending on the color of the rose, but generally speaking she visits to bring you good news.

ROSE OF JERICHO
Selaginella lepidophylla

ESSENTIAL PROPERTIES

new beginnings, abundance, happiness

This incredible desert plant can survive in a dormant state without water or roots for up to two years, and then come entirely back to life—for this reason, she's also known as the "resurrection plant" or "resurrection fern." There is another plant entirely with the same common name and similar resilient properties classified as *Anastatica hierochuntica*, but the green spike moss is the one with Magical properties.

MEDICINAL PROPERTIES

Rose of Jericho can treat infertility, particularly in women, and is good for the lungs and digestive system as well. She can soothe the pangs of childbirth; traditionally, after a baby was born, midwives would submerge rose of Jericho in water so that the plant would be reborn at the same moment.

ROSE OF JERICHO

MAGICAL PROPERTIES

Rose of Jericho is one of the most fascinating plants in the herbal kingdom, as she functions much the same way as the soul does. Just like rose of Jericho, the soul can stay dormant and suppressed for years, but when properly nourished, it can expand into the most brilliant display of love and light. Rose of Jericho calls in whatever is needed for your soul to thrive. She represents rebirth, but also the uplifting happiness that can be felt when you provide your spirit with the right fertilizer to expand to its fullest potential.

PLANT WISDOM

Work with rose of Jericho to set your old self free and rise reborn. She will open the doors to a new self, or a new beginning. She teaches us that we can't expect to know who we will be in the future, because we are always changing—our future self is not set in stone. But rose of Jericho shows us how to celebrate who we are at the present moment. Rise from the ashes, and come forth reborn with rose of Jericho. Only those who have dedicated a longtime practice with her will be blessed with her wisdom in the dreamworld.

ROSEMARY
Salvia rosarminus

ESSENTIAL PROPERTIES

memory, protection

Rosemary is a woody, fragrant, perennial herb. Like so many Magical herbs, she's actually a member of the mint family. She can season foods, is often burned as an incense, and is an ingredient in some cleaning products and shampoos.

MEDICINAL PROPERTIES

For thousands of years, rosemary has helped to relieve muscle pain, improve memory, boost the immune system, and promote hair growth. Rubbing a balm made with rosemary on the skin can repel insects. Ingesting rosemary in excessive amounts can cause vomiting, coma, and pulmonary edema, so don't overdo it.

MAGICAL PROPERTIES

Rosemary is an herb of remembering, improving both physical memory and remembrances of loved ones who have passed on. Rosemary can help you remember your dreams, your past lives, and, perhaps most importantly, the love you have for others. As a protection herb, rosemary is one of the best at fighting evil spirits, and is an ingredient in exorcism spells in many cultures. She is also great for any variety of defensive Magic.

PLANT WISDOM

Connect to your inner knowing with rosemary. She will bring forth knowledge that's been within you since before you were born. If rosemary appears to you in a dream, she has to come to warn and protect you—for there is evil lurking somewhere in your life.

ROWAN
Sorbus aucuparia

ESSENTIAL PROPERTIES

protection, psychic ability, abundance

The rowan tree has long been recognized all over the world, in so many different cultures, as a powerful protector. Most parts of rowan trees are edible and good for a variety of ailments. Her bright red berries are tiny, like holly berries, but unlike holly her fruit can be eaten. Rowan is also called the "Witches tree" and the "tree of power," partly because the berries of this tree have a natural pentagram engraved in them.

MEDICINAL PROPERTIES

The rowan tree's berries have been used for millennia for stomach disorders and bleeding. Her leaves may remedy asthma, colds, arthritis, and sore eyes. It's believed that these curative properties are due to the berries' and bark's astringent nature.

MAGICAL PROPERTIES

Meditating with rowan instantly fills you with a sense of peace and prosperity. If you don't have access to a rowan tree, you can work with rowan's bark, leaves, and berries for protection spells as well as spells for abundance. You can keep her bark in your hands when meditating, or eat her berries in foods to bring peace and abundance.

PLANT WISDOM

Rowan is without a doubt an incredibly Magical and sacred tree. It is wise to grow a rowan tree around your home to keep it protected. Rowan is very territorial—in a good way! She takes pride in the land she lives in, and will guard it for as long as she is alive. Rowan is also a great listener, so sit and chat with her, especially if you feel like something is off. Maybe you've had a streak of bad luck or you've been stuck for a while—if that's the case, place your hands on rowan and ask that she take away anything that she sees latched on to you. She can even clear your auric field of negativity.

To dream of rowan is to dream of a portal to other worlds; she is inviting you to travel into the unknown. Walk to her in your dream and place your hands on her—she will take you on a journey like no other.

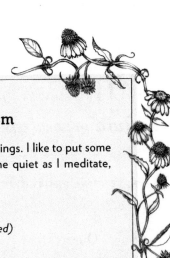

Rowanberry Third Eye Jam

This third eye jam can be used in any food and Magical workings. I like to put some in my tea or on a cracker or toast, eat it, and then sit in the quiet as I meditate, journal, or practice Magic.

WHAT YOU NEED

>   **2 pounds dried rowanberries** *(washed and stems removed)*
>
>   **2 pounds apples** *(peeled, cored, and quartered)*
>
>   **4 to 5 sprigs of rosemary**
>
>   **1 teaspoon chopped fresh basil**
>
>   **1 bay leaf**
>
>   **Jelly bag**
>
>   **½ cup sugar** *(consider brown, cane, or coconut sugars)*
>
>   **Jar with a lid**

WHAT TO DO

+ Place the rowanberries, apples, rosemary, basil, and bay leaf in a large pot—you want to make sure there's room for everything to move, so that you can stir without worrying anything will spill.

+ Cover the fruit with cold water. Bring the mixture to a boil over medium heat, then reduce the heat to low and simmer for 15 to 20 minutes, or until the fruit is soft.

+ Allow it to cool for 5 to 10 minutes, then ladle the fruit into a jelly bag. Leave this suspended over a bowl to drip overnight, or for at least 11 hours. Do not squeeze the jelly bag to extract more juice—just allow it to drain naturally.

+ Once you've finished draining the juice, return it to a pan and add your sugar. Simmer on low heat for 10 to 15 minutes, or until the sugar has dissolved.

+ Once the sugar has dissolved, increase the heat and bring the mixture to a boil. Boil for 5 minutes, and then once the jelly has reached the setting point, pour it into a jar and seal.

Rue

Ruta graveolens

ESSENTIAL PROPERTIES

protection

Rue is Queen of the Herbs—a fragrant evergreen that grows wild in fields all over North America and Europe, though she is native to the Mediterranean. She blooms in tiny yellow flowers that can make the world seem as though it is made of sunshine.

MEDICINAL PROPERTIES

Rue is often cultivated for medicinal uses, as a condiment, and sometimes as an insect repellent. She can aid in menstrual problems and stimulate the uterus. Used topically, she can treat arthritis, sprains, swollen skin, tooth-aches, headaches, tumors, and warts. She's an antifungal and can also repel lice. Be careful when working with her, though, as when your skin is covered with rue, exposure to the Sun can cause sunburns. Ingesting too much can cause gastric distress and can even be fatal.

MAGICAL PROPERTIES

Rue protects you from any outside influences that may be causing you harm and leading you to do things you don't actually wish to do. Rue can help you detach from these influences, so you can return to the heart of who you are. Rue further protects you from hexes, curses, and evil forces. Her somewhat "stinky" smell is said to ward off all malicious entities.

PLANT WISDOM

Rue is a protectress, and she will not only protect you from the outside world, she will also protect you from yourself. If you want to work on releasing bad habits, self-harm, self-sabotage, or anything like that, connect with rue, and allow her to reflect back to you all the things you may have neglected or hidden away—all those wonderful qualities about yourself that, when forgotten, lead to not caring for yourself as you deserve. Meeting rue in a dream is pretty Magical—the sense of peace she brings is something I can't really express. It's almost like meditating.

SACRED FIG
Ficus religiosa

SACRED FIG

ESSENTIAL PROPERTIES

meditation, awareness, protection

This plant is sacred to a variety of religions and Magical practices all over the world. Buddhism, Jainism, and Hinduism all celebrate her—though she is known by other names, including bodhi tree and ashvattha tree. In Santería, she is known as alamo. The tree has a distinctive heart-shaped leaf, and has a life span of 900 to 1,500 years—or longer.

MEDICINAL PROPERTIES

According to Ayurvedic tradition, sacred fig acts as an aphrodisiac; she can also cure a cold or cough, improve the skin, and aid a troubled digestive system. Her bark and leaves may be ground into a paste and rubbed over the skin, and decoctions of the roots and bark can be consumed safely.

MAGICAL PROPERTIES

It was under the sacred fig that Gautama Buddha attained enlightenment. Sacred fig is an extremely effective aid to meditation, and can help you attain a trance state—the better to connect with your true self. She heightens awareness of all the energy that is around you and within you, and can protect you from outside forces. The wisdom of our ancestors dwells in this plant, and so I often ask for her guidance on such things as life purpose or the next steps in my journey. I also consult her on any decisions I have trouble making on my own.

If you meet sacred fig in a dream, go and sit with her. If you aren't advanced in intentional dreaming or lucid dreaming, it may seem impossible—but when sacred fig is present, anything is possible, even for a beginner. She often comes with a message from your higher self, and this connection gives you the power to move freely in your dreams.

Grow this beautiful soul in your yard, so you can sit with her for outside meditation. If you're growing her as a houseplant, keep her in your sacred space. I also love to have her in the bathroom, to sit with me when I take a bath. She can be a great support while doing a Full Moon ritual bath; her wisdom and guidance are explosive when the Moon is full. I wouldn't recommend keeping her in a living space where there is a lot of people activity, as she likes her peace just as much as we do.

SAFFRON CROCUS
Crocus sativus

ESSENTIAL PROPERTIES
Moon Magic, abundance, blood Magic, love

Saffron, widely considered the most valuable spice in the world, is the crumbled threads of the stigmas of the saffron crocus. One crocus blossom produces .0011 ounces of fresh saffron and tastes kind of like metallic honeyed hay. This spice, along with being highly fragrant and flavorful, is also highly pigmented, and produces a lovely orange color. It would make for a very expensive dye plant, but it does provide color along with flavor to dishes. These crocuses grow mainly in the Mediterranean, for they prefer well-drained, claylike soil and full sunlight.

MEDICINAL PROPERTIES

Saffron is a powerful antioxidant, and has been shown to improve mood, anxiety, and premenstrual symptoms. It may also serve as an aphrodisiac.

MAGICAL PROPERTIES

Saffron is a powerful love-drawing herb, and is helpful in spells for wealth and abundance, too. I love to sprinkle saffron in my abundance spells, as she will draw in positive energies, aiding in the success of my creative projects. Cook with saffron while setting intentions of love—your food will ignite those feelings in whomever you serve it to, providing of course that your spell is for the highest good of everyone involved. But I work most often with saffron in blood Magic. I often harness the power of my sacred menstrual blood in my healing work, my spiritual development, and when I'm communing with my ancestors. Saffron's ability to connect to the Moon's energy makes her a perfect partner in any Moon Magic you do, and of course our feminine cycles are profoundly tied to the Moon.

PLANT WISDOM

Saffron is a jack-of-all-trades in the plant kingdom—she can handle just about anything you ask of her! I grow her outside where she can soak up the Moon's energies, and then bring her blossoms in when I need her help. Saffron flowers can make your home feel very healing and peaceful, making it a place of refuge.

Dreams of saffron are intense. She shows you the things you have hidden or have refused to face—she wants you to work through them, so that they no longer hold you back. She will be there to help you.

Saffron Blood Magic Purging Ritual

This ritual is perfect for purging, for releasing toxic energy. It helps you let go of what no longer serves you. This will be quite intense, and the effects can take up to a week to be felt fully. You'll likely experience lots of tears and life changes, so be prepared. This ritual calls for menstrual blood, but if that is not available to you, you can either prick your finger or use saliva instead—it won't be quite as powerful, but it will work.

WHAT YOU NEED

Cedar or frankincense incense

Several handfuls of salt

A bowl of water

A bowl with a small amount of salt

3 red candles

½ tablespoon pau d'arco

1 tablespoon tobacco

A handful of rose petals

1 tablespoon saffron

A few drops of menstrual blood *(or blood from your finger, or saliva)*

WHAT TO DO

+ Cleanse your space and lift the energies surrounding you by burning cedar or frankincense incense. Leave it burning while you perform your ritual.

+ Create a salt circle large enough for you to sit within it. As you sprinkle the salt, set your intentions for protection.

+ Set your bowl of water and bowl of salt in the circle.

+ Light your red candles and place them inside the salt circle. Arrange them in a triangle, with one directly in front of you, one behind you to your right, and one behind you to your left.

+ Sit quietly for a moment and relax your mind and body. Envision the things you wish to release. If you're uncertain, ask the plant spirits present (pau d'arco, tobacco, rose, and saffron) to help you navigate.

+ Add the pau d'arco, tobacco, and rose petals to the bowl of water. Thank each of them for being present with you.

+ Add the saffron, and ask her for her guidance. Thank her for her help.

+ Hold the container of blood in your hands. Pour your love into it. Ask that it help you purge and release. Pour your blood into the water, followed by a pinch of salt from the bowl of salt.

+ Lift the water bowl to your heart center. Take a deep breath and feel the healing, love, and fire entering your body. Raise the bowl to the sky and say, "I call on my guides, ancestors, and angels to come through and help me surrender to my own healing." You can adjust this phrase to whatever feels right to you.

+ Lower your bowl to the ground and sit in silence, meditating. Feel, sense, taste, and listen to the spirits twirling within and all around you.

+ When you've finished, blow out your candles and pour your bowl of water into the earth. Once you've cleaned up, sip some soothing tea such as chamomile or yerba buena to calm your mind.

SAGE
Salvia officinalis

ESSENTIAL PROPERTIES
healing, wisdom

Sage has a long history, recorded as far back as the Egyptians, for use in a wide variety of medicinal and Magical ways. She too is a member of the mint family, and can be utilized as a spice, an herb, a tea, or burned as a smudge stick, depending on your needs.

MEDICINAL PROPERTIES

Sage serves many medicinal functions, though she is most widely recognized for promoting mental clarity and possibly longevity. She is a diuretic, a topical anesthetic, an antiseptic, and a styptic, meaning she can stop bleeding. Though Plant Witches and other herbalists have known and understood sage's value for centuries, modern medicine is still catching up: Recent clinical studies have been focused on the positive effects of sage on mental functioning in humans.

MAGICAL PROPERTIES

There is a reason it's called "sage advice"—sage has long been associated with wisdom and determination. She helps you find clear answers to even the most difficult of questions. Sage is a truth seeker, and will assist you to find purpose and uncover secrets. She is also a powerful tool for both physical and spiritual healing.

PLANT WISDOM

Sage is sacred, especially to Native Americans, who have treasured her as part of their culture for centuries. She comes with infinite wisdom, and her messages are unique to every single person she works with. She can provide you with anything from ancestral connection to deep spiritual healing. Sage asks that you take the time to work with her to experience something special and unique, something you could never have anywhere else. Dreaming of sage is rare, but if you are in need of healing, or if you wish to clear sadness from your home or from yourself, invite her in and ask that she bring her healing powers into your spirit.

SAGO PALM
Cycus revoluta

ESSENTIAL PROPERTIES
resilience

Despite her name, sago is not actually a palm at all, but an ancient kind of plant known as a cycad that has been around since the prehistoric times—yes, since the dinosaurs! A male sago produces a golden cone, which may grow

more than two feet tall. The
female produces a beautiful,
big golden flower that slowly
opens when it is fertile. She
does not flower yearly, but
rather every second or third
year. On the years she doesn't
flower, she produces a new set
of spring leaves.

SAGO PALM

MEDICINAL PROPERTIES

Sago palm's bark and seeds
can be made into a poultice for healing sores and swellings—but the seeds are
poisonous, so be careful. The juice of young sago palm leaves can be used to
treat flatulence and vomiting, and the pollen is a narcotic.

MAGICAL PROPERTIES

Working with sago palm will help you find your resilience, so you are able
to get through difficult times and rise back up again to achieve great things.
Keep her by your altar and/or in your sacred space when working on your
abundance or success spells. Having her by you while you are trying to finish
a project will keep you motivated, inspired, and productive. She is also great
at helping you make tough decisions; meditate with her, exchanging breaths
as you tap into the core of your question, and she will show you the direction you need to take. You can also seek her advice by inviting her into your
dreams.

PLANT WISDOM

The ancient medicine and wisdom of this sacred plant is often overlooked;
instead she is treated as any other decorative plant. But she is so much more
than that. In my home, sago palm is a goddess—I speak with her and care for
her each and every day. Having conversations with her is like indulging in the
richest piece of chocolate you've ever had. Her wisdom and perspective on life
can shift the way you think about just about everything.

SAINT JOHN'S WORT

Hypericum perforatum

ESSENTIAL PROPERTIES

protection, psychic ability, clarity

Saint John's wort is a ground cover that grows easily and well—so easily, in fact, that she can take over your garden if you let her. She is also called *fuga daemonum*, meaning "chase away demons" and another name is *sol terrestris*, meaning "Sun on Earth."

MEDICINAL PROPERTIES

Saint John's wort is well-known for her ability to treat mild to moderate depression and the symptoms that tend to go along with depression, including nervousness, anxiety, fatigue, lack of appetite, and difficulty sleeping. People have been working with Saint John's wort for more than 2,400 years—the Greeks, Romans, and Native Americans all knew she could help treat reptile bites, cramps, or superficial wounds.

MAGICAL PROPERTIES

Saint John's wort is a powerful protector, shining her bright light into the shadows, detecting whatever evil may dwell there, and chasing it away. Keep her in your garden to create a protective barrier around your home, and keep her in your home to protect those within it—you can hang her over your windows to keep evil from entering. Saint John's wort is also fantastic for divination work, as she opens your psychic gifts while also keeping you safe. I do not recommend using her for communication with spirit unless you are quite experienced, but I do recommend keeping her with you when working with divination tools like tarot or oracle cards, or however you connect to your higher self.

PLANT WISDOM

Working with Saint John's wort will bring you a sense of who you are, exposing truths hidden within. Connect with her to bring clarity, helping you see beyond the layers that hide your most unique and powerful self. Dreaming of her symbolizes abundance, particularly in happiness and peace of mind.

SANDALWOOD

Santalum

ESSENTIAL PROPERTIES

psychic ability, wisdom

The sandalwood plant has many benefits, from the medicinal to aromatic to Magical. Sandalwood is highly prized because she can maintain her fragrance for decades, and that fragrance is a distinctive warm, almost creamy scent.

MEDICINAL PROPERTIES

Long used in Ayurvedic medicine and traditional Chinese medicine, sandalwood oil can help with colds, urinary tract infections, digestive issues, muscle issues, mental health, liver and gallbladder problems, and hemorrhoids. It is also useful for a variety of aromatherapies, particularly to promote a sense of calm. Sandalwood is reportedly an antibacterial, an anxiety reliever, and a mental stimulant.

MAGICAL PROPERTIES

Sandalwood is one of the most well-known and powerful plants in history, and her healing and Magical properties have been treasured for centuries. Sandalwood helps you to release ties to the past, or anything that is no longer serving you. She grounds you, and shows you the lessons learned from difficult situations, allowing you to move on with peace of mind. Additionally, sandalwood supports psychic development and personal growth.

We've all been in situations where we repeat the same mistakes and get the same results. Why can't we learn our lesson? Oftentimes it's because we are not as in tune with spirit as we should be. Life got in the way. Working with sandalwood is like going through a file cabinet of classes you've taken in life but were too busy fooling around to truly receive their wisdom. She forces you to sit down and finally learn from your mistakes, to truly understand why you haven't been able to learn in the past. Invite her into your dreams after meditating with her, to amplify and develop your gifts.

SARSAPARILLA
Smilax aristolochiifolia

ESSENTIAL PROPERTIES
abundance, happiness

Sarsaparilla is best known for flavoring drinks and foods—especially root beer! She has also been turned to for centuries to treat a variety of ailments by a number of cultures. Sarsaparilla is a climbing vine, but it is her root that is prized for Magical uses.

MEDICINAL PROPERTIES

Native Americans have used sarsaparilla root for a variety of medical uses, as it is valued for its healing powers. Until the early 20th century, it was used to treat syphilis in the United States as part of the official pharmacopeia. It can be used for treating psoriasis, rheumatoid arthritis, and kidney disease. Its ingestion can also increase urination to reduce fluid retention. It is believed to inhibit premature aging.

MAGICAL PROPERTIES

Place sarsaparilla in your home, especially in your kitchen, and she will grant good health to all who live there. Place her in your closet to bring out a different perspective on life, a brighter one that will amplify your spiritual practice. Work with her when you are ill and are in need of better health, and she can motivate you to take better care of yourself, showing your heart how you would feel if you practiced true self-care. For abundance spells and intentions, keep her near you or place her on your altar. You can also include her in your spellwork for manifestation.

PLANT WISDOM

Sarsaparilla ignites happiness within you, which in turn elevates your frequency, attracting abundance into your life. Her roots are so wild and happy it is contagious, and they love life with such a passion it illuminates those who work with her. Dreaming of sarsaparilla indicates a deeply rooted trauma that may be affecting your health. Ask her to help you heal.

SEA BUCKTHORN
Hippophaë rhamnoides

ESSENTIAL PROPERTIES

hex-breaking, protection, luck, energy clearing

Sea buckthorn, not to be mistaken for buckthorn (*Rhamnus*), produces orange-yellow berries, which have been used over centuries as food, medicine, and skin care. This amazingly resistant plant is able to withstand temperatures as low as -43°C (-45°F). Sometimes referred to as the holy fruit of the Himalayas, sea buckthorn can be applied directly to the skin or ingested.

Sea Buckthorn Luck Spray

You can use this luck spray whenever you're doing spells for luck—spray it on your altar, or outside the building when you're going in for an interview, when you're about to take an exam, or even outside a restaurant when you're about to go on a date.

WHAT YOU NEED

1 cup water

2 teaspoons sea buckthorn

1 teaspoon sea salt

Orange peel

1 to 2 drops lemongrass essential oil

Spray bottle

WHAT TO DO

+ Bring the water to a boil, and then add all the ingredients except the essential oil.
+ Simmer for 10 to 15 minutes.
+ Strain and let it cool, then stir in your essential oil.
+ Add the mixture to your spray bottle. When ready to use, simply spray the air and say, "May luck find me here."

MEDICINAL PROPERTIES

Sea buckthorn is a popular plant in Ayurvedic and traditional Chinese medicines, and can treat arthritis, ulcers, and gout. There is some evidence that she is also effective in countering memory and concentration loss due to aging. She promotes heart health, protects against diabetes and stomach ulcers, protects your skin, supports a healthy liver, and offers so many more benefits.

MAGICAL PROPERTIES

There is a legend that says making a circle of sea buckthorn branches and dancing within it under a Full Moon will call an elf to appear, one who may grant a wish. Placing sea buckthorn branches in your doors and windows can offer protection from Magical attack and can bring good luck to those who live in this home. Sea buckthorn is also great to work in spells for legal matters, as she will bring luck in your favor. Simply place the leaves in your wallet or use the bark in your workings.

PLANT WISDOM

Oddly enough, when this plant speaks, she isn't as tough as she may seem. She's gentle, understanding, and has a wisdom about her that is so enchanting. She teaches you how to defend and protect yourself and to learn self-care, because in your journey the person who is present the entire time is you. Sea buckthorn reassures you of your worth and capability. Dreaming of eating her berries symbolizes spiritual growth, while dreaming of cutting her down indicates that a dark Magic has been placed against you.

SHEPHERD'S PURSE
Capsella bursa-pastorsis

ESSENTIAL PROPERTIES
healing, protection

Shepherd's purse, belonging to the mustard family, is a common weed found in many parts of the world. Her fruit's flat, triangular shape is what inspired her name. The mucilage in her seeds trap nematodes, making her a very handy plant to keep in your garden.

MEDICINAL PROPERTIES

Shepherd's purse can treat heart and circulatory problems and low blood pressure, though she can also help clear up bladder infections, ease headaches, and act as an astringent and as an antidiarrheal. She may also treat menstrual issues, and she contains substances with both anti-inflammatory and antioxidant properties. Be careful, though, as she can cause drowsiness if taken in excessive amounts.

MAGICAL PROPERTIES

Shepherd's purse is a healing herb that is most commonly known for stopping bleeding—both literally and spiritually. She can stop the bleeding of the spirit by repairing holes in your aura. When these cracks are repaired, the spirit can come back to full strength.

PLANT WISDOM

Shepherd's purse can assist you on any healing journey, particularly when you are working to heal someone else. Having her with you will help you identify and sense what they need, and amplify your ability to help them. You will dream of shepherd's purse only if you've been a longtime devotee, but once you begin working with her you won't want to stop! Her dreams bring what I call add-ons—every time she visits you in a dream, she will add to your gifts as a healer.

SICILIAN SUMAC
Rhus coriaria

ESSENTIAL PROPERTIES
protection, love

Some species of sumac are poisonous, so make sure you're working with *Rhus coriaria* specifically. This small tree grows clusters of tiny fruits. They are a deep, dusky red and when dried may be ground into a lemony-flavored spice that is often used in Middle Eastern cuisine. The leaves and bark of Sicilian sumac contain high levels of tannins, making them useful for dyeing purposes.

MEDICINAL PROPERTIES

Sicilian sumac ranks very high among antioxidant-rich foods. She can neutralize free radicals that can cause cancer, heart disease, or signs of aging. She is also a great addition to an anti-inflammatory diet. Sicilian sumac can give you more energy and help maintain your body's metabolism. Her boiled fruit can serve as a remedy for painful menstruation, and you can steep her roots and berries in boiling water to make a wash for sores.

MAGICAL PROPERTIES

Sicilian sumac carries a profound, fiery energy that comes from both her color and her passionate nature. If you need to bring the element of fire into your spellwork, add Sicilian sumac. You can also place her on your altar to represent fire. Sicilian sumac's fire is protective, like flames warding off the darkness. Sprinkle her on your love candles to ignite passion. If you are seeking a more fiery love with someone else, use a red candle, but if you're looking to find that passion within yourself, use a pink candle. Add saffron crocus (see page 284) to any creativity spells to bring passion there as well.

PLANT WISDOM

Sicilian sumac is incredibly versatile. She teaches the importance of seeking different perspectives, and never allowing yourself to be closed into a box—or closing yourself in. So often we feel we are nothing more than the titles we give ourselves . . . mother, lawyer, gardener, even Witch. We contain multitudes. Sicilian sumac understands this, and helps us to see that all the different parts of us are still us, and make up a harmonious whole. We are expansive beings, and no box or title will ever hold us in or describe us perfectly.

SKULLCAP

Scutellaria

ESSENTIAL PROPERTIES

peace

This plant's name refers to the shape of her flower, which resembles a miniature medieval helmet. She grows near marshes, and is a member of the mint family. Skullcap blooms with brilliant, vibrant colors that will make any garden stand out.

MEDICINAL PROPERTIES

In traditional Chinese medicine, skullcap can treat hepatitis, inflammation, and diarrhea. Native Americans worked with her to treat various gynecological issues, but nowadays she is most often called upon to ease muscle tension and anxiety.

MAGICAL PROPERTIES

Skullcap is one of the most powerful relaxants in the herb kingdom, for both the physical and spiritual body, making her an excellent choice for transitioning between one state of being and another. Skullcap can also facilitate commitment in relationships.

PLANT WISDOM

Skullcap brings a stillness to our lives, a place of quiet where we can simply *be* and grasp all the deliciousness of our presence. If you're someone who is always on the go and have very little time for yourself, invite her into your dreams. She will show you what you are missing in the rush of it all, bringing clarity and perspective to what is truly important to you.

SLIPPERY ELM

Ulmus rubra

ESSENTIAL PROPERTIES

protection, love

The twigs and leaves of the slippery elm are slightly furry, and the inner bark is slimy—hence her name. She is also called red elm because when her leaves first emerge, they have a distinct reddish tint.

Slippery Elm Truth Spell

Slippery Elm's specialty is revealing the truth, especially when it comes to those who have ill intentions for you.

WHAT YOU NEED

Black candle

1 handful slippery elm

Small bowl

WHAT TO DO

+ Light your black candle and dress it with your saliva by rubbing a thin layer of spit all over the outside of the candle.

+ Place slippery elm in a small bowl next to the candle, and ask her to expose any ill will or negative people in your life. Blow out the candle after thanking her for her help. Within the next 2 to 3 weeks, you will catch each of these people in action, 1 by 1.

MEDICINAL PROPERTIES

The inner edible bark of slippery elm is a demulcent, which means it can form a soothing film over mucous membranes. This doesn't last very long, only about a half an hour, but during that time it will relieve pain, particularly a sore throat or a canker sore. Slippery elm can also relieve the symptoms of irritable bowel syndrome.

MAGICAL PROPERTIES

Work with slippery elm to open up your throat chakra and find your voice. If you're a creative person but can't seem to find your voice in the work you're doing, connect with her.

PLANT WISDOM

Slippery elm can see the truth of all that is, but she is a romantic at heart. She tells tales of love, especially stories of soul mates or love that is eternal. If you sit with her, she can tell if you and your lover are in fact soul mates, meant for each other—if all of a sudden her leaves start to sway and rustle, she is giving you her blessing. Ask her into your dreams to find the truth within yourself, the truth of who you really are, with the purest wisdom that you possess.

SNAPDRAGON
Antirrhinum

ESSENTIAL PROPERTIES

protection, opening the door between realms

Lovely and beneficial, snapdragon's flowers, leaves, and seeds all have uses. The seeds can even be pressed as an alternative to olive oil. She got her name for the shape of her flower—which, when gently pinched, looks like a dragon's mouth opening and closing.

MEDICINAL PROPERTIES

The snapdragon's flowers and leaves have anti-inflammatory properties, and are also considered a stimulant. You can make the leaves and flowers into a poultice to use on tumors, ulcers, and hemorrhoids. And while the flowers are bitter, they are a good source of vitamins.

MAGICAL PROPERTIES

Long ago, snapdragons were planted around the home to ward off Witchcraft, and you can do the same thing using the oil from her seeds. You can reverse a hex or a spell gone wrong with snapdragon, as she will help you see the truth of a situation—particularly if someone is lying to you. This beauty calls in spirits, amplifies energies, and is a great divination companion. Work with fresh snapdragons when traveling in the spirit world during meditation, and with them dried to conjure communication. Place daisy petals in the sculls or "mouths" of dried snapdragons, and hang them by the front door to keep evil from entering.

SNAPDRAGON

PLANT MESSAGES

Snapdragon brings a cleaner direction to your intentions. Most often we think we know what we want, but then when we get it, we may find it wasn't really what we wanted at all. Snapdragon will be your companion when setting intentions and planning your future and spells, letting you see beyond the mind to what you truly want—a superpower, for sure. Invite her into your dreams to travel back into your past, where you can observe messages you may have missed and learn from them.

SOLOMON'S SEAL

Polygonatum

────────────────────── ౭

ESSENTIAL PROPERTIES

shadow work, self-awareness, blood Magic

Solomon's seal is a flowering plant with a variety of medicinal and Magical uses. It is said that she was given her name because the scars on her roots resemble the seal of Solomon, the ancient Hebrew king. Solomon's seal is a food staple in China, where the root is used to make tea, or fried with sugar and honey as a treat. She has helped the people of China survive times of famine.

MEDICINAL PROPERTIES

Solomon's seal can treat pain, fever, inflammation, lung disorders, allergy, and weakness. She can be an aphrodisiac, though she is best used with the aid of an herbal practitioner. She is believed to restore mental vitality following a period of stress or exhaustion, and is also used topically for bruises, boils, hemorrhoids, and redness of skin.

MAGICAL PROPERTIES

Solomon's seal is one of the most useful plants in a Plant Witch's collection. She can help with changing a habit you want to break, and when you're having trouble with a difficult decision. Placing Solomon's seal in your planner will keep you focused on your goals and plans, and keep you from breaking good habits. She digs into the root cause of your self-destructive behaviors and shines her light so you can address it. Her new stems have shades of dark red, and for this reason she holds strong energies in blood Magic, primarily in working with new beginnings, shedding the old self, and connecting to your ancestors.

Shadow work is Solomon's seal's specialty. She illuminates the dark spaces where we have hidden parts of ourselves, the "good" and the "bad," and gently reflects them, allowing us to fully see ourselves as a whole. And then, once we have allowed ourselves to see clearly, she will help with what needs to be healed, teaching us to embrace ourselves entirely, even the parts that scare us the most.

Invite her into your dreams to navigate your inner world. It took me a little while to make this happen, but after I worked with Solomon's seal for a couple of years, she entered my dreams and showed me my inner world—and let me tell you, it was a powerful experience! She set me on a path to awakening more of my power by illuminating my truth.

SPIDER PLANT
Chlorophytum comosum

ESSENTIAL PROPERTIES
abundance, energy clearing

Also known as airplane plant and spider ivy, this common houseplant has elongated foliage that is either solid green or variegated with white. Spider plant reproduces in the summer, producing tiny white flowers on long stems, and offsets that grow off to the side like little baby spiders—they're very cute! Spider plants have so many leaves in a small area that they are fantastic for filtering the air in your home.

MEDICINAL PROPERTIES
This plant has no known medicinal properties.

MAGICAL PROPERTIES

Spider plants birth new babies by the dozens when you take good care of them—and so it makes sense that she's terrific for fertility, abundance, and manifesting work. Transplanting her babies is a spiritual act in itself; make sure you set your intentions as you replant them, and they will grow abundance in your life. Spider plants are energetic filters, kind of like a dream catcher for negativity. Keeping one in each room of the house creates an energetic shield that can capture any negative energies that may have slipped past. Keeping her on the porch keeps your home protected and brings in peaceful energies, for spider plant brings a message of mindfulness.

PLANT WISDOM

Spider plant teaches you to pay attention to every detail with an open heart and heightened awareness. Are you a healer? Place her where you do your healing work on others, and she will help you tap into their energies. Keep her in your sacred space or wherever you practice meditation, yoga, healing, or even where you work on creative projects. Dreaming of spider plants is rare, but when it happens it symbolizes the web of life—in these dreams you are able to explore and see how your future may turn out to be.

STAR ANISE
Illicium verum

ESSENTIAL PROPERTIES
psychic ability, balance

There are several varieties of anise—one is an herb with tiny yellow flowers, and the other is what we are discussing here, the star anise, a completely different plant, an evergreen tree. Both have a licorice-like scent and flavor, and both are common ingredients in cuisines all over the world.

MEDICINAL PROPERTIES

This plant has no known medicinal properties.

MAGICAL PROPERTIES

Star anise naturally grows into an eight-pointed star. This balanced, equal shape speaks to how anise can help balance the forces within you, bringing you into a clear understanding of what is truly right for you. Finding this balance gives you a sense of calm, so that you are able to see beyond what has been blocking you. Star anise loves to wake the spirit in you, and can amplify your work with psychic intuition and inner knowing. Place her on the altar when you want to do spiritual growth work, and add her to your Magical workings if you wish to bring in wealth and luck. Placing star anise at the corners of your home will protect you, creating a safe space for fairies and angels to enter. Star anise's border blocks only ill will, inviting all positive energies to enter.

PLANT WISDOM

Dreaming and meditating with star anise is so powerful. When I work with her, she amplifies my gifts more than I could ever imagine, sending me into states of geometric sacredness. But be wary—she isn't gentle, not even with beginners, so be prepared for some eye-opening truths.

STINGING NETTLE
Urtica dioica

ESSENTIAL PROPERTIES

protection, secrets, happiness

Stinging nettle doesn't mess around—her leaves really hurt. Her stinging hairs are made of silica, which break off into the skin and then exude chemicals, causing a histamine reaction. For this reason, she is known as "devil's claw" or "devil's plaything"—but despite her fearsome sting, she is an extremely useful and beneficial plant. She's an excellent food source, and her stem fibers can be spun like flax, creating a fabric that is as strong as hemp and yet as soft as cotton. You could even dye this fabric with nettle herself, as she produces a lovely green hue.

MEDICINAL PROPERTIES

By the 5th century B.C., Hippocrates had recorded no less than 61 medicinal uses for stinging nettle. You can drink her as a tea to relieve hay fever, clean out a urinary tract infection, boost lactation, and to serve as a general energy tonic if you've been ill or have a chronic condition. Her leaves are delicious and high in protein and vitamins, but always cook them first—you definitely wouldn't want those hairs in your mouth or throat.

MAGICAL PROPERTIES

Stinging nettle carries such strong positive energies that simply having her in your garden amplifies the properties of all the other plants you grow, and placing her in sachets or charms along with other protection plants will amplify those energies tenfold. Sprinkle her in a glass of water, placing one in each room of the house to spread her positivity throughout your home. Drawing a bath with nettle will clear negativity and lift positive energies up into your auric body, leaving you feeling nurtured and loved.

Stinging nettle also brings secrets to light. If you feel someone is keeping something from you, burn stinging nettle while speaking their name, and in just a few days the secret will be revealed.

PLANT WISDOM

Stinging nettle works hard to protect herself, and she will do the same for you—but only if you care for her. You can also invite her into your dreams to help you sleep deeply, feeling both calm and nurtured.

STRING OF PEARLS
Senecio rowleyanus

STRING OF PEARLS

ESSENTIAL PROPERTIES

manifesting

String of pearls is a leafy succulent vine native to dry parts of southwest Africa. This creeping vine produces tiny little beads along a dangling stem—looking exactly like a string of pearls. Like most succulents, she requires very little care, though she does love attention, and grows well in a mixed succulent box or basket. She blooms in the summer, producing daisy-like flowers that are tiny and cute, with a sweet, spicy, cinnamon-like scent. String of pearls is toxic when ingested, causing minor illness like vomiting or diarrhea.

MEDICINAL PROPERTIES

This plant has no known medicinal properties.

MAGICAL PROPERTIES

You can use one of her pearls in any manifestation spellwork, or you can take a full string and make a wish on each pearl. Once you've made your wish, repot each pearl separately, making sure you propagate her properly, and as she grows she will feed your wish.

PLANT WISDOM

String of pearls is lovely and sweet, with a can-do attitude. She combines positivity with grounding vibrations, and sets an example of confidence—she knows she can reach and expand because she has a solid foundation. She roots deep and strong to hold her in place as she explores. I meditate and chat with string of pearls about opportunities that come my way, and she helps me reflect on whether they are right for me and my growth. She teaches us to trust in divine timing, knowing that the world will pave the way when the time is right. Meanwhile, she suggests that we build good foundations, setting ourselves up so that we are spiritually prepared for whatever the road ahead has in store for us. The universe would never allow you to walk a path you aren't ready for—not because you don't deserve greatness, but because the love the universe has to offer is so big you need to be prepared to take it on! String of pearls will help you get ready.

String of pearls appears in your dreams to draw your attention to your goals that you have been ignoring—she reminds you to take action! Remember, things don't just happen for you. You need to put in the work.

SUNFLOWER
Helianthus annuus

ESSENTIAL PROPERTIES

intuition, happiness

Sunflowers are known for their bright, sunny dispositions. Their large, bright yellow-orange flowers resemble the Sun, and are often related to Sun deities. But did you know how incredible these Sun-loving sunflowers actually are? The sunflower bud is a heliotrope, meaning she turns her face to follow the Sun across the sky. When she blooms, coming into her abundant fertility, she loses this ability, keeping her own counsel.

MEDICINAL PROPERTIES

The sunflower is known for her fertility, and women wishing to conceive are encouraged to eat her seeds. While the seed has many culinary and life-sustaining uses, in oil form sunflower is also a very hospitable host to other healing plants and plant-derived healing oils and ointments. If you plant sunflower in your garden, she will extract toxins and heavy metals from the soil—though if this is the case, make sure not to eat her seeds, as they will now be saturated with those toxins. Use sunflower leaves to brew a tea with astringent, diuretic, and expectorant properties, making it very useful for the flu season. You can make the leaves into a poultice to treat sores, swelling, snakebites, and spider bites.

MAGICAL PROPERTIES

Sunflowers have many meanings to many people, but I treasure her for her devotion to inner guidance. She teaches that each and every one of us is on a journey that can at times be stressful or even scary. But sunflower reminds us that we are always capable of walking out of the darkness and into the light. Her gaze is set on the light; she is devoted to her path and never strays from it. We can learn from her example and trust in ourselves, trust that our self-knowledge will lead us to the right path. We can trust that there are no mistakes—just lessons and preparations.

PLANT WISDOM

Sunflower stands tall and proud, bearing a message of authenticity. She proclaims that we must embody our truths. Work with her to learn to stand as proudly as she does—she will lead you to your authentic self. Add her to baths, teas, spellwork—you can even bake with her oil. She isn't generally all that interested in showing up in dreams, but she will visit you if you have lost someone, or if there is a message for you from the spirit world.

TANSY

Tanacetum vulgare

TANSY

ESSENTIAL PROPERTIES

happiness, healing

This yellow button of a flower is a cheerful-
looking thing, and yet she is incredibly
powerful. In medieval Europe tansy was used
in embalming rituals to ward off worms, and
she is still often used in funeral wreaths. In
the Victorian language of flowers, tansy was
a declaration of war. Offered in rituals and
wreaths to the goddesses of death and rebirth, this late-summer flower can be
dried for later use in Imbolc rituals between the winter solstice and the spring
equinox to welcome the spring.

MEDICINAL PROPERTIES

Tansy is known to repel not only mosquitos, but when planted near crops like
potatoes, she can also keep away the potato beetle. In medieval times, she was
taken as a tea to expel worms from the body. Be aware just how powerful tansy
truly is, however; in larger doses she is known to be toxic and not recommended for consumption.

MAGICAL PROPERTIES

If your auric body needs cleansing, take a bunch of tansy and swipe it all over
you, starting from the head and working down to the feet. Many cultures use
plants in this way, and you should make sure to burn the bunch of tansy afterward to get rid of any junk she may have picked up. If your auric body needs
healing, say if you've had a streak of bad luck or are just feeling like you're
stuck and need a reset, repeat this ritual for seven days. Make sure you hydrate

during this time, and stay away from technology, especially social media—just rest and heal.

PLANT WISDOM

Tansy fills your soul with light and joy—just having her in your home is uplifting. Place her in the main room where people often gather. I like to have her on the kitchen table to bring the family into harmony. If someone is sick or sad, bring tansy into their room, and she will share her healing energies.

Dreaming of tansy means a death is coming, either a literal death or a death of a certain time of your life. This seems dark, considering what a bright light tansy is, but where there is light there is always shadow.

TEA TREE
Melaleuca alternifolia

ESSENTIAL PROPERTIES
strength, unblocking, protection, purification

Tea tree, or melaleuca, has been used as an herbal medicine by Indigenous peoples for thousands of years. She is a small tree or shrub in the myrtle family. The oil made from her leaves is herby and camphorous in scent.

MEDICINAL PROPERTIES

Tea tree is used topically to treat a variety of skin conditions, including bacterial and fungal infections, dandruff, and acne. She is also an effective insect repellent, and can be sprayed into your child's hair during the inevitable lice infestations at school. Tea tree oil should not be taken internally, as it can cause drowsiness, nausea, and even hallucinations in sufficient quantities. Tea tree oil has been used since the 1920s, but gained in popularity in the late 1980s and early 1990s, and remains useful to this day.

Tea Tree Resetting Footbath

Tea tree can guide you back to your center with this footbath, allowing you to find whatever has been blocking you.

WHAT YOU NEED

Large bowl

2 to 3 drops tea tree oil

1 to 2 drops witch hazel oil or 2 tablespoons dried witch hazel

1 bunch of abre camino

1 orange, sliced

2 acorns

3 pine cones

Black candle

WHAT TO DO

+ Bring a big pot of water to a boil. Once it is hot, but not uncomfortably so, pour the water into a bowl large enough to hold your feet.

+ Add all the ingredients. Light your black candle, setting your intentions for resetting and unblocking.

+ Sit quietly with your feet in the bath for at least 10 minutes, allowing tea tree to guide you as you meditate.

MAGICAL PROPERTIES

Diffuse tea tree essential oil during any Magical workings on clearing blockages, or while you meditate to discover what has been blocking you. Anoint any amplification talismans, crystals, Magical tools, or jewelry with tea tree oil to add to their power. You can also add it to a bath, particularly a footbath, to soak in and reset.

Tea tree is known as the "oil of the angels" for good reason—she can help you connect to those spirits who are there for you in the darkest of times. Tea tree can also give you strength and protection when you need it. But I want to focus on her unblocking ability—she can help you overcome whatever obstacles you are facing, allowing you to access more power and tune in to your higher self. In dreams, tea tree often appears in winged form, either as a bird or an angel, but you will know it's her by her scent. She has likely come to give you a message about your health.

THYME

Thymus vulgarus

ESSENTIAL PROPERTIES
protection, courage, new beginnings

In ancient Greece, thyme's bright evergreen sprigs were thought to be born of the tears of Helen of Troy. Ancient Egyptians embalmed with thyme, and in the Middle Ages women gave knights and warriors sprigs of thyme to bring them courage in battle.

MEDICINAL PROPERTIES

Thyme is such a powerful antimicrobial that before the advent of antibiotics such as penicillin, physicians would heal wounds with thyme. Today, she is a common ingredient in a variety of mouthwashes, including Listerine (though she is not the compound that is responsible for that burning sensation).

MAGICAL PROPERTIES

A common household herb, thyme is another plant that opens the gates between worlds—she is particularly inviting to fairies. Thyme is protective, and will clear any negative energy that may have attached itself to you.

Thyme will bring peace to a sad or angry space, and supports overall renewal. Working with thyme will elevate your practice, giving you the confidence you need to believe in your Magical workings.

PLANT WISDOM

Thyme's powerful vibration resonates down to the bones, inspiring you to get to work and make Magic happen. Dreaming of thyme symbolizes worry—you are anxious about something, but thyme is there to tell you that there is a method to the madness, the journey, and the timing. She encourages you to be patient and trust fully.

TOBACCO
Nicotiana tabacum

ESSENTIAL PROPERTIES
healing, banishing

Tobacco is native to North and South America. It is often stated that English colonist John Rolfe "discovered" tobacco, but that is of course untrue. As with many plants, Native Americans used and worked with tobacco long before colonists invaded their land. Tobacco is sacred to many cultures and religions, and in many Native American cultures it is used to promote calm, peace, and the ability to speak to others and with the ancestors. Unprocessed, chemical-free tobacco also often incorporated into ceremonies and healing practices.

MEDICINAL PROPERTIES

Though tobacco is commonly smoked by people around the world, it can be fatal if ingested incorrectly or too often. That said, tobacco can relieve pain and anxiety temporarily, and tobacco was and still is used in many cultures to dress wounds. In addition, chewing tobacco can relieve toothache.

Tobacco Clearing Spray

This simple and effective spray can be used to clear and protect entryways such as your front door, and over the altar after you have finished a spell.

WHAT YOU NEED

    1 tablespoon loose tobacco

    1 tablespoon ground sage

    Peel of 1 orange, cut into small pieces

    1 teaspoon sea salt

    8-ounce glass jar

    Spray bottle

WHAT TO DO

+ Place all the ingredients in your glass jar. Fill the jar with hot water and allow the potion to cool, uncovered.

+ Once the potion has reached room temperature, cover the jar and place it in your refrigerator.

+ When you're ready to use it, strain the potion and add it to a spray bottle, spraying any area that needs clearing.

MAGICAL PROPERTIES

You do not need to smoke tobacco to work with her. Try sprinkling tobacco in front of your door to protect your home. You can also place tobacco leaves over your bed to invite spirits to visit your dreams. Meditate with tobacco by lying down and placing tobacco on your womb, beneath the belly. She will take you back to your roots, and guide you through a deep healing experience.

Although tobacco is an important part of Indigenous cultural traditions, it is possible to work with her even if you are not part of those cultures—if you are respectful. Out of that kind of respect, I ask that you not work with tobacco for connecting with your ancestors, unless your culture does so traditionally. However, you can absolutely incorporate tobacco into your banishing or protection Magics without fear of offending her or anyone else.

TURMERIC
Curcuma longa

ESSENTIAL PROPERTIES

peace, creativity, love

We all know turmeric to be the delicious beige root with brilliant yellow innards, related to the ginger family. She is a staple in Indian, Southeast Asian, and Middle Eastern cooking.

MEDICINAL PROPERTIES

Turmeric is known to have wonderful effects on the brain—she can improve mood, lift depression, and even work to offset the effects of Alzheimer's. Turmeric is fantastic at detoxifying the body and purifying the spirt.

MAGICAL PROPERTIES

Turmeric's power is all about confidence and well-being. She clears away stagnant energy, allowing high-vibration energies the space to move freely. Turmeric is both grounding and uplifting, creating a peaceful sense of balance. Turmeric is also associated with passion—work with her to increase lustful energy.

Turmeric Passion Bowl

This spell will bring passion into your relationship, into a project you've been working on—it can even help you find passion in your relationship with yourself.

WHAT YOU NEED

Large bowl

1 tablespoon turmeric, fresh or dried

A handful of red roses

1 whole red chili pepper, fresh or dried

11 sunflower seeds

3 to 5 cups water

1 tablespoon Himalayan pink salt

WHAT TO DO

+ Add all the ingredients to a large bowl.

+ Place it under your bed to invite passion into your relationship with yourself or your partner.

+ You can also keep this bowl next to you while working on a project.

PLANT WISDOM

Turmeric's wisdom is ancient, and rings true to so many beings on this Earth. She tells us, *You are sacred.* Her guidance helps us to remember to put ourselves first, knowing that we will succeed only if we take care of ourselves. Turmeric will be there for you, cheering you on as you make your way through this life. If turmeric appears in your dreams, this means there will be a rise in passion in your life, either in love or in your creative endeavors.

VALERIAN
Valeriana officinalis

ESSENTIAL PROPERTIES

purification, protection, opening the door between realms

There are many varieties of valerian, and some form of her has been used since ancient times. Though it is her root that is most often used for healing, valerian blossoms are delicate, sweetly scented little balls of love. She attracts pollinators, and cats often respond to her in the same way they do to catnip.

MEDICINAL PROPERTIES

Valerian is best known for her ability to help us sleep. Her root in particular is used for medicine, and she can be brewed as a tea. However, if nightmares are your concern, keep some of her leaves in your pillow to keep those frightening visions at bay. Valerian can also reduce anxiety and stress, as she has a powerful, grounding energy.

MAGICAL PROPERTIES

Valerian promotes harmony, peace, and a calm mind. She is great to work with for purifying new objects and new home spaces because she removes negative energy. Keep valerian by your brightest windows or spaces to amplify her purifying energy. Bring her to meetings, gatherings, and social events to keep yourself grounded and protected from the wild energy of other people's thoughts, emotions, and vibes that can invade your auric field. I always keep some in my hand when I approach an important conversation with my partner so we don't let our emotions get the best of us, and instead remain clear and focused on the topic.

PLANT WISDOM

Valerian is a grounding herb that will protect you as you open communication to other worlds and realms. She does this even while you sleep—keep her by your bed and she will meet you in your dreams, preventing you from flying away into places that aren't beneficial for you. She will also keep you from dreaming silly nonsense, instead opening you up to vivid and meaningful dreams. She brings wisdom for those who need to come back home to the self, remaining present in the body—daydreamers, this is your plant! Work with her to get things done, to bring those daydreams into reality.

VENUS FLYTRAP
Dionaea muscipula

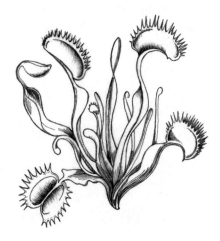

VENUS FLYTRAP

ESSENTIAL PROPERTIES
protection, manifesting, banishing

This famously carnivorous plant catches her prey with a literal trap of her leaves. She secretes a sweet-scented nectar that lures insects in; then her tiny hairs are triggered and her jaws snap shut—and they do so incredibly quickly, in about one-tenth of a second.

MEDICINAL PROPERTIES

A juice made from Venus flytrap can stimulate the immune system, and researchers are studying if she may be useful in treating cancer, particularly Hodgkin's disease and non-Hodgkin's lymphoma.

MAGICAL PROPERTIES

Feed Venus flytrap with insects. As you do so, bring to mind a negative emotion or experience that has been haunting you. As you place the bug into one of her traps, release the negativity from your mind and let her take it from you. Place her on your altar or next to you when you are working on manifesting spells, such as bringing in money, luck, love, and so on. Keeping her by your windows protects your home from unwanted people and energies.

PLANT WISDOM

Venus flytrap consumes negativity, sinking it inside her and replacing it with tranquility and serenity. Take no part of her that she does not offer freely, but instead use her unique willingness to consume pests as a way to channel negativity out of your life.

VIOLET
Viola sororia

ESSENTIAL PROPERTIES

spiritual development, love

Violets grow wild and easily—so easily that some consider them a weed, though I don't! They are far too useful, and have been valued for both their scent and flavor for centuries. Violets have a place in the perfume industry, and are also good for eating, though they are primarily used to flavor candies.

MEDICINAL PROPERTIES

Both the flowers and leaves of the violet may be eaten, and will calm a cough or sore throat, and may ward off headaches as well. They can also be used to relieve constipation. Violet's healing can calm inflammation—of the body, the heart, and the mind.

MAGICAL PROPERTIES

It should surprise exactly no one that violet is a lover—her leaves are shaped like hearts! Work with her leaves and the petals she produces to craft powerful love spells and potions, but remember, forcing someone to fall in love with you is against the natural laws of this world, and will only end up hurting everyone involved. Instead, work with violet to cultivate a love that is growing already, naturally.

PLANT WISDOM

Violet's wisdom is that of spiritual devotion. Bring her into your life to fuel your spirit and reawaken your love for your spiritual practice. She helps you to be more devoted, holding you accountable to your own practice. We all need her in our lives! When you dream of violet, you are receiving a powerful message from your guides, so look around in your dream for clues and signs. You could even try to talk to her in your dream, for she herself may well be the guide who wants to speak with you.

WILLOW
Salix

ESSENTIAL PROPERTIES
healing, energy clearing, protection

The willow makes a majestic arc, bending from her top to bow to the ground, closing and completing a splendid loop. A single branch that falls in moist ground can regrow an entire tree. Willow branches make excellent dowsing rods, helping you to find water running underground, or energy lines like ley lines.

MEDICINAL PROPERTIES
Willow bark contains a chemical called salicylic acid, which is extremely similar to that used to make aspirin—and indeed, willow bark was used as a powerful pain reliever until aspirin's invention, and is still used by naturopaths.

MAGICAL PROPERTIES

Clear your home of unwanted entities by spiritually sweeping it with a bundle of willow branches and leaves. You can also boil her leaves and add that water to your bath—if you do, prepare for a healing like you've never felt before. You may find yourself weeping, purging emotions that have been hidden. Take these tears and place them in a jar, keeping it on your windowsill during a Waning Crescent Moon so that the Moon's energy can take your tears into its light and heal those waters. You can then use those tears for powerful self-love or general healing spellwork.

PLANT WISDOM

Willow is my favorite tree of all time. There was a willow tree in the cemetery where I used to play as a child, and when I needed guidance, she was my parent. If you are under a willow tree, you are instantly cloaked by her, hidden away under her arms. In this realm, no one will disturb you. I built an altar there under her branches, and she taught me how to keep myself safe, and keep both spiritual and physical intruders out. If you are suffering, she will take you into her embrace and create this safe space for you. You can place her branches on your altar, over your bed, or anywhere you want to keep intruders from entering. She can also help you forget your pain so that whatever is going on in your life, you have moments of peace and love.

Dreaming of willow happens most often to children who are going through hurt, pain, and trauma, though adults in those circumstances may dream of her as well. She will also visit those who self-harm, bringing healing but also a kind of escape from the real world. She offers dreams of a happy existence, speaking to you of better days on their way, and the importance your being is to the Earth. She understands your pain, and keeps you holding on.

WITCH HAZEL
Hamamelis virginiana

ESSENTIAL PROPERTIES

opening the door between realms

Witch hazels are small trees or large shrubs, depending on who you ask. They have fragrant flowers that glow like fiery embers in the Sun. In this case the "witch" in witch hazel doesn't refer to Magical practitioners—it's derived from the middle English word *wiche*, which means "bendy" or "pliable." Her branches, like that of her cousin the willow, make for powerful dowsing rods, telling the secrets of the underground rivers that flow beneath our very feet.

MEDICINAL PROPERTIES

As an antimicrobial and antibacterial, witch hazel makes a very good toner. If you're struggling with acne, try her out! She can also help with scalp sensitivity, and is useful for treating minor wounds, scratches, and insect bites.

MAGICAL PROPERTIES

Witch hazel harnesses the energy of the Sun; work with her when you need a fire element or want to amplify fire energies—so any spellwork that involves love, passion, self-love, creativity, or power. I especially love to work with her while I'm doing candle Magic. Witch hazel can also help you connect to your center, your core. This space is where we hold powerful energies, but is unfortunately often ignored, which can lead to anxiety, foggy mind, and even health issues. Work with witch hazel to tap into this space and you can learn to use this energy for spiritual work, even spells. This energy from the center core is grounding, and is great for manifesting money, good health, success, and healing.

When you've been working with witch hazel for a few months, she will grant you energies that open portals, particularly to those of the spirit realm, fairy realm, and demigod realm. Reaching a particular being from any of these areas will be much more effective when you've got witch hazel helping you. Witch hazel does not visit in dreams, but you can form a relationship with her either through meditation, or simply by working with her in your Magical and spiritual practice.

WITCHGRASS
Panicum capillare

ESSENTIAL PROPERTIES

banishing, protection, manifesting

Witchgrass is well-suited to her name—she is easy to overlook if you're not seeking her out. She grows all over the United States, and can reach as high as three feet. Her blades are green to purplish in color, and her seeds arc out like a loose broom.

MEDICINAL PROPERTIES

Witchgrass seeds are edible, and can be cooked whole or ground and used as a flower, much like millet. You can make an infusion of the leaves to use as an emetic. The roots are quite tasty—mild and slightly sweet. They contain mucilage, and so can be soothing to sore throats.

MAGICAL PROPERTIES

To banish negative forces in your life, speak to witchgrass about what it is you wish to banish, and then send her into flame to turn that negative force into ash. For protection, you can simply place her over your door or windows to keep out intruders or ill-willed people or spirits. You can also speak your intentions or prayers for protection by braiding witchgrass—I like to keep the braid over my fireplace or stove, as the fire element keeps the protection ignited. You can also work a braid to bind yourself or someone else, preventing harm from being done. It is very important that you do not use witchgrass to bind for any negative reason—the witchgrass will turn those intentions around toward you instead.

PLANT WISDOM

Manifesting with witchgrass is so much fun. She takes you into a trance state where you can spiritually experience what it is you wish to bring into your life. Gather enough witchgrass for two braids, and then braid them both while speaking your intentions over and over. When you've finished, place one braid over your altar or in your sacred space. Take the other braid and bury it in the ground, asking Mother Earth to create roots for your intentions. If you dream of witchgrass, that means that someone is gossiping about you or spreading ill will. When you wake up, take some time to bind that gossip by braiding her.

WOLFSBANE
Aconitum napellus

ESSENTIAL PROPERTIES
protection

Also known as devil's helmet, wolfsbane is the queen of poisons. She stands several feet high and has bright-purple drooping flowers that attract attention atop her slender form. She's stunningly beautiful, but she's a real killer—literally. Wolfsbane is highly toxic and has been understood as a poison since ancient times—she was once spread around the boundaries of a farm to poison predators threatening livestock . . . including wolves threatening sheep.

MEDICINAL PROPERTIES

Extracts have been given orally in traditional medicine to reduce fever and for pain, inflammation, and high blood pressure; but do your research and use extreme care if you choose to touch or ingest this plant.

MAGICAL PROPERTIES

If you grow wolfsbane, she will build a protective auric field around your home, one that is almost impossible to break through. However, you must devote yourself to her and work with her often in order for her protection to remain strong.

PLANT WISDOM

This plant is ideal for those who dance to their own tune. She is an observer, hiding beneath her cloak and watching the world around her. She is quiet, but still very powerful. Working with her will help you shut out external noise so you can tap into your inner wisdom. She teaches us to be still, to find ourselves—and she shows us that we are never lost. We are always right where we are. Invite her into your dreams, but don't expect her to visit right away; as I said, she is an observer, and she will work to uncover your truth before meeting you in your dreams. But once she is there, she will connect with you in a way that is unique to you, as she meets every one of us with our own individual message.

WORMWOOD
Artemisia absinthium

ESSENTIAL PROPERTIES

protection, amplification, psychic ability

This ancient silvery beauty is said to have grown in the path of the serpent as it exited Eden. Wormwood is often mistaken for sagebrush due to her similar appearance and scent. She might be most famous for the visions caused by drinking absinthe, a vision-inducing liquor that is made from her oil.

MEDICINAL PROPERTIES

Wormwood can treat fever, digestion problems, liver disease, depression, loss of appetite, muscle pain, and memory loss. She can also treat Crohn's disease and, when made into a salve, can relieve itching from insect bites. However, wormwood can be dangerous if overused (for longer than two weeks), and pregnant women should avoid her.

MAGICAL PROPERTIES

Wormwood's Magical uses are multifold. Soaked in wine for several days, she is known to present visions, astral projections, and divination. When immersed in olive oil, grapeseed oil, or avocado oil for three Full Moon cycles, she becomes a powerful anointing oil that can be used for protection, spell reversal, and communication with spirits. Place the flowers in the trunk of your car to keep you from traveling into dangerous areas, and to keep you safe from stalkers. Wormwood may also be used in spells to send harmful magic back to its sender. When burned in combination with mugwort, bay, or blue lotus, she serves as a bridge of communication, allowing you to call up spirits.

PLANT WISDOM

Most often, I work with wormwood to fine-tune my clairsentience; she makes it so that when I have visions, I am able to walk around, touch and move things, look for messages, and so on. When I was younger this was difficult to do, and my mother would place wormwood in my pillow to help me navigate my visions and be able to feel and sense objects to get even more information. Invite wormwood into your dreams to help you navigate your dreamworld, especially in times when you are having trouble sleeping.

Wormwood's message to you is *Mind over matter*—or rather, *Spirit over matter*. She reminds you that you are limitless and powerful, so long as you truly believe, do the work, and take risks, even when you are afraid.

YARROW
Achillea millefolium

ESSENTIAL PROPERTIES

psychic ability, clarity

Yarrow has clusters of ferny foliage with flower heads composed of many tiny, tightly packed flowers. The showy flowers come in an array of beautiful colors and can be mistaken for Queen Anne's lace. They are now found all over the world, bringing blooms from early summer to fall.

MEDICINAL PROPERTIES

The leaves and flowers of the yarrow plant can be used to bring down a fever, to relax hay fever, and to bring on menstruation (so be careful if you think there's a chance you might be pregnant). Yarrow can treat the common cold, dysentery, and stomach issues, and chewing on the fresh leaves can relieve a toothache.

MAGICAL PROPERTIES

Placing yarrow on a coffin or on a grave helps the spirit let go and cross over. Putting yarrow in your braided hair creates an energy web around you that helps you tap into your inner wisdom. Work with yarrow often to develop your psychic gifts. Make yourself a cup of yarrow tea and stir it with a cinnamon stick—this will warm the bones and release hidden truths, so you can learn something new about your being.

PLANT WISDOM

Whether your goal is to open the heart or the third eye, yarrow will aid you to be more perceptive and attentive, and she can help you allow yourself to be loved and cared for. Yarrow helps you release the dark, release the ghost you're keeping within. She helps you to let go of the things that are keeping your truth from shining through. It isn't easy to let go, let alone to surrender, but yarrow can help you surrender to your truth, your purpose, and your presence here on this Earth. When you dream of yarrow, she will bring you to your truest form, opening a world of *a-ha!* moments that will guide you through life.

Yerba Buena
Clinopodium douglasii

ESSENTIAL PROPERTIES
purification, peace, clarity

Not to be confused with spearmint or yerba santa, this is *Clinopodium douglasii*, a rambling, low-growing herb with dainty, delicate flowers—though she does smell a bit like spearmint. It's not surprising that multiple plants go by this name, since it simply means "good herb."

MEDICINAL PROPERTIES

Yerba buena is a pain reliever, particularly when used to relieve headaches, toothaches, and joint pain. Yerba buena tea has calming effects on the mind and nervous system as well, and yerba buena has long been used to relieve abdominal pain, colic, and diarrhea, and aid in indigestion.

MAGICAL PROPERTIES

When burned, yerba buena clears and purifies. If you like to purchase antiques, I suggest clearing their stagnant energies with yerba buena before bringing them into your home. But if that's not practical, make sure you keep the windows open while you cleanse with yerba buena, and leave them open for half an hour afterward before burning juniper to bring in peaceful energy.

Yerba Buena Clarity Bath

This bath will purify your mind, body, and spirit, allowing for clarity as your open third eye can zoom in to the depths of your soul.

WHAT YOU NEED

    4 cups water

    1 tablespoon yerba buena, fresh or dried

    1 teaspoon dried yerba buena

    1 teaspoon dried lovage

    White candle

WHAT TO DO

+ Set the water to boil and add 1 tablespoon of fresh or dried yerba buena. Allow the mixture to boil for 10 minutes.

+ Let this cool while you run your bath, then strain and add to your bath water.

+ Mix the teaspoon of dried yerba buena with the lovage.

+ Light your candle and use it to set your dried herbs aflame.

+ Inhale the smoke as you relax in the bath, setting an intention for what it is you wish to see.

PLANT WISDOM

Keep yerba buena around to clear energies that can linger after a fight or an argument—she will maintain a sense of peace. I tie a sprig of yerba buena to my showerhead along with eucalyptus and mugwort—as they steam, they spark my third eye while I indulge in the medicine of water. Dreaming of yerba buena symbolizes a clear path ahead of you, letting you know that the next cycle of your journey won't be as bumpy as the last. But if you dream of receiving yerba buena as a gift, it symbolizes the coming of a purge, of a letting go or surrender.

YERBA MATÉ
Ilex paraguariensis

ESSENTIAL PROPERTIES

amplification

The Guarani Indians in the highlands of Brazil, Paraguay, and Argentina enjoyed yerba maté well before her popularity today. Nowadays, she is most often consumed as a caffeine tea, but she will do more than just keep you going through those languid mornings. A cup of yerba maté tea may be as strong as a cup of coffee, but with the added benefits of herbal tea, plus the warmth and happy-buzz of chocolate. She's pretty great.

MEDICINAL PROPERTIES

Yerba maté's phytochemicals will also stimulate your brain, heart, and vascular health. She can improve diabetes and high cholesterol, and has been used to treat depression. She contains vitamins A, B_I, C, and E, as well as magnesium, calcium, zinc, sulfur, iron, and many more, making her just about the most beneficial herb available.

MAGICAL PROPERTIES

Yerba maté can make you feel like the world is your oyster—nothing can get in your way. Sprinkle some yerba maté into your bath on days when you have low energy, or when you're not in the mood to do anything, and she will lift that funk right off you. We all need her energy in our lives, and when we combine yerba maté with our Magical craft, our workings become exponentially more powerful. Add her to your spellwork or keep some yerba maté sprinkled on your altar to create a positive energy bubble.

PLANT WISDOM

Yerba maté works particularly well on your womb center. If you're carrying old energy, say from old lovers who treated you badly, or if you are simply feeling less intimate or sexually inspired than you'd like, lie down and place some yerba maté above your sacral chakra. Rest in silence, meditating with her as she clears away whatever has been clogging you up and sparks some new energy. Work with her wisdom as often as possible, especially if you have big plans. You can invite her into your dreams to create dreams within dreams; this is how she will show you the infinite opportunities life has to offer you.

Yucca
Yucca filamentosa

YUCCA

ESSENTIAL PROPERTIES
purification, protection

Yucca got her name from my ancestors, the Taíno people, though she is a staple in food, medicine, and spirituality for many native peoples. She is native to North America, Central America, and the Caribbean, and has around 40 species and 24 subspecies. She is also known as Adam's needle. Almost all of the yucca plant can be used as food, though the stems or trunks can be toxic unless handled properly.

MEDICINAL PROPERTIES

Yucca roots are not only delicious and highly nutritious, they also offer a variety of benefits to your general health. Yucca can reduce blood pressure and cholesterol and can relieve migraine headaches. You can also make her into a balm to help with sprains and joint pain, and to calm dandruff. According to a study

Yucca Root Cleansing Bath

This cleansing process will either clear you before spellwork, or dissolve any residual effects of a casting after a Magical practice.

WHAT YOU NEED

3 to 4 yucca roots

1 tablespoon grated ginger

1 garlic clove, smashed

1 teaspoon Himalayan pink salt

Yucca powder

3 to 4 yucca leaves

White candle

Charcoal

WHAT TO DO

+ Cut your yucca roots into halves and add them to a pot of boiling water.

+ After 5 minutes, add the ginger, garlic, and salt. Boil for another 5 minutes.

+ Remove from the heat, strain, and allow to cool.

+ Chop the yucca leaves into small pieces and mix them with the yucca powder to make an incense.

+ Run a bath, and add the yucca tea.

+ Light your candle, and place your yucca incense on your charcoal to burn.

+ Relax in the bath and allow yucca to clear all that is attached to you. If you feel that an excess of negative energy has latched on to you, or if you need to banish evil eye, you can repeat this bathing ritual every day for 3 days.

done by NASA, yucca is one of best plants for filtering the air, so keep her in your home to improve air quality.

MAGICAL PROPERTIES

For purification, you can cleanse yourself by taking a few yucca leaves and tying them together at their base. Using a sweeping motion over the body, sweeping from the top of your head and out the bottoms of your feet. If you feel an excess of energy, for instance if you're anxious, stressed, or are having trouble focusing, cut a piece of yucca root and rub it over your belly, then meditate while holding the root. She will draw that energy out of you.

PLANT WISDOM

My ancestors worked with yucca, and so she is near and dear to me. Simply having her in the home protects those who live there—and she will shake her leaves if there are ill-willed spirits near. The more you work with yucca, the more she will speak to you, physically, spiritually, and energetically. If your ancestors worked with yucca, she will visit you in your dreams and help you speak with them there. If not, she will bring you peace and harmony while you sleep.

ZZ PLANT
Zamioculcas zamiifolia

ESSENTIAL PROPERTIES

wisdom, self-awareness, spiritual development

ZZ, also known as Zanzibar gem and eternity plant, is a wonderful houseplant as it can tolerate low light and requires infrequent watering. It's a charming plant, with tall, woody stems studded with oval leaves. Like many other houseplants it contains oxalate crystals, so use caution with pets.

MEDICINAL PROPERTIES

Several Indigenous peoples, particularly in Africa, work with ZZ plant to relieve stomach aches. The juice from the leaves can soothe an earache, and a poultice made from the plant can serve as an anti-inflammatory.

MAGICAL PROPERTIES

ZZ plant grows in a steady fashion, and can bring to light the areas in your life that deserve to grow in the same way—with patience and steadiness. I work with her each and every time I study a new plant, read a new book, or take classes online, as she supports me in my growth and learning. I also love to keep her by me when I meditate with other plants, as she helps me absorb their messages. Placing a ZZ plant in your office, workplace, or in a classroom will help those around her be more productive and alert.

PLANT WISDOM

ZZ plant is a powerful support for children. Her energies support learning, developing, and growing, and she can teach children how to focus and really absorb the information they receive. She can offer them comfort, and help them understand their true selves, so that as they navigate the shifts and changes of growing up, they always know that they are the same being deep within.

A BENEDICTION

Don't forget we are more than just flesh.
More than just bones. More.

Better than we think.
Better than we believe. Better.

Stronger than we hope.
Stronger than they say. Stronger.

Continuing Your Journey

As I sat down to write this, a hawk flew overhead, bearing a message for you, dear reader and fellow Plant Witch. The hawk came to remind you that we all carry the heartbeat of Mother Earth. The Magic you see in the world is simply a reflection of the Magic that lives within you.

This is your journey, your spiritual practice, and your life. In your work with Plant Witchery, make sure to do what feels right to you. All I've tried to do here is inspire you, leading you on the first steps of a path where, soon enough, you will begin to receive wisdom yourself. You are fully capable of tapping into all the Magic that exists in this world—and you can do it by creating your own practice. There are no rules or processes that you have to follow; your Magic is yours alone. Your practice will grow and expand as you build a relationship with your Magic, and as you explore the ways in which it will work uniquely for you.

Think back to the beginning. Think back to the time when all our ancestors had was the Earth, the stars, the animals, and themselves. And they were powerful. Nothing else was needed, because they knew what power there is in each of those things. Everything has a spirit, everything has a voice, and everything carries a message . . . including you. You carry a message that the world needs to hear. Speak it loud and clear.

You can find your message by listening within. The world outside isn't the only world that exists. Be still. Connect to your spirit and allow yourself to tap into your other world, the inner world, the world where your truth lives. Take a walk within and visit the spaces you've left untouched.

You may find things there you didn't want to look at, for we all have our shadows. But this is how you heal, and how you show up to make your offerings to others. The hurt, the pain, the falls, the obstacles, and, most important, the abilities you conjured to get through it all *are Magic*. Put spirit before fear, prayer before worry, and your light before breaking, and you will be a force for good in this world.

Pray for the Earth, pray for our sisters and brothers, pray for love to rise over the shadows clouding the skies. Pray for the waters to speak in tongues, pray for the trees to sway fiercely, and pray for our mountains to wake the echoes of our Mother's belly. You carry light, medicine, wisdom, Magic, and the blood of our ancestors, all living loudly within your bones. Show up for our Earth, our people, and, most important, show up for yourself with compassion, love, and unity. Remember the ancient songs that tremble our spirit.

LIST OF PLANTS BY ESSENTIAL PROPERTIES

abundance

alfalfa, allspice, angel wings, apple, ashwagandha, banana, basil, bay laurel, bayberry, bergamot, birch, angel wings, cat's claw, cattail, chamomile, chicory, cinnamon, cinquefoil, clove, comfrey, daffodil, dill, dracaena, echinacea, fiddle-leaf fig, geranium, grape, High John the Conqueror, hollyhock, jade, lemon balm, lipstick plant, mandrake, maple, monstera, peony, pine, rose of Jericho, rowan, saffron crocus, sarsaparilla, spider plant

amplification

ashwagandha, carnation, chickweed, dragon's blood, echinacea, grape, lemongrass, pennyroyal, wormwood, yerba maté

animal Magic

hops

art Magic

elm

awareness

blackthorn, devil's shoestring, dogbane hemp, lavender, sacred fig

balance

air plants, alocasia, anise, calamus, calathea, chickweed, elm, enchanter's nightshade, jack-in-the-pulpit, maple, ponytail palm, star anise

banishing

butcher's-broom, centaury, cherry blossom, chinaberry, croton, devil's shoestring, honeysuckle, oak, pipsissewa, tobacco, Venus flytrap, witchgrass

blood Magic

saffron crocus, Solomon's seal

clarity

areca palm, cactus, calathea, dogbane hemp, eucalyptus, eyebright, garlic, honesty, hyssop, liverwort, nutmeg, Saint John's wort, yarrow, yerba buena

control

calamus

courage

allspice, alocasia, arrowhead, bloodroot, borage, fennel, lungwort, thyme

creativity

adder's-tongue, banana, bay laurel, damiana, eucalyptus, eyebright, feverfew, grape, hollyhock, jasmine, lipstick plant, maple, monstera, orange, passionflower, turmeric

energy clearing

abre camino, angelica, cedar, chinaberry, dumb cane, eucalyptus, fiddle-leaf fig, morning glory, oregano, sea buckthorn, spider plant, willow

faith

poinsettia, prayer plant

feminine energy

burdock, dracaena, jasmine, magnolia, moonwort, raspberry

friendship

daisy, jade

freedom from cares

air plants

happiness

bergamot, blessed thistle, calendula, catnip, copal, cornflower, daisy, fiddle-leaf fig, geranium, lemon balm, lipstick plant, pau d'arco, ponytail palm, rose of Jericho, sarsaparilla, stinging nettle, sunflower, tansy

healing

adder's-tongue, alfalfa, althaea, angelica, arrowhead, ashwagandha, bleeding heart, burdock, butcher's-broom, cactus, carnation, cedar, centaury, chamomile, echinacea, elder, eucalyptus, eyebright, feverfew, hawthorn, hellebore, hibiscus, hickory, hydrangea, hyssop, lavender, liverwort, lungwort, marjoram, pau d'arco, peace lily, pine, prayer plant, sage, shepherd's purse, tansy, tobacco, willow

hex-breaking

sea-buckthorn

intuition

cinquefoil, fern, ginkgo, hoya, iris, lavender, motherwort, rose, sunflower

love

adder's-tongue, angel wings, avocado, basil, birch, bleeding heart, bloodroot, angel wings, calendula, caraway, catnip, cattail, chamomile, chickweed, cinnamon, cinquefoil, clove, clover, cornflower, daffodil, damiana, dill, dragon's blood, goldenrod, hawthorn, hibiscus, jasmine, lovage, marjoram, monstera, myrtle, orchid, orris root, oxalis, passionflower, raspberry, rose, saffron crocus, Sicilian sumac, slippery elm, turmeric, violet

luck

alfalfa, allspice, angel wings, blessed thistle, catnip, Chinese evergreen, clover, daffodil, devil's shoestring, High John the Conqueror, jade, sea buckthorn

manifesting

alfalfa, apple, bay laurel, bergamot, black cohosh, cattail, dill, enchanter's nightshade, pipsissewa, string of pearls, Venus flytrap, witchgrass

meditation

sacred fig

memory

rosemary

Moon Magic

honesty, moonwort, saffron crocus

new beginnings

birch, cherry blossom, clove, enchanter's nightshade, grape, High John the Conqueror, holly, hollyhock, ivy, morning glory, passionflower, Queen Anne's lace, rose of Jericho, thyme

opening the door between realms

acacia, altamisa, apple, calendula, cherry blossom, chicory, dandelion, datura, elder, foxglove, gladiolus, juniper berry, mint, oak, oxalis, parsley, peony, pine, prayer plant, primrose, Queen Anne's lace, snapdragon, valerian, witch hazel

peace

agrimony, chamomile, Chinese evergreen, coltsfoot, datura, elm, hellebore, hibiscus, hops, lavender, peace lily, skullcap, turmeric, yerba buena

prevent thievery

caraway, comfrey

productivity

areca palm

prosperity

pothos

protection

acacia, African violet, agrimony, ague, aloe vera, angelica, arrowhead, basil, belladonna, birch, black cohosh, blackthorn, blue lotus, burdock, butcher's-broom, cactus, caraway, cedar, centaury, cinquefoil, clove, clover, cornflower, croton, devil's shoestring, dill, dragon's blood, dumb cane, elder, fennel, fern, foxglove, garlic, gladiolus, heather, hellebore, holly, honeysuckle, hoya, hyssop, jack-in-the-pulpit, juniper berry, liverwort, mandrake, maple, motherwort, mugwort, mullein, oak, orchid, oregano, orris root, parsley, pennyroyal, peony, raspberry, rose, rosemary, rowan, rue, sacred fig, Saint John's wort, sea buckthorn, shepherd's purse, Sicilian sumac, slippery elm, snapdragon, stinging nettle, tea tree, thyme, valerian, Venus flytrap, willow, witchgrass, wolfsbane, wormwood, yucca

psychic ability

ague, althaea, anise, belladonna, blue lotus, borage, butcher's-broom, cat's claw, centaury, coltsfoot, cornflower, ginkgo, goldenrod, hazel, honeysuckle, hoya, lemongrass, lilac, mint, mugwort, myrtle, oxalis, ponytail palm, rowan, Saint John's wort, sandalwood, star anise, wormwood, yarrow

purification

air plants, altamisa, chinaberry, copal, fennel, hyssop, juniper berry, orange, oregano, pau d'arco, tea tree, valerian, yerba buena, yucca

purity

magnolia

reflection

cattail, peace lily

resilience

dandelion, holly, sago palm

secrets

never-never plant, pennyroyal, stinging nettle

self-awareness

belladonna, bloodroot, fern, ginger, iris, mulberry, Solomon's seal, ZZ plant

self-love

African violet, avocado, basil, borage, chamomile, lovage, never-never plant, peace lily

shadow work

adder's-tongue, blackthorn, datura, holly, mullein, Solomon's seal

spiritual development

apple, cedar, cinnamon, gentian, hickory, iris, lilac, moonwort, pothos, violet, ZZ plant

strength

alocasia, arrowhead, ashwagandha, birch, black cohosh, blessed thistle, cactus, calathea, chickweed, fennel, ginger, hickory, nutmeg, oak, parsley, tea tree

success

allspice, areca palm, cinnamon, clove, pothos

unblocking

abre camino, cat's claw, chicory, ginger, High John the Conqueror, tea tree

truth

orange

weather manipulation

heather

wisdom

acacia, bay laurel, cinquefoil, hazel, lilac, maple, oak, pine, prayer plant, sage, sandalwood, ZZ plant

wishes

dandelion, grape, poinsettia

About the Author

JULIET DIAZ is a Seer and an Indigenous Taíno Cubana from a long line of *curanderos* (healers) and *brujas* on both sides of her parents' lineages. She is a *bohuiti* (healer) of her tribe, Higuayagua. She's a mother of two boys, three cats, and over 400 plants.

When Juliet was three-years-old, signs of her natural gifts like cosmic channeling, seeing, plant whispering, healing, energy reading, and communication with spirits and other realms began to shine through. She believes Magic lives within us all and feels passionately about inspiring others to step into their truth. Juliet has devoted her life to helping others weave light, medicine, and magic into their spirits, helping thousands of people come back to themselves and heal. Her Sacred Soul Healing service merges together all of her gifts and the different healing modalities she has learned from her ancestors, elders, and spirit guides. She's the creator of Sagrada Collective, a virtual sanctuary.

She has a master of science in herbal medicine, and countless certifications in an array of healing modalities. Featured in major publications like *National Geographic*, *The Atlantic*, *Wired*, and *Spirit and Destiny UK*, Juliet is the author of the genre-defining book *Witchery: Embrace the Witch Within*, published by Hay House.

www.iamjulietdiaz.com
Instagram @iamjulietdiaz

www.thesagradacollective.com
Instagram @thesagradacollective

HAY HOUSE TITLES OF RELATED INTEREST

YOU CAN HEAL YOUR LIFE, the movie, starring Louise Hay & Friends
(available as a 1-DVD program, an expanded 2-DVD set, and an online streaming video)
Learn more at www.hayhouse.com/louise-movie

THE SHIFT, the movie,
starring Dr. Wayne W. Dyer
(available as a 1-DVD program, an expanded 2-DVD set, and an online streaming video)
Learn more at www.hayhouse.com/the-shift-movie

ALCHEMY OF HERBS: Transform Everyday Ingredients into Foods and Remedies That Heal,
by Rosalee De La Forêt

WILD REMEDIES: How to Forage Healing Foods and Craft Your Own Herbal Medicine,
by Rosalee De La Forêt and Emily Han

WITCH: Unleased, Untamed, Unapologetic,
by Lisa Lister

All of the above are available at your local bookstore,
or may be ordered by contacting Hay House (see next page).

We hope you enjoyed this Hay House book. If you'd like to receive our online catalog featuring additional information on Hay House books and products, or if you'd like to find out more about the Hay Foundation, please contact:

Hay House, Inc., P.O. Box 5100, Carlsbad, CA 92018-5100
(760) 431-7695 or (800) 654-5126
(760) 431-6948 (fax) or (800) 650-5115 (fax)
www.hayhouse.com® • www.hayfoundation.org

———

Published in Australia by: Hay House Australia Pty. Ltd.,
18/36 Ralph St., Alexandria NSW 2015
Phone: 612-9669-4299 • *Fax:* 612-9669-4144
www.hayhouse.com.au

Published in the United Kingdom by: Hay House UK, Ltd.,
The Sixth Floor, Watson House, 54 Baker Street, London W1U 7BU
Phone: +44 (0)20 3927 7290 • *Fax:* +44 (0)20 3927 7291
www.hayhouse.co.uk

Published in India by: Hay House Publishers India,
Muskaan Complex, Plot No. 3, B-2, Vasant Kunj, New Delhi 110 070
Phone: 91-11-4176-1620 • *Fax:* 91-11-4176-1630
www.hayhouse.co.in

———

Access New Knowledge.
Anytime. Anywhere.

Learn and evolve at your own pace
with the world's leading experts.

www.hayhouseU.com